HOLY MAN

HOLY MAN

FATHER DAMIEN OF MOLOKAI

GAVAN DAWS

UNIVERSITY OF HAWAII PRESS

HONOLULU

Published originally by Harper & Row, Publishers
University of Hawaii Press edition 1984
88 87 86   4 3 2

ISBN 0-8248-0920-3

Designed by Sidney Feinberg

Library of Congress Cataloging in Publication Data
Daws, Gavan.
   Holy man: Father Damien of Molokai.
   Bibliography: p.
   1. Damien, Father, 1840–1889. I. Title.
BX4705.D25D38   282´.092´4   [B]   73–4075

To the memory of my friend Larry Windley
who knew about Hawaii and about pain
and who was a wise and happy man

CONTENTS

Foreword, ix

CHAPTER ONE
THE TRAITS OF HIS FACE
1

CHAPTER TWO
I AM GOING IN YOUR PLACE
17

CHAPTER THREE
GOD'S ATHLETE
53

CHAPTER FOUR
A PECULIAR GOLGOTHA
123

CHAPTER FIVE
STIGMA
215

Notes, 253

Bibliography, 281

Index, 289

A section of photographs follows page 114.

FOREWORD

The research for this book was carried out in several places: in Tremeloo, Belgium, where Damien was born and where there is a museum named for him; and in Louvain, where he began his religious life with the Sacred Hearts Fathers and where his remains are now buried; in Rome, at the archives of the Congregation of the Sacred Hearts; in Hawaii, where he spent the last twenty-five years of his life. Some supplementary reading was done in London, mostly at the British Museum.

Everywhere I went I was kindly received. For help of all sorts —making research collections available on the most liberal of terms, tracing obscure documents, locating the originals of contemporary pictures and photographs, verifying medical and scientific data, assisting with subtleties of translation, and giving the completed manuscript a critical reading—I have many people to thank.

First among these are several Sacred Hearts Fathers, who were more than patient with the attempt of a non-Catholic—indeed a non-Christian in the strict sense of the word—to make historical and biographical sense out of the life of a man who may one day be the Congregation's first saint. I thank in particular Reverend Father Amerigo Cools, archivist of the Congregation, whose help was invaluable. My thanks also to his fellow priests, Reverend Fathers Telesphore Bosquet, Harold Meyer, Henry Systermans, and Angel Lucas.

Also helpful in ways large and small were Jacob Adler, Janet
Azama, Asa Baber, Janet Bell, Patrick Boland, O. A. Bushnell,
Emmett Cahill, Agnes Conrad, Father Daniel Dever, James Doug-
lass, Cornelius Downes, Leon Edel, Lela Goodell, Francine Gray,
Ira Hirschy, John J. Hulten, William Illerbrun, Donald E. Johnson,
Yasuto Kaihara, Harold Kent, Elizabeth Larsen, Richard Marks,
Robert McGlone, Boone Morrison, Robert Moser, Mary Muraoka,
Paki Neves, Laila Roster, Robert Schmitt, Norman Shapiro, Olaf
Skinsnes, A. A. Smyser, Michael Speidel, Christopher Strawn,
Frank Waitherwerch, Vincent Yano, August Yee, and Klaus Well-
mann. My thanks to them all.

Permission to quote from the letters of Charles McEwen Hyde
was granted by Harvard College Library. Permission to quote
from the letters of Peter Young Kaeo in the Hawaiian Mission
Children's Society Library was granted by Mrs. Thomas H. Davis.
Permission to quote from material in the W. D. Alexander Papers
in the Hawaiian Historical Society Library was granted by the
trustees.

My wife, Carolyn Kato Daws, shared the early, tedious work of
months of microfilming scores of thousands of pages of manuscript
documents. Later, she checked references, typed the manuscript,
and helped read proof.

Part of the expense of travel and of copying documents was
defrayed by small grants administered by the University of Hawaii
Foundation; I thank the donors.

The index was prepared by Delight Ansley.

A note on language. At one time or another, Damien wrote in
five languages: his native Flemish; French, the language of his
Congregation; Latin, the language of his Church; English, one of
the official languages of the Hawaiian kingdom of his day; and
Hawaiian, the other official language and the day-by-day language
of his parishioners. In translating Damien into English, I have tried
to maintain the tone of his writing, which was by no means elegant. He was stiff and formal in his approach to language, a writer
of purposeful letters who took no particular joy in words. As for

what he wrote originally in English, I have transcribed it exactly. It happens that this was the language he was least at home in. He was not sound in its grammar or its spelling. So he turns up on the page idiosyncratically—but always comprehensibly: he wanted to make himself clear.

Concerning the use of the terms "leper" and "leprosy," current practice, increasingly, is to avoid the word "leper." The argument is that it carries all the stigmatizing overtones of ancient, ignorant usage, and that it is inappropriate to the twentieth century, which has—or ought to have—a more enlightened and humane approach to people with the disease. It is a complicated situation, one that causes considerable dispute. I have used the word "leper" occasionally, where the context demanded it, in quotation marks. Damien and his contemporaries, of course, used the word habitually. Where I have quoted them directly, I have left the word as they wrote it. As for "leprosy," there has been something of a move to substitute the term "Hansen's disease," after the discoverer of the leprosy bacillus; but "leprosy" as a descriptive term is still acceptable to the medical profession. I have followed this usage.

G.D.

For when I was in sin it seemed very bitter to me to see lepers, and the Lord Himself led me among them, and I showed mercy to them. And when I left them, what had seemed to me bitter was changed into sweetness of body and soul.

—*The Testament of St. Francis of Assisi*

"Sometimes I wonder whether Damien was a leprophil. There was no need for him to become a leper in order to serve them well. A few elementary precautions—I wouldn't be a better doctor without my fingers, would I?"

"I'm not as suspicious of leprophils as you are, doctor. There are people who love and embrace poverty. Is that so bad? Do we have to invent a word ending in phil for them?"

"The leprophil makes a bad nurse and ends by joining the patients."

"But all the same, doctor, you've said it yourself, leprosy is a psychological problem. It may be very valuable for the leper to feel loved."

"A patient can always detect whether he is loved or whether it is only his leprosy which is loved. I don't want leprosy loved. I want it eliminated. . . . We don't want to waste time with neurotics, father."

—GRAHAM GREENE, *A Burnt-Out Case*

Ordinary and gifted men in many ways are similar. We all have our oedipus complexes, our fights with this or that authority. Some few, though, seem to take their struggles very seriously, and take their time in solving them. I suppose we call them "gifted" or "great" when they find a way to offer the rest of us what they have, what is "wrong" with them as well as valuable and rare in them; and that "way" will be a craft or a message or a style which turns secret preoccupations into an open, lively message or vision felt to be irresistible by others.

—ROBERT COLES, *Erik H. Erikson: The Growth of His Work*

CHAPTER ONE

THE TRAITS
OF
HIS FACE

I

The settlement doctor came to see him the day before he died—not with the thought that anything could be done about his condition, which was beyond hope (his grave, indeed, was already dug), but rather to take his photograph. Until lately, he had been strong enough to be carried outside each day for a brief spell of sunshine; but at last this became too much for him, and he was forced to lie in his upstairs room, "nailed to his bed," in the phrase the others used for the deathly ill. Even then, he insisted on sleeping on the floor as usual, on a straw mattress with a single blanket thrown over it, wearing only an old shirt; and in his last exhausted days the others had the greatest of trouble persuading him to submit to a gentler rest. Now at least he had clean linen, and pillows for his head; but by the time of the doctor's visit he was no more than half conscious, so weak that he could not prop himself up for the picture-taking.

The camera stood on a tripod at the foot of the bed, draped in a photographer's black cloth. One of the others held him in place, head and shoulders and arms, then moved back at the right moment so that the image on the glass plate would show him alone. It took more than one attempt to get a satisfactory effect: a terrible tiredness in the ruined face, an infinite remoteness in the eyes, the beaten hands slack and open on the quilt, letting go of life.

His work at the settlement had been to help men die, thousands of them over the years. Now he was dying, just as they had done.

His sight was failing; his voice was choked off; the mute weeping mouths of his open sores were closing, sealing themselves over with a black crust. The signs were unmistakable: he had seen them so many times on his rounds among the sick that they had become intimately familiar in their sequence and in their meaning, like the Stations of the Cross. He wanted to die at Easter, so he said, to go through crucifixion, death, and resurrection with Christ. The photographs were taken on Palm Sunday, the beginning of Holy Week. At eight o'clock the next morning, Monday, April 15, 1889, four days short of Good Friday, he was dead—forty-nine years of age, almost twenty-five years a missionary priest of the Roman Catholic Church, sixteen years pastor of a congregation of leprosy victims, and four years and some months himself marked and known as a sufferer.

II

It was as "Damien the Leper" that the world knew him. That the world came to know him at all was singular enough. Kalawao settlement, the place to which his mature vocation led him—the place where he died—was hidden away on an all but inaccessible peninsula of Molokai, a sparsely populated and little-visited island of the Hawaiian chain, itself the remotest archipelago of the northern Pacific, as distant in fact and feeling from the European cities of Damien's young manhood as any place in the world.

In Damien's day, in the Christian world, the victim of leprosy was still the "leper" of the Old Testament—the outcast of all the earth, "unclean, unclean." The church no longer performed the rites of death over his living body, stretching him beneath a black pall, throwing graveyard dirt upon his head and feet; but he was severed from society just the same, the only difference being that now it was the state which saw to his segregation. In the Hawaiian Islands, he was sent to Kalawao settlement, a community that existed only because leprosy existed. There on Molokai he was put ashore, out of the way of the well, buried alive in loathsomeness, watching as the surf of the years chafed away at his prison wall of dark tumbling sea rocks, waiting while the slow rotting of his body killed him.

Damien went to Kalawao not as a diseased man under constraint, but as a priest, ready to serve the sick and to save their souls if he could—eventually, as matters turned out, to take the mortal afflictions of others upon himself. In this he was a rare man, rare for Hawaii, rare for the world; but still not unique. The Christian tradition of succor for the outcast was as old as Jesus, who showed a special compassion for the diseased. In imitation of Christ, holy men would cradle leprosy sufferers in their arms; saints might kiss the open sores. This impulse was still producing vocations in Damien's time. Other men and women of religion locked themselves away in places as cut off from the world as Kalawao, to work among the victims of leprosy and to die of their disease. By and large, such deaths went unnoticed. Self-sacrifice is silent, often enough; saintliness may be the affair of one man and his God. Public remark is another thing; and it was the special fate of Damien not only to die of leprosy but to have his death seen as somehow representative, so that he came to embody for the whole world what it was to be a "leper," his affliction signifying what the open sores of one man might mean to all men.

That was why the settlement doctor wanted to take pictures of Damien on his deathbed. It was not done out of clinical interest —any one of the thousand disfigured Hawaiians at Kalawao would have served just as well. For that matter, there were in the world some millions of victims of the disease to be identified, inspected, and described if science would be advanced by it. But Damien, marked as mysteriously as any other man who came down with leprosy among friends and neighbors and strangers who were spared, was marked again, this time most singularly, as the doctor understood: among all the world's leprosy victims, Damien was uniquely the Leper of all the world.

III

The story of Damien's life and the history of the disease that killed him played back and forth upon each other constantly, coming together coincidentally to begin with, then in a way that seemed almost fated. Damien was born in 1840, at the beginning of the decade in which for the first time leprosy was given a full and reasonably accurate medical description. He came to the Hawaiian Islands in 1864; Kalawao settlement was founded a year later. Damien committed himself to live and work there in 1873, at the moment when the Norwegian scientist Gerhard Henrik Armauer Hansen was successfully identifying and describing the bacillus of leprosy, *Bacillus leprae.*

Hansen's was one of the earliest accomplishments of its kind in what was then a new science called bacteriology. The techniques he used were extended and refined in the 1880s and '90s, bringing within the prospect of ultimate control a whole range of deadly bacterial diseases: tuberculosis, typhoid fever, diphtheria, syphilis. This was a great era in scientific medicine. Only slowly did it become apparent that while many bacilli associated with serious disease could be isolated by laboratory techniques, cultivated, prepared in a vaccine, and used for inoculation, *Bacillus leprae* could not. Leprosy was resisting the best efforts of science, which meant that one of the oldest known human diseases, and the one universally regarded as the most frightful, remained essentially unpreventable and incurable.

If there was any mitigation of this apparently infinite harshness, it was that leprosy seemed—in gross terms—to be an affliction of the few rather than of the many. Several million living human beings might have the disease; but several hundred million did not, and—according to educated opinion—never would have. As late as the 1860s, leprosy was held to be somehow transmitted along hereditary lines: an awful curse, to be sure, but by its nature limited in the number of victims it might attack.

In the two decades after Hansen discovered *Bacillus leprae*—

the period of Damien's life at Kalawao, his death, and his immediate posthumous fame—it was scientifically established in Europe that leprosy was not hereditary at all, but contagious. Damien's own case, in fact, was used as prime evidence of contagion at work. A growing fascination with his life turned to horror at his approaching death, and this translated itself into a general consternation about what leprosy might do to other white men.

For most Europeans, consideration of the disease had not really been urgent since the Middle Ages, when leprosy had retreated from the white man's continent, persisting in epidemic form only in isolated pockets to the extreme north and south, especially in Norway and the Mediterranean countries. In the non-Western world, however, and especially in the tropics, the disease continued to be a widespread scourge: white men simply were not conscious of it. But, as the European imperialists of the nineteenth century continually expanded their dominion, it became only a matter of time before leprosy was brought once more within the white man's imperium—close to home in a new way, so to speak.

Even then, as long as Westerners could comfortably maintain that leprosy was hereditary, and at the same time primarily a disease of the dark-skinned, the primitive, the poverty-stricken, living their mean lives and dying their sordid deaths well away from the great and flourishing centers of Western civilization, there was no cause for alarm. But if leprosy was in fact contagious, and if—as Damien's life and death among the Hawaiians seemed to show—the contagion was capable of passing between races, from dark-skinned man to white-skinned man, then perhaps Western imperialism was creating an empire of leprosy, in which Westerners themselves might be consumed.

"Half a century of territorial conquest," wrote one Britisher from the heart of the greatest empire of all, "commercial enterprise, and colonization scheming, with their foreign labour importations from every quarter of the globe where leprosy exists, has revived the belief that the malady is contagious—a belief that goes on extending every day the more we know about it." There had never been such a movement of goods and peoples across the earth and its oceans. In the midst of it all, imperialism was building up a kind of free trade in disease. Sugar and bananas handled by leprous West Indians; tea and ginger from China; codfish from New Brunswick; rags from countries bordering the eastern Mediterranean—anything and everything unloaded on the docks of the home countries might be contaminated. Worse, foreign-born seamen themselves might bring the dreadful disease ashore. The "Indian lascar" or the "coolie" would surely find his way from the waterfront to some den of "insanitary promiscuity" in the city, a place of the kind that had "always been a favorite starting point for foreign epidemic invasions from cholera to pest, and must afford a ready passport to leprosy." Lazarus, covered with sores, licked at by dogs, was crossing the world to lie at the rich man's gate.

Not surprisingly, there was a moment of panic, in which public and private fears were merged. Empire was pictured as a powerful, self-confident man stricken, if not by disease, then by the awful fear of it—as if the white man's hand so firmly taking hold of all the world had picked up a taint capable of infecting the whole body.

The rich man of the West suddenly found himself beleaguered in a war he had not expected to have to fight. "Militarily speaking, the enemy has been long within the lines, and no danger has been till now suspected." One response was to invoke power, the same sort of power that had created empire in the first place. But for all that "repression" and "control" were conjured, nothing in nineteenth-century colonial administrative practice suggested a way to cure empires of leprosy, any more than nineteenth-century medical investigation succeeded in finding a way to cure individuals. Colonial officials might arrest and segregate the diseased, count up numbers of deaths, and write reports. Doctors and nurses might bandage sores. Researchers might experiment: Hansen and others went so far as to inoculate themselves with leprous material to see if they could find out how the disease was transmitted. They did not succeed. Leprosy would not be repressed; it continued to control its own territory; it threatened, indeed, to extend its dominion.

If the disease would not reveal itself to science, much less yield to political authority, then the imperial world would somehow have to come to terms with it in all its repulsiveness. The best way —the only way—seemed to be to cloak it in religion, cover it with faith. The Christian missionary, after all, with his special vocation, might penetrate farther into the mystery of leprosy than any doctor or government official. Crossing into leprous territory to treat with those who lived and suffered there, offering the love of Christ as redemption from the shame and squalor of heathenness and its diseases, the missionary became the conscience of the materialist age of expansion. If nothing could be done to heal the leprous body, at least the leprosy of the soul might be cleansed.

And so Damien appeared to many of his contemporaries in Europe as the most benign of imperialists, a man who went on behalf of his civilization to the ends of the earth, to do good among dark-skinned unfortunates there. The kingdom he sought to extend was that of Christ, and on its tragic frontier he died.

IV

One of the triumphs of empire was its communications system, putting the different parts of the world more readily and closely in touch than ever before. Disease might make use of this ease of access to travel the world in the nineteenth century; but information—news—moved even more quickly. In 1889, something that happened in mid-Pacific could be known in Europe—if it was worth knowing—within a month. The word of Damien's death on April 15 was brought from Kalawao on Molokai to the port town of Honolulu on the island of Oahu. From there it went by steamship to San Francisco, where the newspapers had it on May 9. The telegraph took the story overland to New York in time for the

papers of May 10; and the London press got the details from the
Atlantic cable the next day.

The *Times* of May 13 carried a leading article linking the moral
drama of Damien's life and death with the imperial theme of uplift
accomplished in far places by Europeans and observed approvingly from a distance by other Europeans. The settlement at Kalawao, which might have been no more than "a scene of loathesome
and despairing riotousness," had been transformed by the vision
of Damien into "nothing less than a model colony. He was not
content that it should simply not be a moral sewer; it was to be an
ideal society, fitted to be a pattern and an example throughout the
Pacific. He insisted that life should be upright and pure, and that
the brand of leprosy should be turned into a cross of honour."
Damien's vision, indeed, had "invited the gaze of the world," and
the diseased of Kalawao had "worked and lived since he came
among them with the invigorating sense that they were no longer
hidden away in darkness. . . . If they needed more than the narrow
resources of Molokai or the pity of Hawaii could yield, they could
tell their wants in a voice which for years had thrilled through the
hemisphere."

The settlement doctor's deathbed photographs turned out to be
well conceived after all—the nearest thing, indeed, to an inspira-
tion. The Hawaiian government, regarding the pictures as "highly
sensational and objectionable," wanted them suppressed down to
the last one. But they were not to be suppressed. They sold widely
in Honolulu; and on the basis of this encouragement to pious
commerce, they were printed up "in large numbers" to be sent
abroad with other earlier photographs of Damien. Thousands of
Londoners bought copies; and when they were displayed in Bir-
mingham, so many people came to crowd against the shop windows that police had to be called to clear the streets.

This might have been nothing more than the typical moment
of notoriety commanded by, say, a spectacular murderer at his
execution; or a suicide who left an instructive message; or the
victim of an unlikely and interesting accident—anyone who hap-

pened to catch the public fancy by the gruesome manner of his leaving life. The *Times*, however, was ready to grant the dead priest, in advance, far more than a moment's hold on the mind of the man in the street. Damien, said the editorial writers, was in his life and death "one of the noblest Christian heroes," who had "well earned both his rest and a beatification which no probation of sixty years is needed to confirm." The man of the moment, then, was also the incarnation of all that was timelessly good in his faith —the very saint of his age.

V

Europeans of the late nineteenth century could be led willingly enough to want a saint such as Damien—partly, at least, because they could watch the working-out of his fate from a secure distance. In the days of his fame he was adequately remote, never closer to his European admirers than the far side of the earth. Dead, he became even more consummately a sainted figure. People could marvel in safety at his photograph, assured that at least this one leprous form would never rise to touch and disconcert them. And the press could proceed with its popular beatification, using the rhetoric of sanctity to abstract Damien from time and place, elevating him from history to eternity.

Closer to where he died, in the Hawaiian Islands, Damien had been appraised differently, this time by another man of God: the Reverend Doctor Charles McEwen Hyde of Honolulu, a Protestant clergyman, an American—a New Englander—middle-aged, eminently respectable, well regarded, well housed, well connected, influential for good among the white businessmen of the capital. Dr. Hyde, in his own mind no less than Damien a frontiersman of the West's imperial Christian conscience, had strong opinions about the quality of Damien's sanctity; and he was not unwilling to make his views known upon request. In the midst of the chorus of praise that followed Damien's death, an acquaintance of

Dr. Hyde named H. B. Gage, also a Protestant clergyman, wrote from California asking for a balanced and reliable judgment on the phenomenon. "Dear Brother," wrote Hyde, "In answer to your inquiries about Father Damien, I can only reply that we who knew the man are surprised at the extravagant newspaper laudations, as if he was a most saintly philanthropist. The simple truth is, he was a coarse, dirty man, headstrong and bigoted. He was not sent to Molokai, but went there without orders; did not stay at the leper settlement (before he became one himself), but circulated freely over the whole island (less than half the island is devoted to lepers), and he came often to Honolulu. He had no hand in the reforms and improvements inaugurated, which were the work of our Board of Health, as occasion required and means provided. He was not a pure man in his relations with women, and the leprosy of which he died should be attributed to his vices and carelessness. Others have done much for the lepers, our own ministers, the government physicians, and so forth, but never with the Catholic idea of meriting eternal life."

In other words, Damien's reputation was so much puffery: he was really nothing but a fraud and a lecher who brought his disease upon himself and deserved his death. Gage decided that all this ought to be more widely known. On his own initiative, and without consulting Hyde, he arranged to have the letter printed verbatim in a Protestant periodical in San Francisco. Not surprisingly, Hyde's strong language was picked up for reprinting elsewhere. Within a few months, his letter was in the papers as far away as Sydney, on the other side of the Pacific, where some months later again, early in 1890, it came before the eyes of Robert Louis Stevenson, who happened to have a profound personal interest in the subject.

Stevenson was just then at the high point of his popularity as a writer, a world figure, as widely known and as affectionately regarded as any author in the English language. In his lifelong battle with tuberculosis, he was at a low point; and this was what had brought him to the Pacific—he was traveling in search of a climate. He had spent several months in the Hawaiian Islands, and some weeks after Damien's death he had visited Kalawao: one notable sufferer interested in the fate of another. Stevenson too was incurably ill; his lungs were being eaten away; he strained for breath and coughed blood. At about that time, writing to a distant friend also isolated by poor health, Stevenson remarked: "There are Molokais all over the world." He carried his own with him. In the midst of life, he was in death; and Kalawao, morbidly fascinating to him as to others because Damien was newly buried there, moved him to his depths.

For this reason if for no other, Dr. Hyde's letter would have enraged Stevenson, who, bearing his own miseries superbly well, still did not like to see the worthy suffering of others devalued. With this apparition of a man named Hyde in his life, other, fiercer things stirred too. There was a kind of word magic at work. The piece of writing that had made Stevenson famous, not so many years before, was a short novel about a man who presented to the world a solid exterior and yet harbored an interior being of crawling horror. Stevenson called his story "Dr. Jekyll and Mr. Hyde." The theme was that of virtue subject to a metamorphosis capable of destroying body and soul in grisly and uncontrollable awfulness. Stevenson had dreamed the plot; and he was led to acknowledge parts of his waking self in the ferociously divided personality of the fiction. Now, as if in a waking bad dream, here was another Hyde rising to confront him—not a Mr. this time, but a presumptuous Dr., parading a self-congratulatory respectability and simultaneously alleging the most dreadful delinquencies in Damien, whose soul, so it seemed to Stevenson, was consumed by goodness just as his body was eaten by leprosy.

In the light of the letter to Gage, Dr. Hyde could hardly appear to Stevenson as anything but a monster of virtue, the basest perversion of a true man of God. The fiction of Dr. Jekyll and Mr. Hyde had been drafted in three days of nonstop work. Now, with the letter of Dr. Hyde before him in Sydney, Stevenson locked himself in his room and took up his pen. He was writing to kill

Hyde, on paper at least; to be rid of this being who degraded "better men" to his own level. "With you," he declared, "I rejoice to feel the button off the foil and to plunge home." In one growling, hair-tearing session, Stevenson put on paper a six-thousand-word polemic. Without informing Dr. Hyde (in which he was like Gage), he had it printed at his own expense in Sydney as an Open Letter; and then sent off copies to Honolulu, and others to Scotland and England, for reprinting in the press.

Stevenson half-expected Hyde to sue him. This did not happen; and so the Open Letter went in pursuit of Hyde's own words around the world. The affair fed on itself—an attack by one minister of God upon another, followed by a famous novelist's defense of a dead man who could not defend himself: a man twice martyred, once by leprosy, once by slander, and now urgently in need of vindication in this world if not the next. If there had ever been for Damien a possibility of decent obscurity in death, it was from then on conclusively denied him.

VI

Dr. Hyde had called Damien a "coarse, dirty man, headstrong and bigoted." "Coarse"—that might well have been so, Stevenson conceded in his Open Letter; but not all saints were refined. If Damien was "dirty," he was dirty among the victims of leprosy rather than clean at a safe distance. To be "headstrong" was to be strong of head; Stevenson added "strong of heart" and thanked God for such strengths in Damien. The "bigot," the Catholic, was a man who believed in his own religion "with the simplicity of a peasant or a child," the point being that "in him, his bigotry, his intense and narrow faith, wrought potently for the good, and strengthened him to be one of the world's exemplars and heroes." Merely by going to the settlement and staying, Damien guaranteed reform, because "public opinion and public interest landed with the man at Kalawao." As for the gossip of sexual immorality, the insinuations were disgusting in themselves, but not nearly as disgusting as Dr. Hyde was for repeating them.

"In how many points of fact we are at one," Stevenson remarked in a passage of relative calm, "and how much our appreciations vary." "There is something wrong here," he concluded, "either with you or me." And since it was Stevenson's hand that held the pen, Dr. Hyde would be the one impaled upon the point of moral right.

Stevenson saw in Hyde (and by extension in his fellow Protestants) a double failure of charity. "Your church and Damien's were in Hawaii upon a rivalry to do well: to help, to edify, to set divine examples." Hyde had, "in one huge instance," failed, and Damien succeeded. This in itself was not unpardonable: "We are not all expected to be Damiens; a man may conceive his duty more narrowly, he may love his comforts better; and none will cast a stone at him for that." But then for Dr. Hyde to vilify the dead Damien —that *was* unpardonably unchristian. "I marvel it should not have occurred to you that you were doomed to silence; that when you had been outstripped in that high rivalry, and sat inglorious in the midst of your well-being, in your pleasant room—and Damien, crowned with glories and horrors, toiled and rotted in that pig-sty of his under the cliffs of Kalawao—you, the elect who would not, were the last man on earth to collect and propagate gossip on the volunteer who would and did."

Just the same, the printing of Hyde's letter had perhaps actually accomplished something, so Stevenson observed: it had opened the way for a discussion of Damien the man. Until Hyde wrote, Damien had been "too much depicted with a conventional halo and conventional features." If only Hyde's letter turned out to be "the means of substituting once for all a credible likeness for a wax abstraction," then the world might finish by owing him something despite himself.

To be sure, the bounds of controversy were set wide enough apart—wax abstraction as against leprous lecher; there was room between for any number of different representations. To begin with, there was the general problem of finding a way to look steadily at leprosy, somehow arriving at a sensible, humane alternative to either blind revulsion or uncritical sympathy. And certainly, as long as the two letters of Hyde and Stevenson were current, it would be hard to look at Damien without first looking at what had already been said about him by the two partisans, one generous, the other notably less than that, neither of whom had necessarily got all his supposed facts correct. All this merged itself with the eternal difficulty of reconciling, in a single human, the aspect of a saint with the attributes of a man. For Stevenson, who in contesting Hyde's worst allegations never insisted upon a waxy flawlessness in Damien, the way to do it was simply to let the truth be gathered and assessed. Then it might be recognized, in a harmony rising above contradictions, that Damien's "imperfections" were no more than "the traits of his face, by which we know him for our fellow." There was something hopeful in the thought, for all men as for the "leper-priest"; because, as Stevenson said, if Damien was indeed a man, "with all the grime and paltriness of mankind," he was still "a saint and a hero all the more for that."

CHAPTER TWO

I AM GOING
IN
YOUR PLACE

I

Damien was his name in religion. He did not acquire it until his twentieth year. Born on January 3, 1840, he was baptized Joseph, youngest son and seventh of the eight children of Frans and Anne-Catherine De Veuster, small farmers with land and a house of modest substance at Tremeloo, a village near the provincial city of Louvain in Belgium.

The De Veusters were Flemish-speakers, rural people with neither especially broad horizons nor high worldly expectations. The father, Frans, was an adequate provider, and by the standards of his time and place an adequate Christian as well, meaning that he was a Catholic who confessed and went to communion perhaps four times a year. The mother, Anne-Catherine, was more devout, more intimately involved in religion; and the children, Joseph among them, took homely instruction in holiness from her. She kept a book of saints' lives about the house, an impressive volume, two feet by eighteen inches, written in Old Flemish and printed in gothic characters. It fascinated the children; and they would often insist that she stop work and read aloud to them, especially stories of hermits, devoted Christians who turned their backs on the world, and ancient martyrs, ready to suffer death for the faith.

Farm and Church, rusticity and religiosity—Joseph grew up watching his brothers and sisters make their accommodations with these two worlds in one. Three of the De Veuster children before him, two girls and a boy, chose to give their lives to the Church;

Joseph's own religious vocation was the fourth and last in the family.

When he was only three, the oldest of his sisters, Eugénie, aged seventeen, decided to prepare for life as an Ursuline nun. At four, Joseph himself wandered away from a noisy *kermesse*, a country fair, to which his parents had taken him, and was found, after some mildly anxious searching, all alone in a church, praying before the altar.

He had his share of childish sociability and competitive playfulness, clinging with other small daredevils to the back of horse wagons passing through the village and being jolted off onto the rough road, skating on thin ice along the frozen winter river and once nearly falling through. He had as well something of a taste for solitude and stillness, and when this came over him he would go off into the fields and sit all day with the shepherds and their sheep. He was ready to put himself out for others; he would go without sleep all night nursing a sick cow for a widow neighbor. He was open to being made a fool for childish charity, giving up his school lunch to a young man who turned out to be as much a confidence trickster as a beggar.

At the age of thirteen, Joseph was big and strong enough to do a day's work on the farm; and, being considered adequately educated for that, he was brought home from school. It was expected that his life would follow much the same path as his father's: work in the fields, and a certain amount of travel to buy supplies and negotiate the sale of crops.

At about the same time, his studious brother Auguste, older by less than three years, with whom he had once played at being hermits in the forest, left Tremeloo to become a seminarian in a religious order. The next year, Eugénie died of typhus in her Ursuline convent; and another of Joseph's sisters, Pauline, his favorite, prepared to take her place among the Ursulines. When Joseph was seventeen, Auguste began his novitiate under the religious name of Pamphile, in the Congregation of the Sacred Hearts of Jesus and Mary at Louvain.

Joseph worked on the farm for five years. His body was growing into its man's shape and strength, stocky, strong, healthy, apparently inexhaustible. He was a more than efficient farm boy; but it was turning out that the hard labor of the fields did not use him up, or rather did not fulfill him. Farming was not the right kind of work for him; it was not what he really wanted his life to mean. He was, in fact, already testing the daytime toughness of his body against the nighttime sensitivity of his soul. His mother discovered that he was putting a hard board in his bed each night, refusing himself the indulgence of comfortable sleep, practicing a silent mortification of the flesh.

In the spring of 1858, when Joseph was eighteen, he left home temporarily, to go back to school, this time under French-speaking masters in the town of Braine-le-Comte, with the idea—his father's idea—that a little more learning would be useful in the business of dealing in grain. The aging schoolboy approached his new studies as he did everything else, conscientiously. At the same time he was getting ready, now that he was away from his parents, to make a test of himself, part of his passage from boyhood to manhood—from being the seventh of eight children to being himself. He was beginning to ask serious questions about youthful familial obedience, and was arriving at new answers about ultimate allegiance, just as his older brother and his two Ursuline sisters had done. There was hardly a time just then when he did not have something serious to think about in relation to faith, through their example. Auguste, Brother Pamphile, was well along in his novitiate with the Sacred Hearts Fathers; Pauline was ready to take her vows as a nun. Joseph wrote home to his mother and father in a mood of respectful urgency, pointing out that Pauline had had "the happy advantage of accomplishing the most difficult task to be undertaken on earth." "I hope," he went on, "that my turn will come to choose the road I must walk. Would it be impossible for me to follow my brother Pamphile?" And, to make the personal immediacy of the issue known to his parents, he underlined the words *my turn.*

He spent the summer of 1858 learning more French, this time with Pamphile at Louvain, within the walls of the monastery of the Sacred Hearts. Back at Braine-le-Comte in the fall, he listened to a priest preach a persuasive mission; and what he heard strengthened his conviction that his religious vocation was real. He stayed up at night a great deal, praying. Eventually, putting together his appetite for hard physical work with his urges to self-denial, solitude, and silence, he decided that he would become a Trappist. Pamphile spoke against this and in favor of his own Congregation; and without hesitation Joseph changed his mind.

His choice for the Church was made. If the formal decision waited, in a sense, upon the ratification of his parents, who were responsible (as Joseph said repeatedly in his letters home) for everything he was and might become, still he had already redefined for himself the question of what he should do with his life, where he must put his loyalties. He was on the verge of crossing from the farm to the Church, abandoning a worldly occupation for a religious vocation, leaving one family for another, setting about not his father's but his Father's business.

This was what Eugénie and Pauline and Auguste had done before him; and no doubt Joseph did it in part to be like them. But he felt his vocation to be passionately his own, one that he was born for. Even more, if he wanted his own way for his own passionate reasons, he was sure they were God's reasons too. He was confident enough of this to use God to threaten his parents (and particularly his father, who wanted him for the farm) if they should attempt to hold him back. Do not stop me, he wrote on Christmas Day, 1858, "because to forbid your son to follow the will of God in choosing a condition of life would be an ingratitude that would bring down cruel punishments on you. Are you not afraid of making an irreparable mistake if I lose a vocation for which God has destined me since my childhood, which would make me unhappy forever? Because, you know, the choice of a life to which God calls us decides our happiness after this life. So my vocation has nothing in it to make you sad."

The De Veusters really had no choice but to agree. Pamphile had already written to Joseph saying that the Sacred Hearts Fathers would certainly accept him, and that discussions with the superior at Louvain should not be delayed beyond the first of the new year, so that Joseph's novitiate could begin immediately. Joseph decided not to go home from Braine-le-Comte to Tremeloo. He went directly to Louvain; his father met him there, and left him with Pamphile at the monastery.

Joseph's new life, *"my turn,"* was of course not his alone. Pamphile, part of the old family, was at Louvain, representing the continued presence and perhaps the reassurance of shared origins. For the moment, at least, the younger brother found himself still following in the footsteps of the older. But with Joseph, brotherly emulation quickly became a kind of holy competition. In the new family, the Congregation of the Sacred Hearts, Joseph was to use his brother at first as a point of reference, but then more and more as a point of departure, with his own achievement being measured by the distance between them.

II

Joseph, admitted to the Congregation as a postulant, was not regarded as a suitable candidate for the priesthood. His education was considered wanting. His command of French, the language of the Sacred Hearts Fathers, was no more than adequate for everyday affairs; as for Latin and Greek, the languages of theological discourse, he had none. A place was found for him among the choir brothers, whose duties included the daily singing of the Holy Office, and who might be assigned, depending on aptitude, to teaching, secretarial work, the care of chapels and infirmaries, or manual labor. On February 2, 1859, Joseph took the religious habit under the name of Brother Damien.

He was by no means unintelligent. In his own way he was very thoughtful. He was capable of sustained hard work. And above all, he wanted to be what his brother seemed certain to become—a priest. So when Pamphile, perhaps not altogether seriously at first, offered to teach him some Latin, Damien responded enthusiastically, and covered so much ground in such a short time that his superior, impressed, reconsidered the limited designation of choir brother and gave him permission to study for the priesthood.

Damien, like Pamphile before him, was committing himself to several years of preparation. After he completed his postulancy, he would begin a novitiate of eighteen months, during which he would learn the life of the Sacred Hearts Fathers. The last few months of this period would be spent in France, where he would take the binding vows of the Congregation at the mother house in Paris. Then he would return to Louvain for the prescribed ecclesiastical studies, a year or two of philosophy, three or four years of theology. After that, eventually, he would be ordained a priest, and assigned a field of work.

In these first years within the Congregation, as he passed from his late teens to his early twenties, Damien's qualities as a young man and a man of God began to define themselves. Damien the student was modest, occasionally daunted by the dazzle of better-endowed men, but industrious, eager to learn, able to cope in his own way with what his teachers put before him. It was not in him to become a true scholar: if there was an intellectual in the De Veuster family, it was Pamphile. Damien had not much taste for the abstract. With him, things to think about were often turned into things to do. Once, after a conference, he carved the key words of the discussion into his wooden desk top to give them the texture of reality—Silence, Recollection, Prayer.

Life generally in the Congregation delighted him. The rituals of the Sacred Hearts moved him deeply; at prayer, he overflowed into audible sighs. Day by day, he found a great deal to be openly happy about; he laughed so much, indeed, that Pamphile thought it wise to caution him against excess. The laughter was, as much as anything else, the natural overflow of a physical vitality more than able to meet the demands being made upon it. When he and his colleagues went on pilgrimage at midnight to the shrine of Our Lady of Montaigu, and everyone slept early against the walk that would last till dawn, Damien stayed up all night. He would take his weekly night watch of adoration before the altar at the inconvenient hour of two or three in the morning, and not feel the need to go back to bed afterward. At mealtime, he chose to eat at the second sitting, when food tended to be short; and he gave up his share of meat to others uncomplainingly.

He had physical resources he knew he could rely upon. His body, well put together, was perhaps his greatest asset. He was by no means handsome: shortish—about five feet eight and a half inches, heavy-set—a hundred seventy-five pounds, broad-featured, somewhat pale-skinned, more than a little short-sighted, and more so in one eye than the other. But people were struck by his physical presence. He was somehow attractive; he glowed with health. And with amiability. It was easy to like him; he was pleasant company, not self-important or overbearing. If he was sometimes a little too impulsive for total decorum, his impulses were seen as simple and good. The one thing that always upset him was to hear the novices arguing among themselves; that, he said, was unworthy of servants of the Sacred Hearts.

He was not considered a complex person. *"Le bon petit gros Damien,"* the others called him, meaning that he was a good young man, stout and strong physically and temperamentally, and perhaps a trifle thick. They did not look for difficulties with him.

He shared sleeping quarters with his older brother; and Pamphile, waking at night, would find Damien's bed empty. His younger brother was continuing the old mortification of sleeping hard, on the floor, rolled up in a blanket.

III

Each member of the Congregation of the Sacred Hearts of Jesus and Mary and of Perpetual Adoration of the Most Blessed Sacrament of the Altar was pledged to imitate the life of Christ in four ways: His childhood, by education; His hidden life, by adoration, half an hour regularly each day and one hour a week at night; His apostolic life, by preaching and missionary work; His crucified life, by mortification and penance. In the fall of 1860, Damien, having completed his novitiate, was ready to take the solemn step of professing his vows as a full member of the Congregation. His earlier passage, from the farm to the Church, had brought him to a spiritual point of no return. Now he was to pass irrevocably from an old to a new life of poverty, chastity, and obedience.

For this ceremony of transition, the Sacred Hearts chose to borrow from the funeral rites of the Church: candlelight, smell of incense, touch of holy water, sound of chanted prayer, solemn silence, and the insistent, overmastering presence of death. With the other professing novices, Damien prostrated himself before the altar and was covered with a black mortuary pall. Lying dead to the world of his past—dead to his old self—he was sprinkled with holy water, and rose reborn into a state of existence consecrated to the service of God.

The ceremony took place on October 7 at the mother house of the Congregation on Rue Picpus in Paris. When it was over, Damien signed the official register. In his hand, the pen made strokes of unusual force and boldness, eye-catching, almost disconcerting in their deliberateness: more imposing by far than the modest personal inscription he had always used at the foot of his letters to his parents—more substantial, indeed, than any other signature set down that day in the records of the Sacred Hearts Fathers.

I V

Damien discovered in this ritual encounter with death a great part of the meaning of his own life. With the long, cloistered, inward-turned novitiate behind him, and the blackness of the mortuary pall cutting him off from the world of the moment, he had been brought close to what lay in the depths of his own personality, and at the bottom of the human condition in general. An awareness came upon him of the powers and problems of existence, of life and of death, and of how the two were inextricably linked; and he was the stronger for the sense of integration he experienced.

The ceremony of the burial pall, once accomplished, gave him a feeling of self-enlargement, of magnification, and not in his signature alone. He felt himself impelled, out of his new full membership in the Congregation, to speak authoritatively to his parents as a man of religion. It was as if his new closeness to the sacramental and teaching powers of the Church had reawakened for him, in his twenty-first year, the associations of his baptismal name, Joseph, earthly father of the Holy Family.

Writing from Paris at the turn of 1861 to wish his parents flourishing good health in the new year and a long, tranquil old age, he went on to speak of the death of one of his colleagues, and then to reflect on the general uncertainty of life. Perhaps, he mused, before the year was out a dear father, a well-loved mother, or even one of his brothers or sisters would be dead. For the sinful soul, the uncertainty of the morrow must produce some "sharp rendings of the heart." But for Christians or men of religion such as Damien, "who consider ourselves to be exiles here below, and who yearn only for the moment of the dissolution of our body to be able to enter our true home, there is, it seems to me, a subject of joy and contentment, in thinking that every moment we are closer to the supreme hour, when we will be able to hear these consoling words: Enter, blessed ones, upon the kingdom I have prepared for you."

Within a few months, as it happened, his grandmother died. The news came to him at Easter, while he was at table. "A sudden trembling seized all my limbs," he wrote to his parents. "I quite changed color and even had trouble keeping myself in the refectory. Happily, the first emotion not only calmed itself but even changed to joy by a small reflection I made upon these words—

Whatever God does is well done." His grandmother, after all, he said, was ripe for heaven; the family from which Damien had separated himself would be reunited with her there. "In order to obtain this blessing, dear parents, let us begin preparing ourselves today for a good death, let us not lose an instant more of the little time we still have to live."

The next time he wrote home, in the late summer, it was to urge his father, on the occasion of the grain harvest—the gathering-in of the year's work—to labor less over his crops and more over his soul. Sixty years of farm work was enough, said Damien. "I believe it would be as advantageous for your present life as for your future to separate yourself a little from worldly affairs so as to apply yourself better to the important business of your salvation, the only matter which is absolutely essential. As your youngest son, dear father, you will allow me to give you a piece of salutary advice, to contribute from my side as much as my position allows and to fulfill in relation to you a duty which to me is indispensable." Attend to the sacraments; pray day and night; do nothing except to the glory of God; meditate on His great love, on the gravity of sin, on death, on the last judgment, says the son to the father—and, he adds, to the mother too, "in my position as man of religion to the whole family."

The De Veuster family, of course, had another man of religion, senior to Damien. Pamphile was ordained a priest at Louvain in 1863, while Damien was still involved in his ecclesiastical studies. When Pamphile offered his first Mass before a congregation that included the De Veusters and their relatives, Damien, following along behind as always, but concerned as always to be the "man of religion" of the family, seized the opportunity after the service to distribute scapulars, tokens of devotion, to all who had assembled to wish Pamphile well. Pamphile, the mildest of young men, remarked that Damien had not said a word to him about doing anything like this, and had further told everyone that the scapulars were souvenirs from the new priest—which Father Pamphile found admirably tactful.

V

If, as Damien said, earth was no more than a land of exile for the man of religion, there was still the question of where he himself would pass his days until, in his words, the dissolution of the body freed him to enter his true homeland in heaven. It would not be the farm, that was settled; the beginnings of his imitation of Christ had already taken him away from Tremeloo. Preparation for the priesthood had led him to Paris, but that was not the place either: the city was intensely part of the world, and when he walked its streets the world was too much with him. Damien was notably unresponsive to the attractions of the metropolis and all its great workings. Paris had no charm for him, except momentarily, when he first arrived there from Louvain. After that it struck him as somehow vaguely "melancholy," and he left it to those more "inquisitive" than himself. Even the forest where he and the other novices took a weekly stroll was too much for him. The government was spending money to "beautify" the woods with avenues and little waterways; a thousand laborers were there every day; and on top of that all sorts of "ladies and gentlemen, horsemen and carriages . . . come at every moment to annoy and torment you."

By his own admission, Damien knew nothing of the world's affairs; he did not even read the newspapers. There was something in him that pulled him away from the civilization of great nations and capital cities, back beyond the more modest culture of villages and open fields, to the idea of the missionary life. The far side of the world was where he wanted to go, the distant and difficult country of hermits and martyrs.

Between the early expression of his wish to be a Trappist and his admission as a postulant in the Sacred Hearts, he had inquired about a place as a student in the American School at Louvain; and had he been accepted there he might have been sent later to Indian territory in North America. During his ecclesiastical studies, he used to pray every day before a picture of St. Francis Xavier, apostle of the East, the missionary supreme, asking for intercession so that he too might be sent on a mission. After he heard the Vicar Apostolic of Tahiti, Bishop Tepano Jaussen, speak during a visit to Paris on the need for Sacred Hearts workers in the missions of Polynesia, he wrote home to his parents: "Probably he will take some of us back with him. Would you be pleased if I was among them?"

VI

The question of his field of work was raised, urgently and decisively, late in 1863. The Sacred Hearts mission in the Hawaiian Islands needed workers. Among those chosen at Louvain to make the long journey to the Pacific was Father Pamphile. At twenty-six years of age he was to do, under his vows of obedience, what Damien, twenty-three and only at the stage of taking minor orders, ardently wished to do. The older brother was committed to leave Europe, the younger condemned to stay.

Arrangements were made; passage was booked for the end of October on a merchantman that would carry six Sacred Hearts priests and brothers and ten Sacred Hearts Sisters to Honolulu. At this point, an epidemic of typhus broke out in Louvain; and Pamphile, visiting the sick and dying to offer them consolation, caught the disease himself. Sickness—typhus indeed—had once before raised questions of life and death and religious impulse in the De Veuster family, when Eugénie had died in her convent and Pauline, Damien's favorite, had taken her place. Pamphile, this time, was not going to die; but he was not going to be able to leave on the Hawaiian mission, either: it was October already, and he could not possibly recover in time for the sailing.

The question was, who among the Congregation at Louvain might go instead. Once before, Damien had asked whether it would be possible for him to do what Pamphile had done, when it would be *"my turn."* He had put the question then to his parents; this time he asked it of the father-general of the Sacred

Hearts, the highest authority in the Congregation, bypassing his superior at Louvain and writing directly to Rue Picpus in Paris.

There was nothing disobedient in this. The Rule of the Congregation permitted it. Still, his superior was less than pleased to receive a notice directing him to release Damien to the Hawaiian mission. Damien was at table when the news came. The superior threw the letter down in front of him, saying, "You are young and very green, Damien, to start before receiving the priesthood." Damien did not stop to reflect on this. What mattered was that he was going where Pamphile could not. He hurried to his brother's sickbed, and Pamphile lay watching while, to his "utter astonishment," Damien kept waving the letter, "crying out in a transport of delight, 'I am going in your place.' "

For Damien, life had suddenly ceased to be a matter of following Pamphile—a younger brother entering the Congregation after the older, learning Latin from him, handing out scapulars at his first Mass. In the all-important imitation of Christ in His apostolic life, Damien was outdistancing Pamphile. It was now, most conspicuously, *"my turn."*

"Without waiting for dinner," wrote Pamphile, "he set off to say goodby to the family." There was very little time for that; just enough, in fact, for a last visit with his mother and a sister-in-law to the shrine of Our Lady of Montaigu, where Damien prayed to be allowed twelve years in the missionary vineyards. Then he went back to Paris for a three-day retreat, and finally made the long train ride to Bremerhaven and embarkation.

The wrench of severance from family and homeland was great, so Damien wrote. But Christ had said, "Go teach all nations," and He was especially with the missionary. Boarding ship, Damien felt strongly and consciously apostolic.

Before leaving Paris on his way to the coast, he had had his photograph taken, wearing a black habit, full-face, solemn, bespectacled, at twenty-three still very young-looking. He sent a large framed print to his parents, and another to Pauline. At his order, the photographer made up twenty small prints as well, and

Damien was very explicit in his instructions about where they were to go—one each to his parents for their prayer books, one each to his brothers at home on the farm, several to friends in the district, and ten to Pamphile to distribute among the colleagues Damien was leaving behind in the Congregation in Louvain. The unexpected evangelist wanted to impress upon those who knew him precisely what he was doing. The photograph showed him standing, crucifix held to his heart, closely imitating the attitude of St. Francis Xavier in the picture before which he used to pray every day in the hope of being made a missionary to far places. Damien was taking up the apostolic life, and he wanted to accomplish great things.

VII

Damien and his fellow missionaries were 148 days aboard ship between Bremerhaven and Honolulu, from October 23, 1863, to March 19, 1864. Their ship, the three-masted merchantman *R. W. Wood*, put in at no ports along the way. Christmas was celebrated with a High Mass not far south of the equator on the long Atlantic leg of the journey. Three weeks into the new year, the *R. W. Wood* was at the turning point of the voyage, Cape Horn, the hazardous passageway into the Pacific. Here, in 1843, a ship carrying a Sacred Hearts contingent to the Hawaiian Islands had been wrecked in a storm, drowning twenty-four missionary priests, brothers, and sisters, and their bishop. On board the *R. W. Wood*, in fine weather, the Office of the Dead was recited in their memory. Soon afterward, frighteningly high winds and waves came up; and for ten days of "true purgatory," in Damien's words, the ship was driven farther and farther south. Then abruptly the wind reversed its direction, from northwest to southeast; and after one more day of mountainous waves, the weather turned fine and the seas remained calm for seven thousand miles, from the South American coast to the warmth of the low latitudes, and north across the equator almost to the Tropic of Cancer and the Hawaiian Islands.

Honolulu, where the *R. W. Wood* dropped anchor in the early spring, was a busy enough little port town, center of the declining whaling industry of the North Pacific and the rising sugar business of Hawaii. It was the seat of an uncertainly independent native monarchy, and the metropolis for a hinterland population of perhaps sixty thousand Hawaiians, spread over eight major islands. The native population, exposed for less than a century to the ways of the Western world, was variously emancipated from the constraints of traditional life, or simply deracinated. The Hawaiian, living an inevitably disturbed village life in the rural districts, or huddled in the port towns in a kind of low approximation of civilization, looked backward to a traditional life of high barbarism, by the world's brutal standards reasonably elegant and generally tranquil. Looking forward, he could foresee with some certainty and no enthusiasm at all a loss of political and cultural independence at the hands of the white expansionists of the later nineteenth century. The capital of the kingdom had become the home of an increasing—and increasingly self-assertive—white population, mostly American.

For Damien, the voyage to the islands had been a considerable experience—seasickness, mortal fear now and then, monotony in long stretches, relieved by the warmth of religious fellowship. He had tried his missionary art on the crewmen of the *R. W. Wood*, mostly German Protestants, without success; and he had found ways to be useful to his colleagues, as sacristan and as recommender of improvised remedies for seasickness. The point of the journey, of course, was to arrive at the commencement of the work of a lifetime. Glad to have set out, glad to have endured, gladder yet to have made his longed-for landfall, Damien wrote to his family: "It would be impossible for me to tell you of the immense happiness of the missionary, after a voyage of almost five months, during which he was obliged to live with heretics and even unbelievers, who close their ears to the first words they are told about our Holy Religion, when he sees the new country which

he must water with his sweat each day in order to win these
uncivilized souls to God."

VIII

Hawaiians, as subjects for salvation, did not seem daunting. Damien's first impressions were scattered but pleasant: a great and
genial bustle at the waterfront, with endless handshakes for the
new arrivals from crowds of brown-skinned natives; a surprisingly
large Catholic cathedral in Honolulu, where Hawaiian communicants sang superbly at a welcoming Mass; good feeling everywhere.

One-third of the native population was already Catholic.
Damien would be going into the field among the largely uncon-
verted, as soon as he could be ordained. His studies at Louvain had
been cut uncomfortably short. Monsignor Louis Maigret, his
bishop at Honolulu, might well have preferred an already-
ordained priest. With things as they were, however, it seemed
more important to get workers into the field than to maintain ever
more polished students at the seminary. Damien and the two
student brothers who arrived with him were sent to the mission's
college at Ahuimanu not far from Honolulu to prepare for ordination within two months. Damien took his subdiaconate on March
26, then his diaconate; and on May 21 he became a priest.

As Father Damien, he wrote to his brother Father Pamphile
about the saying of a first Mass: the memory of such an occasion
at home, when Pamphile officiated; the actuality of his own experience in Honolulu; and the difference between the lives of priests
in the two places. "You will remember the sweet emotions you
experienced the day when you had the happiness to go to the altar
for the first time, and sacrifice the Holy Victim of our salvation. It
was the same for me, with one difference, because you saw about
you relatives and Brothers well used to the practice of religion,

while those who surrounded me were new Christians. . . . In spite of the hardness of my heart, it seemed to me that it would melt like wax, when for the first time I passed the bread of life to a hundred people there. Indeed I was impressed by this thought: that several of those whom I saw, dressed in white, coming modestly to the Holy Table, perhaps used to prostrate themselves before idols."

Writing to Pamphile, he used French, the language of the Congregation. In a letter to his parents, he used Flemish, the language of his first family, of his childhood. He was Father Damien now, robed in office, more than ever able to speak of himself as the man of religion of the family; yet for the moment he was very much the child of his parents again, by no means instructing them in their religious duties as he had taken it upon himself to do during his novitiate, but begging the aid of their prayers. With the mission field an immediate and pressing reality, his task seemed to him suddenly enormous, and he felt himself to be all agitation and insufficiency.

"Here I am a priest, dear parents, here I am a missionary in a corrupt, heretical, idolatrous country. How great my obligations are! How great my apostolic zeal must be! What purity of habits, what rectitude of judgment, what prudence in action I must show! Alas! dear parents, I who in my childhood saddened you so much by capriciousness unworthy of a Christian—how will I carry out the obligations of a missionary priest? Ah! do not forget this poor priest running night and day over the volcanoes of the islands in search of strayed sheep. Pray night and day for me, I beg you! Have prayers said for me at home, for if God withdraws his grace from me for an instant, I would immediately be plunged into the same mud of vice from which I want to rescue others." After all this, he concluded reassuringly: "Do not worry about me in the least, for when one serves God, one is happy anywhere." And he signed his letter as he would do habitually from then on: "J. Damien De Veuster, *prêtre-missionnaire*"—missionary-priest.

IX

When Damien spoke of running night and day across the volcanoes of the islands, he was exaggerating, but not greatly. He had
been assigned with his fellow voyager, Clément Évrard, also
newly ordained, to the island of Hawaii, the last of the group along
the chain to the southeast, and the biggest, with enormous mountain peaks and slopes housing volcanic fire pits, most of them
dormant or extinct, one still highly active. Much of Damien's first
parish was lava flow, ancient or recent.

The two young priests left Honolulu with Bishop Maigret early
in June, 1864, aboard the little steamer that ran somewhat erratically between islands. Maigret was to bless a church on the west
coast of Hawaii; and while he was there, he would see the recruits
to their stations on the east coast.

Along the way, the steamer put in at the island of Maui; and the
missionaries went ashore to visit some colleagues. Damien was
pleased at the prospect of being able to talk to priests with some
experience on the outer islands. As he said, sensibly, "The advice
of veterans is not to be scorned by a young missionary who, even
if he had studied and learned by heart everything the theologians
had written, often would not know how to act with Christians
newly emerged from barbarism."

Damien had just enough time ashore to say a Mass before the
boarding whistle blew. Not wanting to go without carrying away
some words of wisdom from the Maui priests, he "naïvely" (as he
said) offered up a prayer on the subject of this wish. As the steamer
was leaving the bay, it caught fire—not seriously enough to cause
loss of life, or even any real danger; still, it was damaged, and it
put back to port, out of action indefinitely.

Bishop Maigret wanted to get on to Hawaii. He had an appointment to keep, a church to bless. Damien, for his part, was happy
to stay where he was, talking to those experienced priests and
practicing the Hawaiian language. A week went by, then two, and
no ship going in the right direction put in. One Sunday, Damien

went out into the country by himself to say Mass, and heard confession there in Hawaiian for the first time. When he came back
the next day he found his traveling companions gone, picked up
by a passing schooner.

Damien was stranded for several more days. Finally able to get
passage, he was put ashore on Hawaii close to where the bishop
was to have blessed the church, only to find that Maigret had left
for the other side of the island, where Father Clément was to be
installed. Damien took another several days to catch up, covering
much of the distance on foot. Father Clément was settled, he
found; but once again Maigret was gone. Damien walked with a
guide another three and a half days to his own district. There at
last he came upon the bishop waiting with the two priests who
served districts adjoining Damien's on the east coast of Hawaii.

Damien's inadvertent introduction to Hawaii—hard and lonely
traveling over long distances—was a good one in its way. The
island was enormous—"as big as Belgium," Damien wrote to Pamphile, not too accurately: Hawaii was about four thousand square
miles in area, Belgium more than two and a half times bigger; but
then Damien had never had to walk across his homeland. The
landscape of the island was endlessly varied and beautiful, and
often very rugged. Damien's own district, Puna, one of the six
traditional land divisions, with a scattered Catholic population of
no more than about three hundred and fifty, was built up from the
outpourings of the active volcano Kilauea.

"I regret not being a poet or a good writer so as to describe our
new country for you," wrote Damien to Pamphile, just after he
arrived in Puna; and he went on to talk prosaically about how the
volcano worked. He had not yet seen it himself—even if Kilauea
erupting was one of the great sights of the world, he was not in the
field to see sights—"but from what the other Fathers say it seems
there is nothing like it in the world to give a correct idea of hell."
Especially amid the volcanoes, he told Pamphile—and himself—
he would need the pure love of God, the ardent zeal with which
the best of priests burned for the salvation of souls. When Damien

did get a chance to see the fire pit for himself, it was as he had been led to believe—"terrible." An old Hawaiian happened to be there making an offering to the traditional goddess of the volcano. Damien seized the opportunity of preaching him a "little sermon" on hell. As always, in Paris or in Puna, Damien's was a moral landscape.

X

A few months in Puna taught Damien at first hand what he had heard in advance from the Maui missionaries: that life in the field was nothing like life in the novitiate in Europe. Damien remarked upon this to the father-general of the Sacred Hearts late in 1864, in the annual letter which all members of the Congregation were duty-bound to write. "Instead of a tranquil and withdrawn life, it is a question of getting used to traveling by land and by sea, on horseback and on foot; instead of strictly observing silence, it is necessary to learn to speak several languages with all kinds of people; instead of being directed you have to direct others; and the hardest of all is to preserve, in the middle of a thousand miseries and vexations, the spirit of meditation and prayer."

Physically, at least, Damien found himself well equipped for the life he was leading. God, he said, had given him the strength of body to cover long distances without too much fatigue. One of his colleagues spoke of a "zeal" which "does not allow him to spend a whole day in one place. God grant that it lasts a long time." Father Clément Évrard, his closest but still distant neighbor, had an even more formidable area to cover: the double district of Kohala-Hamakua, something like a quarter of the whole island. He was not nearly as strong as Damien. Eight months there was as much as his body could take. He and Damien discussed exchanging posts, if their superiors would allow it. The idea was sensible; the formal obediences were given; and early in 1865 Damien left Puna for Kohala-Hamakua.

His new district was awesome in size: a thousand square miles, perhaps a little more. Again, the population was scattered: perhaps two thousand Hawaiians in all, fewer than half of them Catholics. To make a tour among them, preaching and hearing confession, would take six weeks at a time. This did not seem an impossible task to Damien. It did mean endless traveling. When a Hawaiian asked him where he lived, Damien pointed to his saddle and said, "This is my home." It was true enough. Again, his body was able to meet the demands made upon it. "I am always in the best of health," he wrote after almost two years in Kohala-Hamakua. "It seems to me that, physically, I am now perfectly adjusted to the active life of the missionary."

For the most part, his district had no roads. He got himself two horses and two mules, and used them as much as he could. But there were large areas where not even the animals could go. One of the villages where he had parishioners could be reached only on foot, by negotiating ten ravines one after the other, with a two-thousand-foot cliff to climb at the end. Another place was all but inaccessible by land, and difficult to reach over rough water. Once, Damien set off that way with two Hawaiian paddlers in a canoe: "nothing but a log with the middle dug out." Before they pushed off, he took the trouble to say an act of contrition—prudently enough, as it turned out. The canoe foundered and tipped them into the water, and they had to hold on to it and swim it back to land. That was sufficient for the moment. The next week Damien tried the land route. He rode part of the way, walked where he could not ride, swam across a neck of water, and arrived on the fourth day of traveling. In yet another place, he was resting on a mountaintop at night, tired and hungry, when his mule broke its tether and wandered off. Damien was fifteen miles from home in the pitch-black darkness; there were wild cattle about. He heard a dog bark, followed the sound, found a Hawaiian family in their hut, and stayed the night with them.

Wherever he was, he could depend on hospitality—any traveler could. The Hawaiians were more than generous with what little they had: perhaps a fish for supper, always the native staple *poi*, water to drink, a straw mat to sleep on. What Damien brought with him was not much more elaborate. He carried his church on his back, a portable altar which he set up with four sticks pounded into the ground and a board balanced on top with a cloth cover. A conch shell called the faithful; the Hawaiian trade winds blew the candles out during Mass as often as not; he heard confessions in the open, on a wooden stool.

At home—when he was there, in the thatch presbytery by his small wooden church in Kohala—his life was just as simple. "We eat what Providence sends us," he wrote to Pamphile. "The calabash of *poi* is always full; there is also meat; water in quantity, coffee and bread sometimes, wine or beer never. As I have had to work all week and cook on Sunday, you will excuse me if my hands are not as clean as yours, which do nothing, I suppose, but turn the pages of books. Sometimes the plates are not well washed, either. But what matter. Hunger and habit make us eat just the same. For dessert, we smoke a pipe. That finished, quickly back on the horse . . ."

With help from the faithful, Damien began to do some small farming. He kept sheep, pigs, and chickens. Bees gave him honey to eat and wax for candle making. Tobacco grew well, and coffee, and potatoes. Soon he was able to offer a surplus of his navy beans and kidney beans to the Sacred Hearts Sisters in Honolulu.

He was also a considerable builder of chapels. In the months he was in Puna, he and his Hawaiian helpers put up four small buildings where Mass could be said; and in the eight years he spent in Hamakua and Kohala, he almost always had one or another construction project in hand. Using the mission's limited budget, and raising money by selling his farm produce and asking for contributions, he negotiated for materials from Honolulu. In the field, he recruited as many Hawaiians as he could to haul cut and numbered planks up from the beach where a schooner would leave them, or to go into the highlands and log wood and drag it to the building site. He enjoyed hard labor; he carried the heaviest logs himself; he talked happily in his letters about his expenditure of sweat, about being a tool in the hands of the Lord. And he was sure the Hawaiians liked the church more for having helped to build it themselves on their own island.

The time he enjoyed as much as any in his life was when a church building was completed and his workers invited everyone to celebrate. "As it is the custom of the country to give a big feast after bringing an important work to a successful conclusion . . . my neophytes wanted to give one for their friends from the other districts, to match the hard work we did in building and finishing this church so well. Everyone was invited for the eve of the Epiphany. A good number of fat animals has been killed and cooked in the *kanaka* oven, that is to say, in red-hot stones. At a signal, the crowd goes to the church, which unhappily is too small to fit everyone in. After a short prayer, I give them a sermon adapted to the occasion. I praise them first for their courage in putting up a church for Jesus. I urge each one present to build another one privately in his own heart, where Our Lord will be pleased to dwell. After which I exhort them to fraternal charity toward the stranger Christians who have come from a distance. Finally I address a word to those who are not yet Catholics. Sermon and prayers over, everyone goes to the place prepared for the feast, all around the church, on the grass. Something like a thousand people are there to celebrate. As our *kanaka*, even the most civilized, always eat with their fingers, no trouble about knives and forks and the rest of a table setting. Everyone brings his own with him. Just like the ancient Romans, they eat on the ground, legs crossed like tailors: a very economical way. No use for tables, chairs, seats.

"As I had to prepare all my neophytes for communion the next day, I spent the best part of the afternoon in the confessional. There, the sincere conversion of several unworthy sinners gave me profound joy. The next day I was obliged to say two Masses: one in the morning for the communicants, and a High Mass as well, with music. Thus it is that the missionary, amid privation, sometimes experiences an access of satisfaction."

XI

Damien's superiors did not see much of him. Perhaps once a year the bishop would visit Hawaii; far less often, Damien would take ship back to Oahu and spend a day or two in Honolulu attending to some absolutely indispensable business—ordering lumber, say, for a new chapel. Then he would be gone again, back to the field. The bishop and his religious counterpart, the provincial of the mission, were always pleased to see Damien, if only for a short time—that "fine face, broad, glowing with health." And by and large they approved of his work. If they criticized him, it was for excess rather than for lack of zeal. Damien was a man of quick decision and action all round, a speedy builder and a speedy baptizer, and one or two of his plans and policies seemed to the leaders of the mission a trifle hasty.

On his first tour of his first district, Puna, Damien baptized thirty new converts, and in his years at Kohala-Hamakua the baptismal figures for his station were generally higher than any in the islands except for the major town of Honolulu, with all its parishioners and priests. It was said of Damien that if his own preparation for the priesthood had been slower and more demanding, he would have seen the need for more intensive preparation among his converts. On the other hand, what he did see day by day in the field only impressed him with the urgency of saving the Hawaiians —from themselves and from competing versions of Christianity.

The Sacred Hearts Fathers, after all, were not alone as missionaries in the islands. They were not even the first to have appeared there in the name of the Christian God. Protestants, New Englanders, had arrived in 1820. The Sacred Hearts followed in 1827. In the late 1840s a Mormon mission came to compete with them, and in 1862 an Anglican missionary diocese was founded at Honolulu.

The Protestants, with a head start and a record of determined work, still dominated the religious scene in Damien's day. If by the 1860s the first great period of New England evangelism was over, giving way to an attempt to form a Hawaiian native clergy, still the old New England mission family was active, politically powerful, socially assertive, influential in educational policy. The other denominations had to make their way as best they could, against this entrenched sect as against the residue of Hawaiian traditional religion.

The result was a considerably confused religious picture. "Every Sunday about ten o'clock," wrote a Sacred Hearts priest of Damien's time on Maui, "the minister of the Calvinist sect, a pure *kanaka* who did not invent gunpowder and electricity, rings his bell to say his anti-Mass. An English ritualist minister also rings his bell to celebrate his quasi-Mass. In my turn, I ring two at a time over the whole town to say at last the True Mass. . . . Unfortunate natives, in the midst of so many contradictory voices."

The Protestant leaders regarded the Sacred Hearts Fathers in particular as interlopers, and the early New England ascendancy over the ruling Hawaiian chiefs meant that the Catholics in their first years faced opposition which rose every so often to outright persecution of converts and expulsion of priests. Their right to remain and to preach and convert was established only in 1839, by the commander of a French man-of-war, at gunpoint. The first written constitution of the Hawaiian kingdom, published in 1840, contained a clause on religious toleration. But in daily practice open hostility continued into Damien's time—arguments over the acquisition of land for church use, the running of schools, matters of protocol and precedence on state occasions. Between white Protestant and white Catholic there was an apparently incurable lack of cordiality, with much deliberately imprecise name-calling back and forth, in private and in public—"Methodist," "Jesuit," "heretic," "idol worshiper."

Damien, a good child of his own Church, did not like Calvinists, and in the field he had to contend with them in strength. On his way to the island of Hawaii in 1864, he had been told to treat his mission as the very beginning of evangelization in the district. Things were in a sense even worse than that. There had been a

Sacred Hearts worker where Damien was going, but not for several years. Catholicism, barely rooted to begin with, was in decay, Calvinism in the ascendant, with all the teaching and practice that Damien found so abhorrent—"the poison of heresy"—the failure to kneel at prayer, the serving of a sort of bastard communion in which *kalo*, taro root, was used as bread and New England temperance ministers gave the Hawaiians water instead of wine to represent the blood of the Savior.

If history had given Calvinism a head start in the islands, several years in Kohala convinced Damien that things were working the other way, in favor of Catholicism. More and more the old generation of New England missionaries were retiring from the field. A number of them, and a greater number of their sons, were going into the profitable business of sugar planting. The native Hawaiian clergymen who replaced them were not nearly so formidable. Damien, who saw himself always as "on a battlefield," believed that if only the Sacred Hearts mission could recruit more priests, brothers, and schoolteachers for the islands, the majority of Hawaiians would "soon enroll beneath the standard of the Cross."

In the meantime, he took his sectarian pleasures wherever he could. There was a rocky cliff in Kohala, two thousand feet high —one of those ubiquitous barriers between minister and parishioner. The Protestant parson needed two hours to scale it. Damien, so he himself reported, could get to the top in forty-five minutes.

XII

When Damien was just a beginning preacher in the Hawaiian language, inclined every so often to be at a loss for words, he would cover the lapse by taking out his handkerchief and blowing his nose. This was typical of his good-humored resourcefulness: there were not many minor problems he could not solve in a quick, rough-and-ready way. As for his trick with the handkerchief, he did not have to use it for long. He studied Hawaiian, he said, with more enthusiasm than he had ever given to French or Latin or English. His first impression of the language of the islands was that it was simple enough, its five vowels and twelve consonants just strung together to make polysyllables. Soon he was reporting that he spoke like a *kanaka*, a native Hawaiian.

In this he was almost certainly deceiving himself. Very few white men would ever speak Hawaiian like a native. The Hawaiian language, in its fullness, was allusive and evocative and richly ambiguous in its symbolic associations. Damien's written Hawaiian, at least, like his written French and for that matter his written native Flemish, was serviceable, but no more. He was no subtle linguist, not even a reliable speller. Words for him were just another tool in the hands of the workman. Although Damien was pleased with his own linguistic accomplishments, he conceded at the same time that the Hawaiian assistants he trained as catechists could hold their audiences better than he managed to do.

It was true, nonetheless, that Damien got along well enough with Hawaiians. He wanted to, very much; and they were willing for it to happen, up to a point. Again, whatever closeness developed was a rough-and-ready one, a matter of simple sociability rather than any sophisticated or calculated crossing of culture by Damien. He was—for a *haole* among *kanaka*, a white man among Hawaiian commoners—very unassuming in his habits, a Westerner who, outside the special world of his church, did not stand upon the ceremonies of high Western civilization. Damien did not mind closeness with Hawaiians. He would sit on the ground and eat sticky, pasty *poi* out of a family calabash, something that very few American Protestant ministers would do. Damien was also a priest, and this completed—for him at least—a hierarchy of affectionate relationships. He liked Hawaiians for what they were, or rather for what he took them to be. "I like our poor *kanaka* very much, because of their simplicity, and I do all I can for them. In their turn they like me as children like their parents. It is by this mutual affection that I hope to convert them to God. For if they love the priest, they will easily love Our Lord."

This he wrote early in his ministry. Loving son to his parents in

his childhood, when familial affection was taken for granted, loving child of the Church in his adolescence, and lovingly obedient
in his young manhood to the father-general of the Sacred Hearts,
according to the Rule of the Congregation, he saw himself now as
Father Damien, loving parent of loving children, among them, of
course, adult Hawaiian men and women. When he left Puna for
Kohala-Hamakua, it was, he wrote, more of an emotional wrench
than leaving his own family at Louvain to come to the islands.

Over the years, Damien came to see more complexity in Hawaiians. He continued to conceive of them as children. They could be
led satisfactorily in matters such as church building; and there
were good times to be had in their company, when they feasted
on a church holiday, or sang beautifully during a High Mass. But,
Damien concluded sadly, there was another side to the Hawaiian
character, that of the bad child, so to speak: willful, perversely
disobedient, unteachable, perhaps even irredeemable. In deciding this, Damien was, of course, himself a child of his own century
and his own culture. He had no anthropologist's ways of getting
outside himself. He could watch from something of a distance
what went on in a Hawaiian village, and even go some way toward
understanding how a people could be caught between two cultures. Beyond that, he could only regret that Hawaiians chose to
go on being Hawaiian when he—and his Church—offered them
something better.

He was particularly taken aback by the open sexuality of the
native Hawaiian. His own life had led him to make his strenuous
man's body chaste for the love of God. In the traditional Hawaiian
culture there was little to inhibit free sexual self-expression; and
the natives of the nineteenth century, still in general an enthusiastically physical people, balked at Christian self-restraint. "Corruption," wrote Damien, "is so precocious among the young *kanaka!*
The children have scarcely learned how to talk before they know
more than a young theologian still has to find out. The parents take
not the least precaution in talking in front of them about all sorts
of things. They go so far as to explain to them all the infamous

ceremonies of ancient idolatry and other abominable pagan cus-
toms. From all that, you will easily understand our difficulty in
making Jesus Christ reign in these young hearts, so easily led
astray by bad example."

As with the children, so with the child-adults. "Let us suppose
you marry this year two young people. They live two or three
months in peace; then some little discontent crops up; they separate permanently. As neither one nor the other can keep chaste,
each one looks for some way to satisfy his bad impulses. But the
civil law forbids adultery. Hailed before a judge, they are fined a
hundred and fifty francs. There they are, reduced to a kind of
slavery for debt. After some long years, they get a government
divorce. Then, each one remarries as best he can. After which,
what priest could ever absolve them?"

The moral fall went all too often with a physical collapse. "All
too often, alas! out of the unruliness of our youth, come numerous
diseases. Scarcely have our *kanaka* reached the age of virility,
when already, in a good many, the feebleness of the aged appears.
If an illness occurs, there they are on their way to the other world
. . . and with what preparation? Sometimes none at all."

One thing which intrigued Damien in a melancholy way was
that the sick Hawaiian looked instinctively to traditional medicine
for a cure. Damien very rarely tried to describe the workings of
any part of Hawaiian culture; but the practices of the *kahuna*, the
specialist in the ancient arts of healing, were of unusual fascination
to him, and he spoke strongly and in detail about his understanding of what was involved. "The charlatan looks for the cause of the
disease not in the actual state of the patient, but in his previous
actions. Ordinarily it is an unfulfilled promise that brings one or
the other ancient divinity into the sick man's body. The god, called
aumakua, kills him little by little. Out of this comes terror, and
consent to the making of a sacrifice. This sacrifice consists of the
immolation of a pig or a chicken, with a certain intoxicating drink
which the doctor-priest offers first to such and such a god. Then
the sacrificial meats are eaten together, and strong liquor is drunk

with the sick man. Finally the doctor treats his patient with wild herbs."

To Damien, all this was nonsense. The Hawaiian *kahuna* was a charlatan, who knew "no more medicine than my horse." And yet the native healer's use of medicinal herbs was as sound empirically as that of any Western doctor of Damien's day. And the *kahuna* —like Damien himself—understood that a past act might have present consequences; that things of the mind, soul, and body were connected; that food and drink ritually offered and accepted might be spiritually fortifying; that sacramental ceremonies performed with priestly authority might be powerfully cleansing. That is to say, the *kahuna*, among his own people, was a true priest.

Hawaiians were sure at least that Hawaiian medicine was good for Hawaiians. Even Christian Hawaiians, Catholics, went to *kahuna*, and this was galling to Damien. The Catholic Church had its own moral diagnosis and a moral prescription for the ills of men. And, within his own priestly role as server of communion and hearer of confession, Damien drove his own healthy body to the limit, seeking out in others the presence of disease, moral and physical. The point was to cleanse and heal. But Damien could not always accomplish what he so fervently intended. Among his people, all too often, the practice of *kahuna* medicine in particular and the persistence of carnal Hawaiianness in general left the Catholic priest nothing to do but administer a forlorn deathbed baptism.

XIII

So it was not altogether surprising that Damien had what he called "black thoughts." These were made worse by his loneliness, his isolation, priestly and personal. In Puna, he had never had to go more than ten days without seeing a colleague; but when he went to work in Kohala-Hamakua, he was sentencing himself to two or three months alone at a stretch. It was too long, and Damien said so many times. Ordinary conversation with someone other than a Hawaiian, and confession, made to a fellow member of his Congregation—these were essential to the renewal of the spirit, the warding off of those black thoughts, that "insupportable melancholy."

The Congregation formally recognized the problem—priests should not be alone—and Damien quoted Article 392 of the Rule of the Sacred Hearts in his letters to his superiors at Honolulu, asking patiently and repeatedly for a companion. "Please plead the cause of the isolated priest of Kohala . . . it is too hard to go on like this."

The companion he wanted, so he said almost every time he raised the issue, was his older brother. From the beginning, he assumed that Pamphile's missionary vocation had survived the accidental circumstances of his displacement by Damien in 1863, and that his brother would follow him to the islands at the first opportunity. He went so far as to put Pamphile's name before his superiors at Honolulu, with the suggestion that they should call for him.

And yet at the same time there was something in Damien that liked the distance between himself and Pamphile, in miles, and in the contradiction of their lives, which could hardly have been more marked: the younger brother, laboring sweaty and dirty-handed on the lava flows of Hawaii; the older cloistered still at Louvain, where, long since recovered from the typhus that kept him at home in 1863, he had become something of a theologian, a scholar and a teacher, but hardly a doer, a physical man of action.

Damien liked to point out the contrast. His letters to Pamphile were the longest and the most detailed in his sparse man-of-action's correspondence; and it was rare that the matter of the missionary vocation failed to be mentioned. When, after a few years, Pamphile was still in Europe rather than on his way to Hawaii, Damien began talking almost as if his brother's life were an evasion of responsibility. This was said sometimes jokingly, sometimes sharply, in so many words: said again and again.

Damien, all his life, never stopped measuring himself against his brother; it was his way of seeing how far he had gone on his own.

Damien, in fact, was very deeply of two minds. He wanted his brother to be at one and the same time in the islands and in Europe; there and not there altogether. In a letter from Pamphile which arrived in 1867, about three and a half years after Damien left his homeland, came two photographs, one of his sister Pauline, one of Pamphile himself. "At first glance," wrote Damien, "I had trouble recognizing the face of my brother." But then, after "several moments of reflection," he said to himself "with inexpressible joy"—"It is the face of Father Pamphile."

In that letter Pamphile talked about a step forward in his scholarly career. He had been chosen to instruct novices. It was an honor, a sign that the Congregation valued his intellectual accomplishments. Damien's reaction, once he had read the news, was edged. He professed not to know if it was a matter for congratulation. "Instead of being a poor missionary among the savages, there you are raised in dignity." He limited himself to a remark about the "impenetrability" of the designs of Providence. "The best thing is to say unceasingly and with resignation, God's will be done. . . . One can do good anywhere." And now, he said, it is "my turn"—that phrase again—"to give you news of the Hawaiian mission." He spoke of coming across Pamphile's letter at a town on the coast while walking a day and a night to confession; of falling on his head in the dark on a new lava flow; of the difference between his own "hard and painful journeys" and the "pleasure trips" of the priest in Europe—"all this without however bearing you the least envy."

Pamphile continued to advance toward his doctorate in theology; Damien continued to work in the field, and to scratch the itch of his brother's nonappearance in the islands: "What is the good of coveting a doctor's bonnet at the expense of the poor *kanaka?*" If, as it seemed, Pamphile was never going to come to the islands, then, said Damien, he should at least be a missionary "in his heart," preparing novices who would have the character required: intrepid, self-reliant, self-sacrificing.

Pamphile never did come to the islands in Damien's lifetime. When, in 1868, Damien finally acquired a colleague to take Hamakua off his hands, leaving him only Kohala, it was not his brother but a young French priest named Gulstan Ropert. Father Gulstan followed the same track from Honolulu as Damien had done, coming down to Hawaii on a schooner, borrowing a horse, arriving in the district to find Damien away, waiting a week for his return. "Ah!" said Damien to him when they met, "I asked for my brother and you have come instead?" "But," said Ropert, who had a small joke to play, "don't you see that I am Pamphile, your brother? The voice may not be the same . . . but the clothes? Look whose they are." Ropert was wearing a soutane that had been made for Damien's brother, with the name of Pamphile sewn inside. "Oh!" said Damien, *"vox quidem, vox Gulstani, sed manus, manus sunt Pamphilii!"*—"It is only the voice of Gulstan, but the hands are Pamphile's." He was speaking from the Old Testament story of Jacob and Esau, about two brothers, very different in aptitude and temperament, who lived in eternal competition for the favor of an authoritarian father, with one ultimately supplanting the other.

XIV

In 1870 Damien fell ill, for the first time in the islands, with a fever that reduced him, as he said, to skin and bone. He recovered well, to his healthy weight of 175 pounds, and to his former strength, though he remained a little sensitive to bad weather. At thirty years of age, he was still *"le bon petit gros Damien."* That, at least, was how he chose to remember himself in his letters to the Sacred Hearts priests and brothers at Louvain. He kept writing to Pamphile, much the same letter once or twice a year, even though, so he complained, Pamphile did not write to him as often as he would have liked. To his parents he wrote only infrequently, leaving it to Pamphile to translate the brotherly letters written in French about the hardships of the field for their Flemish-speaking mother and father. When Damien did write to Tremeloo directly, it was mostly to reassure his mother in particular that he was happy and in good health.

The question of Pauline, his favorite sister, was worrisome to him. He kept the photograph of her that had arrived in Pamphile's letter early in 1867. Then another letter from Pamphile in 1869 said that Pauline was ill, very likely dying. Then nothing; in fact nothing from Belgium for almost three years. Damien wrote to Pauline in 1872: "Where are you then, dear sister? Have you already gone away to heaven? Not so fast, please!"

Not really knowing if Pauline was alive or dead, Damien told her about his work—how well dressed his Hawaiians were, able to read and write; soon, he said jokingly, they would be more civilized than Europeans. But as they were becoming civilized, so they were dying off. There was disease everywhere among them; death was harvesting more than birth was sowing; the population in his district was dropping all the time, as it was everywhere in the kingdom. The *kahuna*, the medical priests, were still influential. Damien could only hope that a good number of his Christians were dying well-disposed.

In this letter, written to someone who might herself be dead, there was a great deal of death. Damien, since the arrival of Gulstan Ropert, had what he wanted more than anything else, a companion and a confessor for the relief of the insupportable melancholy of isolation; still, the letter to Pauline ended with something very close to "black thoughts." "In general I have much vexation and little consolation. It is only by grace from above that the burden which the Good Lord has deigned to lay on my shoulders feels sweet and light. When sickness comes upon me I rejoice that my end approaches." He was thirty-two.

CHAPTER THREE

GOD'S
ATHLETE

I

In the spring of 1873 Damien made one of his infrequent trips away from Hawaii, to Wailuku on Maui, where a new church was to be blessed by Bishop Maigret. It was a big building, which had taken six years to complete; the priest in charge, Father Léonor Fouesnel, was proud of it. A good many of the other Sacred Hearts Fathers were there for the ceremonies. While they were all together, the bishop raised the question of the mission's responsibility to Catholics on the island of Molokai, and in particular to Hawaiians confined in the leprosy settlement at Kalawao. Molokai, visible on the horizon from Wailuku, was an out-of-the-way island, with a population of only about four thousand natives, a minority of them Catholic. The situation for the Church there had never been satisfactory, and was now—after forty-five years of the presence of the Sacred Hearts mission in the Hawaiian Islands—as bad as ever. Catholics on Molokai were able to see a priest only when one of the Fathers could find time to make a visit from Maui, which was rarely—perhaps no more than a few days in the year. It was not good enough, and the presence of the leprosy settlement made it worse: since 1866, the faithful had been living and dying there in desperate conditions, without the sacraments.

In 1872 a Sacred Hearts brother spent six weeks at the settlement, putting up a church, which was named for St. Philomena. The few-score Catholics at Kalawao used it for prayer, but they remained without a parish priest. Every time a visiting Father came back from Kalawao he brought with him pathetic pleas from the sick and deprived. In all conscience, something would have to be done. At the end of the year, Father Aubert Bouillon of Maui wrote to Bishop Maigret that he would go to Kalawao to stay unless the bishop forbade him. Maigret told him to remain where he was.

Talking over the difficult question of Kalawao with his priests at Wailuku, the bishop said that he did not want to order anyone to take up a post there. A priest owed his superiors obedience, but there were limits; and Maigret was hesitant about the cruelty of sending a missionary alone into such desolation and danger.

Four young priests, Damien among them, presented the idea that they might serve Kalawao in turn, staying a few weeks or months at a time. Maigret found this acceptable. Damien was ready to be the first to go. He and Maigret took ship from Maui, along with fifty leprosy victims and some cattle. Ashore at the settlement on the morning of Saturday, May 10, 1873, the bishop told the Catholics assembled there that they had their priest.

II

Like most of the other Sacred Hearts Fathers in the islands, Damien already knew about leprosy at first hand. He had seen the disease in the Kohala district in the late 1860s; some of his parishioners had already been sent to Kalawao. Damien had no reason to think that leprosy was curable, and it was his understanding that it was "very contagious." Confessing Hawaiians with visible signs of the disease, he had sometimes felt a kind of burning or itching on his own skin at the closeness of the contact. To go to Kalawao was to walk in the valley of the shadow of death; he realized that.

Looking back a few months later, he talked about experiencing an "unequivocal presentiment" about Molokai: leaving Kohala for the blessing of the church at Wailuku, he had heard "an inner voice" telling him that he would never be back. For him, this was unusual. He did not ordinarily hear voices or have revelations. He was not a mystic of that sort. Once, while he was on Hawaii, St. John the Baptist had told him in a dream where to build a church. Occasionally, on tour, he believed he had been led supernaturally to take a particular turning through the trackless country of Kohala, and had thus found a sick or dying man who needed him. For the most part, however, regarding himself as a tool in the hands of the Divine Workman, he did not expect Divinity to use his language in expressing its wishes or commands.

Providence it certainly was that he went to Maui to hear the bishop put his fateful questions; God's will it must have been that led him from Kohala to Wailuku to Kalawao—of all this he had no doubt. Beyond that, God had in a sense willed his whole life to be a preparation for Molokai.

His situation at the settlement would be exceptional—lonely, difficult, hazardous. The Church, in the early years of Christianity, had a name for men who went out of their way to serve God in isolation through singular hardihood—living in the desert, or climbing a pole and remaining there for years in prayer, quite apart from other men and yet mutely compelling their attention. Such notable self-mortifiers were called "athletes." There was in Damien something of the athlete: an aptitude for mortification, no doubt beginning as a private impulse but somehow expressing itself publicly. He had an appetite for doing good for God in difficult circumstances. If this meant that he would be noticed by other men—and inevitably it meant that—then, in all humility, he could not see that being noticed for God was a bad thing, so long as he himself took no credit. So he was quick to take Pamphile's place on the laborious voyage to the Hawaiian Islands, quick to replace Father Clément Évrard in the notoriously difficult district of Kohala-Hamakua. Indeed, his athlete's body was always doing spectacular things for God. Once, when he was still a student of theology at Louvain, and some workmen tearing down an old building belonging to the Congregation were afraid to climb a tall, decaying chimney, Damien went up alone and took it apart brick by brick, while everyone watched. Coming out to the islands on

the *R. W. Wood,* Damien followed the sailors into the rigging to
talk religion. Then there was the climbing of cliffs at high speed
in Kohala, ahead of the Protestant parson; and the carrying of
heavy logs—heavier than his Hawaiian helpers could manage—to
build churches on high places, where they would be seen by passing ships.

There was another cluster of associations in Damien's life which
had to do with athleticism and mortification, bringing together in
a religious context ideas of cleanliness and dirt, health and sickness, wholeness and putrefaction: what might have been called
the pathology of the athlete. The members of the order he had
chosen to join, the Sacred Hearts, were known familiarly as the
Picpus Fathers, after the street in Paris where the mother house
stood. The word *picpus* was obscure in derivation; traditionally, it
was supposed to have come from a time when some kind of plague
in the neighborhood attracted priests who treated the sores of the
sick: *piquer-pus, Picpus,* prick-pus. More ascertainably, the distinguishing practice of the Congregation, perpetual adoration at the
altar, was inaugurated at the mother house when it was founded,
in 1804–1805, close to the Picpus Cemetery, where thirteen hundred mutilated bodies lay—victims of the guillotine of the French
Revolution, in response to whose excesses the Congregation of the
Sacred Hearts was formed.

These associations, of course, were in the mind of every member
of the Sacred Hearts; but Damien was able to carry them unusually far into himself. When, as Joseph De Veuster, nineteen years
old, he renamed himself in religion, he chose to be called Damien,
after an ancient physician-saint, one of two brothers who went
among the sick and were martyred for Christ. The hero of the new
Damien was St. Francis Xavier, a name evoking that of St. Francis
of Assisi, who found the strange sweetness of God's spirit in the
embrace of a leprosy victim, and whose first substantial work was
the reconstruction of a church at Assisi, the church of St. Damien.
As for Francis Xavier himself, he was, like Damien, a young man
supremely insensitive to the beauties of civilization, who burned

to go on a mission to the East, was not chosen, and managed to find a place on board ship only when one of the company fell ill and could not go. Xavier's energies were extraordinary. He was sturdily useful and cheerful on the voyage out; had no appetite for fine food and no aversion to dirty work; was a devoted nurse always to the sick, and indeed sought out leprosy cases to tend; was a vigorous and inventive evangelizer and baptizer; was prepared to go itinerating in strange places with nothing but a breviary and a portable altar and an umbrella against the Eastern heat; and once, most dangerously, went alone into the Malay archipelago to a deadly island named Morotai, where the people were poisoners. This was the hero of Damien: another athlete of God.

If Damien was, without much doubt, almost openly measuring himself against Xavier—having himself photographed in his posture, willing himself to do great things in strange archipelagoes— he was also measuring himself quietly against his brother Pamphile. Again, the context was that of health, sickness, and self-sacrifice: one sickness, Pamphile's typhus of 1863, had put Damien in a position where, ten years later, he could confront the greater disease of leprosy.

Beyond this again, of course, there was the greatest measure of all—the imitation of Christ. When Damien left Kohala to visit his bishop at Wailuku, and to meet his destiny, it was Easter, the time of Christ's death and resurrection. Damien was thirty-three, the age of Christ crucified. In going to Molokai, he was making a crossing of his own between the world of the well and the world of the mortally ill, between life and death-in-life.

At Kalawao he could begin the supreme mortification of the athlete, putting his superbly strong and healthy body at ultimate risk for God's sake. All those years before, professing his vows at Rue Picpus, he had gone beneath the burial pall and emerged filled with the thought of earth as a place of exile, where man waited until the dissolution of his flesh freed him to enter his true homeland in heaven. Now he had found his place of exile, Kalawao, where the dissolution of the flesh was everywhere around. At the settlement, from the beginning, Damien chose to address his congregation not as "my brothers," but as "we lepers."

III

Damien's appearance at Kalawao was part of a larger stirring in the politics of charity at Honolulu. Leprosy, in 1873, three decades after its unobtrusive appearance in the Hawaiian Islands, was belatedly recognized for what it had become—a "national blight," an epidemic disease in a population already threatened by other diseases, a menace to the very existence of the Hawaiian people. Segregation was being taken seriously; the leprosy laws were being applied rigorously. There was resistance—one Hawaiian shot and wounded his examining doctor, escaped, and was recaptured; a good number more fled and hid successfully; but enforcement went on. In the year 1873, as many victims of the disease were identified and shipped to Kalawao as in the seven years since the settlement was opened. There were harrowing scenes at the Honolulu waterfront, as month after month the little ships left for Molokai, loaded with victims bound for exile. Leprosy, in short, was on people's minds as never before; Kalawao was forever in the Honolulu newspapers. The harshness of the segregation law was acknowledged along with its necessity. It was the moment for equivalent gestures of sympathy.

In mid-April of 1873, just as Bishop Maigret was getting ready to go to Maui for the blessing of Father Léonor Fouesnel's church at Wailuku, the editor of the bilingual newspaper *Nūhou* at Honolulu made a suggestion. It was that the Hawaiian monarch, King William Lunalilo, recently crowned, might well pay a royal visit to Kalawao, where his presence would have a "most consoling and inspiring effect" upon his unhappy exiled subjects. "And if" —continued the "respectful" suggestion—"a noble Christian priest, preacher or sister should be inspired to go and sacrifice a life to console these poor wretches, that would be a royal soul to shine forever on a throne reared by human love."

King Lunalilo did not go to Molokai. He sent instead two members of the Board of Health with a letter to be read at Kalawao, assuring the exiles that everything would be done for them consistent with the good of all the Hawaiian people.

Where the king did not go, Damien went; and when it became known that a Catholic priest had landed at the settlement with nothing but his breviary, there was a surge of charitable feeling among respectable white men at Honolulu. A dozen well-meaning gentlemen got up a subscription, raised $130 on the spot, and gave it to Bishop Maigret. In recognition of Damien's sacrifice, several Protestants came to Mass at the Catholic cathedral.

"We care not what this man's theology may be," wrote the editor of the *Nūhou*, three days after Damien went ashore, "he surely is a Christian hero." Among the various churches of the islands, the matter of theology, of course, was of more than passing importance. It was quickly pointed out that a Mormon elder, a Hawaiian, himself healthy but with a diseased wife confined to Kalawao, lived at the settlement and held services. In addition, a white Protestant minister and some Hawaiian subordinates had been conscientiously visiting the leprosy receiving hospital in Honolulu. A Protestant church, named Siloama after the healing waters of the Old Testament, had been built and dedicated at Kalawao several years before the Catholics had built St. Philomena's; and a Protestant deacon from a Honolulu church, a Hawaiian who had contracted leprosy, was now at Kalawao. Finally, the Protestants, ever since the founding of the settlement at the turn of the year 1866, had been paying for twenty copies of the Protestant Hawaiian-language paper *Kū'oko'a* to be sent regularly to Kalawao.

It seemed necessary to have all this put in evidence, because the Honolulu press was acting as if Damien had done something singular. Certainly, whatever he had done created an extraordinary impression. The provincial of the Sacred Hearts mission in Honolulu, writing to the father-general of the Congregation in Paris, had no explanation for the phenomenon; he could do not much more than describe it. The only topic of conversation, he said, was the devotion of Damien, the risk he ran of catching an incurable disease. He was being admired and exalted for his sacrifice in going among the victims of leprosy without a place to live, without the necessities of life. And yet, as the provincial remarked, there was nothing unusual in this among the Sacred Hearts Fathers: it happened whenever one of them went to a district where the mission was not established. And, of course, there had been Sacred Hearts Fathers and brothers at Kalawao before Damien. But "all that had happened without noise, without public admiration. The honor of attracting attention, exciting sympathy, stirring up the press, was reserved to Father Damien."

If the public was, in the provincial's word, "ravished," it was clearly because popular belief had it that Damien was at Kalawao to stay: permanently, alone, voluntarily, without taint of disease in himself or in anyone close to him to take him there. Nothing had been mentioned in public at Honolulu about the plan to have four priests serve the settlement turn by turn while maintaining their districts on other islands. The provincial told the father-general about it: "Without detracting from the devotion of Father Damien, I should tell you in praise of our Fathers that several of them had asked to devote themselves to the service of the lepers. We did not wish to send one priest only to stay on Molokai. Father Damien was not sent there to stay." Bishop Maigret had meant him to remain only a fortnight. But the situation had changed. If there had seemed no reason at first to make the efficient internal arrangement of the mission generally known, the public response to the news about Damien quickly rendered it difficult, next to impossible: it would have been, morally speaking, a disappointment, anticlimactic.

Meanwhile, Damien was writing from Kalawao to say that there was urgent work to do. Having landed with nothing, he needed "a case of wine—books for pious reading and study—some shirts —trousers—shoes—a bell—some rosaries—some catechisms—altar bread big and small—a sack of flour—a lockable chest with a key." Not knowing when or whether he was to be replaced, he asked who would be "the priest privileged to gather the harvest of the Lord," and he put himself forward: "You know my disposition. I want to sacrifice myself for the poor lepers."

"Nothing decided," the provincial wrote to him after he had been ashore ten days, "except that you can stay on Molokai following your devotion until new orders." A week later, the matter more or less decided itself. There would be no new orders; Damien could stay. "Considering the circumstances that led him there," wrote the provincial to the father-general on May 28, "the good effect his appearance has had on the public, and the necessity of administering the sacraments to the dying, we are so to speak forced to leave him there."

IV

The Protestants of Honolulu could hardly have been happy at the ravishment of the public by the self-sacrifice of a Catholic priest. They were embarrassed by it; and yet they could see no clear way to redeem their embarrassment. As the American clergymen of the capital said in discussions among themselves, it was one thing for a lone, celibate Catholic priest to go to live at Kalawao, but quite another for any married man of God such as they to be forced to do the same. He would either have to leave his wife and children behind, which was painful, or take them with him, which was unthinkable.

The general question of leprosy was raised at the annual meeting of the Hawaiian Evangelical Association in June, 1873, by which time Damien had been a month at Kalawao. After prayer and deliberation, forty-eight Protestant ministers, whites and Hawaiians, signed a powerfully-worded statement. With a loathsome, incurable, deadly disease fastening itself upon the "vitals" of the nation, the prospect was that "our Hawaiian people will become in a very few years, a *nation of lepers.*" "Do we consider what this means? It means the disorganization and total destruction of civili-

zation, property values, and industry, of our churches, our contributions, our Hawaiian Board and its work of Missions. It means
shame, and defeat, and disgraceful overthrow to all that is promising and fair in the nation. We are on the brink of a horrible pit,
full of loathsomeness, into which our feet are rapidly sliding."

The members of the Evangelical Association, as pastors and
teachers, saw their pressing duty. "While striving to comfort and
strengthen with the love of Jesus the afflicted hearts of the lepers
and their friends," they must also "teach and persuade all the
people to obey the law of God and segregate the lepers from
among us," and "teach every leper who cleaves to his people and
refuses to go away, that he is sinning against the lives of men and
against the law of God."

Accordingly, the Association's members resolved to preach frequently to their people on the "duty of isolating their lepers,
especially as illustrated by the Mosaic law in the thirteenth chapter of Leviticus." And they resolved to set apart July 18 as "a day
of Fasting, of Repentance before God for our sins, and especially
for those sins which promote the spread of the disease, and also as
a day of prayer to God, to strengthen the King and officers of the
Government in cleansing the land of this disease, and to turn the
hearts of the people to help in this work of saving the nation."

It might have been said of the members of the Association that
they seemed rather more ready to have the Mosaic law enforced
in all its rigor than to follow to the end the idea of the love of
Christ. Jesus had been willing to go among the diseased. So had
Damien. The Christian love of the Evangelical Association seemed
more fastidious, more remote. It might have been said as well of
their statement, with all its references to the preservation of property values and industry and civilization, that it had a ring more
American than Hawaiian, more *haole* than *kanaka*. At all events,
the Association's meeting did not produce a volunteer among the
white ministers for service at Kalawao. When the congregation of
Siloama, the Protestant church at the settlement, asked—not for
the first time—for a pastor, the minister who was found was not

a white man but a Hawaiian. His wife had leprosy; she was at Kalawao; the Board of Health was asked for permission to have the man join her. The Board in turn proposed an alternative: another Hawaiian minister, himself just diagnosed as suffering from leprosy. He would be sent to Kalawao soon in any case. This settled the matter. In Damien's lifetime, no white Protestant minister went to live at Kalawao.

V

At the end of June, Damien came down from Kalawao to Honolulu on the steamer, to see his superiors, to go to confession, and to encourage the people of the capital in their charity toward the settlement. He took back with him some generous gifts; and the distribution, as he remarked, in turn encouraged the sufferers at Kalawao to think of the Catholic priest as "father-general of the poor and unhappy," at the expense of the "heretics," who lost in confidence.

The general question of movement in and out of the settlement had been before the Board of Health in June, at about the time of the Evangelical Association's meeting. The Board came to the decision that only its own authorized agents should be allowed to go back and forth to Kalawao. Damien was not a Board agent, yet here he was in Honolulu. He was not suffering from leprosy, either, yet there he was at Kalawao. And evidently, from complaints that came to the Board from Molokai, Damien was leaving the settlement to preach in the healthy districts of the island. The Board decided in September that, if Damien wished to stay at Kalawao, he might do so; but that, consistent with the segregation and isolation laws, he might not leave.

This meant two things of immediate importance. Damien could not be active in his ministry on all of Molokai, but just at Kalawao; and he could not go to another priest outside the settlement whenever he felt the need of confession. One or two of the Sacred

Hearts Fathers saw the Board's ruling as a Protestant plot to make Damien's life intolerable, forcing him in the end to leave the settlement. It was true that Damien was an embarrassment to the Protestant mission, and that there were men closely connected with the Protestants on the Board of Health: in fact, a majority. But it was also true that Damien was breaking the letter of the segregation law. The question was whether the law ought to be applied to ministers of religion.

If one priest might not leave the settlement freely, neither should another freely enter. Late in September, one of Damien's superiors, Father Modeste Favens, provincial of the mission, was traveling between islands, and his steamer touched at the settlement landing to unload cattle. The provincial wanted to go ashore, but the captain forbade him. Damien came out in a boat, but was not allowed to board the ship. The two priests could do no more than shout at each other from a distance; and so Damien had to make his confession from his bobbing boat, at the top of his voice, in French, receiving a loud absolution from his confessor over the ship's rail.

Some weeks later, one of the Sacred Hearts Fathers from Maui came to a healthy district of Molokai to hear the confession of an old French sailor who lived there. Setting the law of God above the law of the Board of Health, as he said, he went on to see Damien, the "prisoner priest." He took off his soutane and put on a red neckerchief, borrowed a straw hat from a Hawaiian, rented a horse, rode to the top of the *pali,* the cliff on the landward side of Kalawao, and made his way down on foot in the middle of the night, arriving at Damien's door at half past three in the morning. He thought he had managed to come and go without being noticed; but the deputy sheriff of Molokai found out and reported him to the Board of Health, and there was an investigation. The priest admitted that he had not applied for a permit to enter the settlement; but then he knew that the Board of Health would not have given him one in any case.

The situation was at once vexing and ridiculous. Everyone concerned was being put in a bad light. Bishop Maigret went to see the representative of the French government in the Hawaiian Islands; the French commissioner protested on Damien's behalf to the Hawaiian kingdom's Minister for Foreign Affairs; the minister conferred with the president of the Board of Health; and in mid-November the Board relaxed its regulations so as to permit medical men to be admitted to the settlement, and "ministers of religion for the exercise of the functions of their office"—provided always that they had the permission of the Board.

Damien duly made his application, and toward the end of December he received an official letter permitting him to "visit the Leper Asylum on Molokai from time to time as circumstances require." Circumstances—defined by Damien as the imperative call of his vocation—required him to be at Kalawao virtually all the time. But what he wanted, and what the official letter did not grant him in so many words, was permission to come and go. He took this permission for granted; used it generously on Molokai, to serve the healthy districts over the *pali*, sparingly for visits to Honolulu; and was not questioned again by the Board.

V I

At a distance, Molokai was gorgeous. Seen as the English lady traveler Isabella Bird saw it, from the tranquil deck of a passing steamer on a shimmering sunny day, the mountainous island floated "like a great blue morning glory on the yet bluer sea." Closer to, it was still an impressive sight, but of a less uncomplicatedly lyrical kind. Robert Louis Stevenson, coasting the north side on his way to visit the leprosy settlement, found the scenery "grand, gloomy and bleak. Mighty mountain walls descending sheer along the whole face of the island into a sea unusually deep; the front of the mountain ivied and furred with clinging forest; one viridescent cliff"; and midway along the coast, "a low, bare, stony promontory edged in between the cliff and the sea." The "promontory" was Kalawao.

Stevenson came to the leprosy settlement and went away again

by boat. He never took the landward route to Kalawao, a hairpin
Hawaiian trail down the face of the cliff, the *pali*, more than
fifteen hundred feet from top to bottom—it was too severe for
anyone in poor health. Some years before, an American friend of
Stevenson, the writer Charles Warren Stoddard—very likely the
man who first interested him in Molokai and Damien—had made
the precipitous descent. Looking over the brink of the *pali*, Stoddard was struck by exhilaration mingled with vertigo. "The whole
face of the abyss was a cataract of verdure, breaking at intervals
into a foam of flowers, and upon this cataract we were balanced
like the birds of the air." On the way down, Stoddard found himself "dropping, slipping, shambling" across a "sharp flank of the
cliff, that cut the air like a flying buttress," and was afraid. He had
good enough reason to be. Every turn in the *pali* trail was treach-
erous. Rocks easily washed loose in the rain and ricocheted along
the narrow zigzag path. Cattle being driven down to the settlement might put a foot wrong and fall, and the watchers below
would see the body come bouncing a thousand feet down the cliff
face, "like a giant football." Going up was no better. Hawaiians
walking the trail in either direction laid offerings for safety's sake
on their little stone travelers' shrines. Catholic priests started the
hike with an act of contrition. Stoddard's own climb took two
hours; and when, out of curiosity along the way, he had his doctor
companion take his pulse, it was 150.

The tiny promontory at the base of the cliff was an unlikely place
for people to live: four square miles of land, hard to get to, hard
to get away from, cut off from the rest of Molokai by the *pali*, and
ringed to seaward by surf beating constantly on a rocky shore, with
only the roughest of rough landing places at a spot called
Kalaupapa. White men were always surprised to hear that in the
old days, when only Hawaiians lived on Molokai—before Westerners, big ships, port towns, missionaries and disease—Kalawao was
heavily populated. Sweet potatoes grew well, and hogs were fat;
and there was fishing off the coast. But by the time the promontory
came to be chosen in 1865 as the site for the leprosy settlement,

depopulation had reduced the Hawaiians of Kalawao to a few-score farmers and fishermen, still living fairly much in the old way, in thatch huts amid the decaying stone fences and windbreaks that crisscrossed the old family gardens of the flatlands.

Along the north coast of Molokai, the Kalawao side, the weather changed markedly with the seasons. In the drier months of summer, the sea was not too rough; fishing canoes could get out and get back in again. The winter was by contrast an uncomfortable time, with surf high enough to keep boats away from the landings for a month at a stretch. When the sea "swells and flings itself upward," wrote a Hawaiian in the early days of the leprosy settlement, the people of the districts adjoining Kalawao turned away from the open sea to feed on fresh-water fish, seaweed, and sand-crabs. And along the promontory itself, there was "nothing at all from Kalawao to Kalaupapa. In these two places the sea dashes up to wither the grass, a hundred feet more or less in some places. The *a'ama* crabs with yellow backs that run about in the dry grass are all that could be caught."

In such a changeful landscape, a watcher could see what he wanted to, beauty or desolation or both: rocky islets just off the coast in a sparkling sea, green jutting headlands, leaping waterfalls on the *pali* after the rains; or the wind whirling surf spray hundreds of feet into the air along the shore; or nothing more than heavy, saturated clouds creeping along the cliff face, and an obscured and sullen sun amid the weeping of rainstorms.

After the founding of the settlement at Kalawao, the sun rose and set there every day, summer and winter, on leprosy; and the watchers could not help reading the disease into the landscape, with all its pustular swellings and erosions and distortions. Charles Warren Stoddard, looking down over the sheer exuberance of the *pali*, saw the promontory below as "a tongue of land thrust out into the sea; it was sunburnt and dust-colored, blackened at the edges. . . . Near the centre of the lowland was a small, low crater, a hillock with a funnel-shaped hollow. . . . The whole plain was like a crust over the water, with a broken bubble in the midst of it."

Another visitor, out early one morning, watched the rising sun throw the promontory into shadow and bring the *pali* into bold relief. "The huge furrows on the face of the precipice soon come into view, causing one for the moment the vagary that it, too, has assumed a leonine countenance after its many years of vigil over the unfortunates below."

VII

The site chosen for the hospital and the first cluster of huts at the settlement—what came to be known as Kalawao village—was in the lee of a cliff, in a place that never saw an early sunrise, and where the bright light of the afternoon was cut off by the *pali* at five in summer and two in winter. When the sun shone, it was warm at the settlement, even hot; in the shade or in the rain it could be cold; and when the wet winter winds blew in off the open ocean, it was miserable.

For all that, the Board of Health was pleased with Kalawao in general. The important thing was that the promontory was a natural prison. Other sites for a leprosy settlement had been considered at the time of the passing of the segregation law in 1865, one of them near Honolulu itself. But, for the Board's purposes, the advantages of Kalawao were outstanding. The place was certainly "difficult of access," and yet capable—with good farming—of sustaining a large population. So the kingdom's leprosy settlement could be at once isolated and self-sufficient. Some of the land on the promontory was already owned by the government (which helped to decide the placement of the hospital). The Board moved to buy out as many of the remaining Hawaiian landholders as could be persuaded to sell; and the first shipload of confirmed leprosy victims waded ashore through the surf on January 6, 1866.

The Board's plan for segregation and isolation was comprehensive but simple. In every district of the islands, men, women, and children suspected of having leprosy would be rounded up by the police and examined by doctors. Confirmation of the symptoms would be made at a receiving hospital in Honolulu. Indisputable cases would be sent to Kalawao. The settlement would have a resident superintendent, who would be under the supervision of the Board's direct representative, a German sugar planter and rancher named Rudolph Meyer, who lived at Kalae, over the *pali* from Kalawao, but close enough to make regular visits. Under Meyer's efficient remote control, the people of Kalawao would live their lives on the promontory, supporting themselves by their own labor. Once they died out, leprosy would be at an end in the Hawaiian Islands. The Board's expectation was that the process would not take unduly long—perhaps several years.

In fact, the leprosy epidemic lasted more than half a century. That was something which could not have been predicted. Another thing went wrong with the Board's plans, and it happened immediately. The settlement did not become self-supporting. Either the Hawaiians sent to Kalawao in 1866 persisted in believing that they were to be kept there only a few weeks or months until their disease went away, so that work was unnecessary; or they refused to work, saying that the Board owed them a living; or they were willing to work for themselves, but not at all willing to share what they grew; or they were too ill altogether for the hard and steady labor of planting *'uala*, sweet potatoes, and *kalo*, the staple of the Hawaiian diet, the raw material of *poi*.

Within six months, the secretary of the Board was writing in some agitation to the resident superintendent: "Do you mean that we will have to feed them?" The Board found this prospect unreasonable, even immoral, and counseled sternness. "They must fully understand they must work to maintain themselves with these necessities, or else lazy vagabonds must be made to feel the consequences of their idleness."

By way of enforcement, the resident superintendents of the early years did what they could, which was little enough. The first, a Frenchman named Louis Lepart—oddly enough, a former Sacred Hearts brother who had severed his connection with the

mission—carried a gun. The second, Donald Walsh, an Englishman with an unsuccessful past in the colonies, failing eyesight, a
small library of pious books, and a grown son who helped him as
a constable before going mad, tried "British Army discipline."
When Walsh died in 1869, his widow succeeded him—a white
woman who, like her husband and Lepart before him, did not
understand the Hawaiian language.

Each in turn had to face mobs of more than a hundred. Help was
far away, at the top of the *pali*, where Rudolph Meyer lived, or
a day's sail across the Molokai Channel to Honolulu. They went in
some fear of their lives. At the settlement a crowd might form, a
riot threaten, at any time, for no reason or any reason: an argument over a woman, too much homemade liquor being distilled
and drunk, a grievance over the distribution of clothes sent by the
Board, a food shortage.

Often enough in the early years, there really was not enough
food; and when a shipment did arrive, it was an urgent matter to
get a share, especially of *pa'i 'ai*, hard pounded *kalo*. Peter Young
Kaeo, an aristocratic Hawaiian confined to the settlement and well
enough provided for there, with a pleasant small home and a
kitchen garden, wrote home to Honolulu in his acquired English
to his cousin, the Dowager Queen Emma, about the *pa'i 'ai* deliveries, and how he watched "men and women large & small on
their march. . . . What a tilyful sight I did see, some just as much
as they could do to troddle along and eager to lay hold of their
native food Pai, for fear that they might get cheated by some
rascal, which is done here by these bad fellows. When I got to
Kalawao, their the people were, thick on the beach 'Rocks' waiting
for their names to be called."

Where the food went after delivery was problematical. "The
sick," wrote Donald Walsh, "are continually urged on by the others to ask for more food and when given is usually all cooked at
once for the benefit of the whole." The stronger, Walsh found,
were "not kind" to the weaker: "generally their sores are un-
washed unless they can crawl through brambles and bushes and

over stone ditches in some instances 7 or 800 yards." Doing his superintendent's rounds, Walsh found the very ill "in their dark houses, lying on their mats, wrapt up in their bed clothes," in miserable condition. Hut by hut, Walsh listed the inhabitants and what they owned.

No. 4 house: 1 Pot. No Water Cask 1 W Can. 1 Lamp 2 Dishes 1 Knife 2 spoons. This house is cold, filthy and wretched. It leaks. Inmates: Manaku—1 Woolen Shirt 1 pants 1 Grey Blanket. Kaahu—1 Blanket, a gown. Napua—1 Shirt 1 old pants 1 cloth pants. Kepilina—1 Gry Blanket. Kaahu is in the last stage of Leprosy. . . . No. 38 house—1 pint tin. 1 Knife 1 spoon. Kaikolani (woman) 1 Blanket. no clothes. This is the most wretched of all the houses—I do not think she sleeps in it.

The strong did better. "By what means I know not," wrote Walsh, "but the men in the Houses No 14 & 15 seem to want for nothing from the soft slippers to hair-oil." In fact, those who did best at Kalawao, apart from the handful of well-connected people like Peter Kaeo, were the lawbreakers, willing and able to take what they wanted. "They must not fancy that they are outside of the Law," wrote the secretary of the Board. But they were, and they knew it. For victims of leprosy, there was very little in life with consequences worse than what their disease had brought down upon them. It was hard to find anything else to threaten them with: constables, leg irons, a lockup—all this was trivial. They were imprisoned already, and with a life sentence. The government of the kingdom was even considering declaring them legally dead. They were at the settlement to die; the true governor of Kalawao, then, was death. The Hawaiians there had a saying: " 'A'ole kānāwai ma keia wahi"— "In this place there is no law."

VIII

One thing all Hawaiians were clear on: disease, epidemic disease, came to their islands from the outside world. That is to say, the white man brought it with him; it was the white man's fault.

Another thing was clear: in the nineteenth century, disease was killing off the Hawaiians as a people. In turn, and repeatedly, cholera, smallpox, influenza, measles, and venereal disease entered at the ports, especially Honolulu, and scythed the natives down. Over the first century of sustained contact with the outside world, from the 1770s to the 1870s, the native Hawaiian population dropped from something like a quarter of a million to about fifty thousand. That is to say, the white man's presence was killing the Hawaiian.

Leprosy was the latest of the outside world's curses to be laid upon the islands together with the blessings of civilization. No one, white or native, knew exactly how or exactly when it arrived. The first authenticated case was thought to date from about 1840; and the popular belief was that the disease was introduced from China, or at least was first recognized in the islands by Chinese—perhaps both. In any case, Hawaiians called leprosy *ma'i Pākē*, Chinese disease; talking about the perpetual presence of the disease among them, they spoke of a *"ma'i Pākē* ship anchored on the Hawaiian people." And, of course, the *ma'i Pākē* ship and all other ships that connected the islands with the outside world were owned by white men. That is to say, leprosy was the white man's fault.

Certainly the white man, the *haole*, knew about the disease; and without much question his ships brought it to the Hawaiian Islands. Yet, somehow, leprosy left him alone—not entirely, but to a great extent. In the nineteenth century, perhaps a hundred cases in all were diagnosed among *haole*. A white man struck by leprosy in the islands could regard his fate as freakish, and perhaps the more awful in his own mind for that, but as an individual disaster, nothing to do with his race as a whole. Hawaiians turned out to be far more susceptible, lacking immunity to this as to other diseases of the outside world. Leprosy became epidemic among them; and it was that which brought on the segregation law of the mid-1860s. At any time after the law began to be enforced with something like efficiency, there were always between five hundred and a thousand Hawaiians confined to Kalawao. New cases steadily replaced the dying. A short, intensive search of the rural districts could usually bring another couple of hundred cases to light; and, without question, hundreds more cases were never known to the authorities.

The *haole*'s way of dealing with the disease involved no cure—none was available, however many promising treatments were tried—but merely a civil version of the Old Testament ritual of segregation and isolation. The Bible and leprosy made their way to the islands within a few decades of one another; and one measure of the Christian Hawaiian came to be the way in which he submitted himself to the segregation laws. Prepare for Molokai as for the grave, wrote a diseased Hawaiian in the Protestant native-language paper *Kū'oko'a:* make your will; provide for your children; press to your brow the *kiawe* frond, the crown of thorns.

By this sort of test, Hawaiians in general were not good Christians. To the consternation especially of people such as the members of the Hawaiian Evangelical Association, the *kanaka* seemed almost to consider segregation worse than leprosy itself. The Association, resolving in 1873 to preach the rightness of segregation, spoke of the "general ignorance on this subject among the common people, and their consequent apathy and perversity. They refuse to separate their lepers from them. They eat, drink and sleep with them. They oppose their removal and hide them. They listen to the voices of evil-minded men who raise an outcry against the King and his helpers, when they strive to root out the evil thing."

This was one moral diagnosis among many to which the Hawaiian was subjected in the nineteenth century. Yet in resisting the thought of his relative or his friend being taken away, never to be seen again, the *kanaka* was not in his own mind being apathetic or perverse: he was being Hawaiian.

As a people, the Hawaiians were at their weakest in the nineteenth century: they were dying. At the level of family and friendship, in the life they led day by day, they were still strong. Now the *haole* was spreading disease, and his inhuman segregation law was breaking up family and friendship. Not altogether surprisingly, it came to appear more and more to the Hawaiians as if there were a plot against the *kanaka*.

Many things of this kind were said about the *haole* and his designs upon the health of the native Hawaiian. Some *kanaka* claimed that vaccination, which the *haole* said prevented smallpox, was actually meant to cause leprosy. It was believed in some districts that when a man with leprosy was found, he was killed immediately by the *haole* authorities. It was believed, too, that people under observation at the leprosy receiving hospital in Honolulu were dosed with the disease so that they would have to be sent to Molokai; and that even people doing well under treatment by *kahuna* were exiled, not to be cured, "but to kill us all as soon as possible to save money." And finally, once a man died at the settlement, his body was sure to be cut up by the *haole.* The Board of Health acquired another name among the *kanaka*—the Board of Death; and Kalawao was called *Ka Lua Kupapa'u,* corpse pit, tomb.

A good many Hawaiians believed, on the evidence of their own experience, that there were two kinds of disease, *haole* and *kanaka,* and that only *haole* could be cured of *haole* diseases by *haole* medicine. So when the *haole,* having first given the *kanaka* leprosy, then gave him medicine, of course it would not work. Accordingly, Hawaiians at Kalawao refused treatment—some of them, anyway—and made fun of the *haole* doctors. "The day following the visit was paid to us by Dr. Trousseau," wrote Peter Kaeo to his cousin Queen Emma in 1873, "the natives which were supplied with Medicine by the Dr. Smashed the Bottles of Medicine on the rocks, which is in abbundance, poured the Medicine out, and kept the Bottles for Tobbacco or other purposes, strewed the Pills on the ground, like planting Corn, and laughing over it. I do not believe that their is One that has any Faith in the Dr. or his Medicine, which is quite evident by the Yell they utter, and the laughter they give. '*Lā'au ola 'ole*'—medicine that doesn't cure— is the one and unanimous word they say."

This sort of thing only convinced the *haole*—who at the same time were reluctantly conscious that *haole* medicine so far had not succeeded in curing even *haole*—that the apathy and perversity which led to so much leprosy among Hawaiians persisted at Kalawao, turning patients into troublemakers. The Board of Health, reporting to the legislature of the Hawaiian kingdom in 1868 on the relation between leprosy and lawlessness, spoke of Hawaiians at the settlement as exhibiting "the most thorough indifference to the sufferings, and the most utter absence of consideration, for the wants, to which many of them were destined to be themselves exposed." Refusal to work, robbery of the sick and dying—"the terrible disease which afflicts the lepers seems to cause among them as great a change in their moral and mental organization as in their physical constitution."

At least this recognized some sort of pre-existing virtue in the Hawaiian character; and there was, in fact, striking evidence that large numbers of *kanaka* were not merely apathetic or perverse. Over the years, hundreds of healthy Hawaiians, faced with the exile of a friend or relative to Kalawao, chose to go too, to help, to *kōkua*, in the Hawaiian phrase. At Kalawao in the early days, there were as many *kōkua* as there were people with the disease. Sensibly, the segregation laws were adapted to fit the case. It was an overwhelmingly Hawaiian case. Just as no white Protestant minister from Honolulu ever volunteered to live at Kalawao, so there was never—or next to never—a white *kōkua*. (One *haole*, a Frenchman, did go to Kalawao, with a diseased *haole* friend: it was a singular case.) But when another of the handful of *haole* confirmed as a leprosy case and sent to Kalawao began to have his own racial nightmares about being buried alive by unfeeling *kanaka*, he asked for his Hawaiian wife to be allowed at the settlement as his *kōkua*, and she was willing to come, as were those hundreds of other Hawaiians.

The whole question turned on whether leprosy could be lived with. The white man, the *haole*, in substance said no, as he had said all through the Christian era. The Hawaiian—perhaps perforce—said yes, if it could be lived with in a Hawaiian way. One *haole* physician, Nathaniel B. Emerson, son of a Protestant missionary, who was the settlement doctor at Kalawao for a time, and who spoke Hawaiian and knew as much about Hawaiians as any *haole* of his time, was right when he observed of leprosy in the islands: "The roots of this thing are very deep and are intricately interwoven with the whole fabric of the community." For reasons incomprehensible to the *haole,* Hawaiians were not totally repelled by the disease. The touch of the leprous hand did not altogether appall them. They were not, as a people, prepared to turn the leprosy sufferer into a "leper" of the Old Testament sort.

It was, rather, the *haole* who insisted that this should be done. It had to be said that, for all the *haole*'s fear about the safety of his person and his property in the islands, nothing was more obvious than that if the disease was not curbed, the Hawaiian—far more than the *haole*—would be the sufferer. But the Hawaiian did not want to listen to the *haole,* even if what the *haole* said was for the Hawaiian's own good. There was even the suggestion that if the *haole* did not like leprosy, then he should leave the islands. Of course the *haole* did not leave: he stayed and enforced the segregation laws, despite the further suggestion that if he did not relax his rigor his sugar plantations would be set afire.

Nathaniel Emerson, who had grown up among Hawaiians, liked them well enough; they were children, he thought, but likable children. He in turn was well enough liked in his time at Kalawao. But the Hawaiians there did not really take him or his doctoring seriously, for a simple and serious reason: he would not touch them. He used to set their medicines out on his gate post so that he would not have to go near them. He was like the other doctor who, on his rounds in the settlement hospital, would do physical examinations by raising the rags from a diseased body with the tip of his cane. It was the same with the white Protestant minister who visited Kalawao occasionally in the early days, concerned to cure the leprosy of the soul. He preached from the elevated distance and safety of a veranda; he would not touch the objects of his concern. From a *haole* point of view, this was only right and prudent; if the segregation program was correct, then individual self-segregation must also be correct. From the Hawaiian point of view, it meant that the leprosy patient was turned into a "leper," an untouchable. And one of the great needs of the Hawaiian, always, was to touch and be touched, to affirm and reaffirm physically his life and his share in a common humanity.

Emerson and people like him were actually doing far more than the average *haole* could bring himself even to contemplate. But the Hawaiian, distrusting much about the *haole*, could not warm to a kind of service that served mankind and yet lacked, literally, the touch of humanity. The Emersons of the early days, treating *kanaka* as "lepers," were not and never would be real Hawaiian helpers, *kōkua*. However difficult it might be, a *haole*, to be a real helper, would have to be able to bring himself to reach across race, across disease, and touch the leprous Hawaiian.

IX

Peter Kaeo, the detached observer of *pa'i 'ai* deliveries and medicine-bottle smashings, was a member of the minor Hawaiian aristocracy. This, together with the fact that he had some white blood, meant that his formal education at Honolulu in the mid-nineteenth century was considerably Western, as were some of his adult tastes and attitudes. Among the exiles of Kalawao, he was a man apart. There was no one else of his breeding at the settlement, virtually no one with whom he could comfortably associate. He occupied himself with reading, a little gardening, and the supervision of his servants as they worked about his grounds midway between Kalawao village and Kalaupapa landing, keeping his house adequate to the style of the aristocrat he knew himself still to be, leprosy or no leprosy. He gave his cottage the name "Honolulu," because he missed the life of the capital and the society of the royal court so much. He was as lonely as any man could ever be.

He lived for news from home, from Honolulu, from his cousin

Queen Emma; and he answered her correspondence in English—
long, gossipy letters written by a man who had plenty of time:
speculations on royal politics; detailed accounts of what the commoners at the settlement were up to—the "natives," as he called
them; requests for Emma to send him *kalo* directly, because the
quality of the settlement's supply was "disgusting"; wistful reports
on the condition of his diseased foot. He missed his old life greatly,
and would put his lost longings into little poems, half-made-up,
half-remembered, and mail them off to Emma:

> Thou welcome the hour
> That awakened the night song
> Of mirth in your town
> Then think of the one
> That once welcomed it too
> And forgot his own griefs
> To be happy with you
> His grief may return
> Not a hope may remain
> Of the few that have brighten
> His pathway of pain
> But he will ne'er forget
> The short vision that threw
> Its enchantment around him
> Whilst lingering with you.

Evenings were the hardest time of day for Kaeo. He used to go
up onto the high ground, look back across the Molokai Channel,
and pretend that he could see his old house in Honolulu. "Last
night," he wrote to Emma, "I was looking at Oahu and the sky
over it was burning with the setting Sun, and meditating on the
Features that joy use to wear when in your Company, when on
looking again I discovered that Oahu had faded from view, then
I strained my poor eyes to catch again a glympse of Sweet Home
but I strained in vain, for it was completely lost in the dark, so I
sung the Air 'The dearest spot on earth to me' when a man passed
on Horse back and he too struck up a native song, and I could not
help laughing at the impudent chap's mocking me he too, proba-

bly, was endeavouring to avoid the anxietyes that his poor acheing heart was crying for, *Home* like myself, so riseing from my Seat I entered the House and ordered Tea."

Kaeo was Western enough to think that *haole* medicines would help him, and Hawaiian enough to see omens in clouds—once a *mo'o*, a dragon, once a black coffin. Like most Hawaiians, too, he placed a great deal of importance on his dreams, asking the *kahuna* of Kalawao for interpretations, and writing to Emma about them. One night after he had watched a schooner passing at sunset between Molokai and Oahu, he dreamed that he was at home.

"I . . . was dressing to go out but on looking at the Glass, I saw that my Eye Brow was gone, so I felt so shame that I came back to Molokai, then I climbed a Pali with several other natives, and they called out to me not to go any more for fear I would fall, but I kept climbing till I reached the top, then I looked down and saw my perilous position and was so frighten of falling and in my freight woke."

He talked to one of his few acceptable friends about it, "and he said that if this is a true Dream, that I am not going to remain here long, but that I am coming home. Oh happy Lord if ever it does come." It came: aristocratic connections had their advantages, extending even to Kalawao. After Kaeo had been just three years at the settlement, the Board of Health moved to allow him to return to Honolulu. He even took his old seat in the kingdom's House of Nobles; and he died a few years later where he always wanted to live, at Honolulu.

Kaeo had first been examined for leprosy and diagnosed as a confirmed case early in May, 1873, at the moment when Damien was about to leave Wailuku for Molokai. At Kalawao, the two did not have much to do with each other. Kaeo, after all, was an aristocrat and a member of the Anglican communion in the islands, the Reformed Church, the religion of the Hawaiian ruling house; Damien was a Catholic priest and a peasant. Damien did visit Kaeo once, without trying to convert him, as Kaeo remarked

approvingly. Another time they had lunch together, with the
president of the Board of Health, who was at the settlement on
official business. And Kaeo used to come across the priest on his
rounds from time to time. In a casual way, Kaeo liked what he saw
of Damien. As he wrote to Emma: "He is a very nice man."

X

Damien, alone at Kalawao in May, 1873, with nothing but a breviary in his hand and no roof over his head, lived in the open for
some weeks, eating his meals off a flat rock and sleeping under a
pū hala, a pandanus tree, near St. Philomena's church. The pandanus was not a camper's best friend, according to Dr. Arthur A.
St. J. Mouritz, the settlement physician for a time in the 1880s.
"The Puhala tree generally and by preference selects rocky
ground to germinate, its aerial roots and their surroundings offer
a choice nidus for centipedes, scorpions, ants, mosquitoes, roaches;
and fleas carried by mangy cats, dogs, and sheep, who seek shelter
from sun, wind, and rain under its branches." Damien, apparently,
was not discomfited; in any case, his only other choice during his
first days ashore was to share a hut with a leprosy victim; and this
he was not yet ready to do.

It was one thing to volunteer to serve the diseased, but quite
another to take the intimate measure of Kalawao. Damien's ministry became a priesthood of worms, of ghastly sights and suffocating
smells, of the most awful physical and spiritual misery. There were
six hundred leprosy sufferers at the settlement; and, apart from
the healthy Hawaiian *kōkua*, Damien was the only man there with
a sound, uncorrupted body—the only *haole*, certainly.

Other priests making brief visits were reduced, often enough,
to speechlessness or weeping incoherence; later, they would write
horror-struck letters about the experience, full of revolting detail
and exclamation points. Even at second hand the horror was fresh.
One of Damien's visiting colleagues told another how "he saw in

the hospital a young woman aged about twenty, whose right side was nothing but a swarm of worms, thousands and thousands of them. All the intestines were bared, he saw the ribs as in a skeleton, but she was not suffering. He saw a leprous man busy cutting off a joint from his finger with a piece of glass. Finally he succeeded, and threw it tranquilly out the window as if it was cured, saying: there's an end to my trouble. Apparently the blood in the finger was poisoned, and it was as if a worm was devouring him from inside."

Damien told his superiors and his family matter-of-factly what he had been able to learn about the course of the malady among his sad, maimed, disfigured parishioners. "Leprosy is an almost incurable disease. It develops little by little through a corruption in the blood and shows itself first in blackish spots on the skin, especially on the cheeks. In these spots there is no more feeling. After a time, the whole body is covered. Then the sores start, especially on the hands and feet. The toes and fingers are eaten away and give off a fetid odor. Their breath also poisons the air." At the same time, he spoke briefly and unemotionally of his own almost unconquerable nausea, and of headaches that lasted for days.

Less than two weeks after he landed, and before it had been decided that he could stay permanently, he wrote—wanting powerfully to remain—"All my repugnance toward the lepers has disappeared." This was courageous, but in advance of the physical truth. "Many a time," he recalled years later, looking back on the start of his ministry, "in fulfilling my priestly duties at their domiciles I have been obliged, not only to close my nostrils, but to remain outside to breathe fresh air. . . . As an antidote to counteract the bad smell I got myself accustomed to the use of Tobacco whereupon the smell of the Pipe preserved me somewhat from carrying in my clothes the obnoxious odor of our Lepers." To protect his legs from "a peculiar itching which I usually experienced every evening after my visiting them I had to beg a Friend of mine to send me a pair of heavy boots." He asked for a new saddle from Honolulu so that he could ride clean on horseback. And when the lumber for his house arrived, paid for out of charity money raised in Honolulu, he put the building up, a single-roomed shack sixteen feet by ten, and lived alone.

"Be careful not to expose yourself to catching this awful disease," his provincial cautioned him solicitously. "I hope the Good Lord will protect you." That was Damien's hope, too. "I am not yet a leper," he wrote to Pamphile a few months into his ministry, "and with the miraculous help of God and the Holy Virgin I hope I never will be." Still, God had sent him to work among the diseased. Damien, unable to cure the leprosy of the body, able only to attack the leprosy of the soul, learned just the same to be doctor as well as priest. One of the white men at the settlement, William Williamson, had been a helper at the receiving hospital in Honolulu until he had caught leprosy himself; and he taught Damien how to clean and bandage sores, and how to apply salves and ointments and prescribe pills. The diseased body, bandaged or not, went on interposing itself between the soul and the administering of the sacraments; and Damien had somehow to cope with that, to be fearless in imitation of Christ. The smell of the crowd at St. Philomena's became so bad one day that he wanted to run outside; he stayed. At communion time, he was afraid he might not be able to swallow the consecrated wine and the Sacred Host for nausea; he managed to. "Sometimes, confessing the sick, whose sores are full of worms like cadavers in the grave, I have to hold my nose." But he stayed on in the confessional. And administering extreme unction to the dying, his own hands had to find a way to apply the consecrated oil to hands and feet that were nothing but open sores.

From the beginning, he made his rounds regularly. In time, he ceased to have to force himself, and lived and worked cheerfully, and ate with good appetite. "In the morning, after Mass, a woman who is clean of disease comes to get my food ready. My meal consists of rice, meat, coffee, and sometimes ship-biscuits. In the evening, for supper, I eat leftovers with a cup of tea that I heat on my lamp. My chicken coop produces enough eggs for cooking. I hardly ever, it is true, eat more than twice a day; I rarely have a midday meal. You can see that I live abundantly; I don't suffer from hunger. During the day, I am very little at home."

Damien had always been an active catechizer and baptizer, and he never had more work of this kind to do than at Kalawao. He visited each of the sick once a week; this alone took him four or five days, from morning to night. Some Sundays, he said Mass three times at Kalawao; the same day he would cross the promontory to Kalaupapa and say Mass and hold prayer meetings there. A first census, taken just after he arrived, turned up just over two hundred Catholics among the six hundred people confined to the settlement. Within ten days, he had twenty new catechumens; the next week, he performed thirty new baptisms; by the end of July, he was reporting to the bishop that he had almost four hundred catechumens.

"Ordinarily," he said of the Hawaiians, "they listen attentively to the word of Salvation, which I spread among them according to their dispositions. Almost from one house to the next I have to change my tone. Here, I give words of sweetness and consolation; there, I mix in a little bitterness, because it is necessary to open the eyes of a sinner; finally, the thunder sometimes rumbles, and I threaten an impenitent with terrible punishments, which often produces a good effect."

Damien used, indeed, everything he could think of to bring the Hawaiians to his God: sweet words here, harsh words there, thunder there again, and charity wherever it was needed. Gifts arriving from Honolulu he distributed "without distinction," so much misery was everywhere. He was right in his judgment that this would lead the Hawaiians to regard the Catholic priest as the father-general of all. St. Philomena's church became too small for the crowds attending Mass. Damien had to line up the overflow outside at the windows, men on one side of the building, women on the other.

Damien continued his statistical tallying, and reported on it with satisfaction to his superiors. The native Hawaiian Protestant minister, for his part, wrote to the Board of Health that Damien was poaching among dying Protestants for baptisms, and to the *Kū'oko'a* complaining generally about the "diabolical" influence of the Catholic priest. The cemetery was a particular cause for Protestant objection. "The papist teacher saw that corpses are a problem for the people when they are just left in the open to be eaten by pigs. Because he is so intent on converting people to his religion, he ordered several bundles of pickets from Honolulu. They have since arrived, and are now set up here . . . like a net ready to snare the ignorant fish which go the wrong way. That is the kind of cemetery this is." For Damien, of course, the cemetery with its picket fence and big cross—also ordered from Honolulu —was consecrated ground. The graveyard was where everyone at Kalawao would finish, soon rather than late. Best by far that it should be as little a horror as possible, at the end of a life of horrors. "In tears I sow the good seed among my poor lepers," he wrote toward the end of 1874. "From morning to night, I am amidst heartbreaking physical and moral misery. Still, I try to appear always gay, so as to raise the courage of my patients. I present death to them as the end of their ills, if they will make a sincere conversion. Many see their last hour come with resignation, and some with joy. Thus, in the course of this year, I have seen a hundred of them die in very good dispositions." A hundred dead in 1874 with good dispositions; together with those dead in 1873, there were already two hundred graves inside the white picket fence.

XI

Living in a world of the blackest imaginable facts, Damien did not speak of black thoughts. He was even able to make jokes. In a letter to Pamphile in November, 1873, he resurrected an old play on words from his Flemish past for his brother's benefit. "Let me tell you about my health, in the hope that you are the same. For seven months I have been in the hospital." He was managing to make a confession once every two or three months, either by snatching a rare opportunity to go to Honolulu for a day or two, or by arranging to see any priest who might be visiting Molokai from Maui or Hawaii for some special reason. At Kalawao, Damien never referred to the "insupportable melancholy" engendered by loneliness from which he had suffered at Kohala.

Just the same, within a few months of his arrival at the settlement, he began asking for a companion. The reason was simple: physical exhaustion. He could not do all that needed to be done, at the settlement and over the *pali* in the healthy districts. Trying to do too much—everything—he wore himself out. He spoke of himself as a reservoir run dry, a lamp with no more oil. He needed a working companion, so that he would not be completely drained, burned out—so that God could replenish him.

His superiors had a candidate. Once again it was not his brother, Father Pamphile, but a Dutch priest named André Burgerman, a man in his forties—eleven years older than Damien—with long experience in the Tahitian mission of the Sacred Hearts, a talent for medicine, and an undetermined disease of his own, perhaps elephantiasis, though he had had contact with leprosy in Tahiti. Burgerman had asked for the assignment to Kalawao; the father-general of the Congregation had approved. When the new priest arrived at Honolulu, however, Bishop Maigret and the provincial, Father Favens, decided that he should not work in the leprosy settlement itself, but instead serve the rest of Molokai. Their argument was that no matter where Burgerman was on the island, his presence would lighten Damien's load.

The two priests met in March, 1874. Father André, making his first visit to the leprosy settlement, came laboriously down the *pali* trail, was overtaken by darkness, and fell. He slid, could not stop himself, and slid some more, all the way to the foot of the cliff, where he lay unconscious until dawn. In the morning, some Hawaiians found him, conscious again and praying, but unable to get up. They put him on a horse and took him to Damien's house, where he fell off "like a lump of lead," and had to be put to bed for three days. His host fed him hot tea with wine; he ate, slept, and recovered, "thanks to the kind care of Father Damien."

This was as well as the two ever got on. As soon as Burgerman was up and about again, disagreements began. At the wish of the bishop and the provincial, Damien was drawing up plans for a church he would build in Burgerman's district at Kaluaaha. Burgerman had nothing but complaints. He thought the dimensions were too small; he wanted something bigger; he was not confident that Damien could do the construction work properly; he would rather do without a church, he said, than wind up with "junk."

Damien, pressed for time and with no energy to expend unfruitfully, was more than willing to have working brothers sent over from Honolulu to build the church; but none were available. His superiors decided that he should do the construction, and that Burgerman should take his place at the settlement while it was going on. When, in a few months' time, the church was finished, painted white, chrome, red, blue, yellow, and brown, and ready to be blessed, Burgerman climbed the *pali* to Kaluaaha; and, after the ceremonies, Damien descended to Kalawao. "It is good that they should be separated, each one doing his own job," wrote the provincial. "Otherwise they would never get on. I do not think it wise to put one in charge of the other."

XII

About six weeks after Damien first went ashore at Kalawao, the inter-island steamer deposited at Kalaupapa landing a part-Hawaiian named William P. Ragsdale, a notable lawyer and political figure, at one time in the 1860s the official interpreter of the kingdom's bilingual legislature—a most engaging man, mercurial, now and then downright unstable, given in his early life to public foolery, but at the same time really no fool, in fact highly intelligent and well educated. Until a few weeks before he appeared at the settlement, Ragsdale had been practicing law at Hilo on the island of Hawaii. One day, picking up an overheated oil lamp, he burned himself, but felt nothing. He saw a doctor, and the lack of sensation in his hand was diagnosed as a sign of leprosy.

This was at the height of the Board of Health's segregation campaign in 1873, the same one that sent Peter Kaeo to Kalawao —and led Damien there. Ragsdale made his own grand and tragic gesture—he was celebrated for his sense of theater—and wrote to the sheriff of Hawaii, giving himself up to the law. "I feel it my most painful and heart-breaking duty to inform you of my full conviction that I am afflicted with the fearful disease called *Leprosy,* and I therefore surrender myself to you so that I may be disposed of as by law directed. . . . No one can fathom the *intensity* of my *grief* in being compelled to separate from my bereaved family; but others have suffered the pangs . . . and therefore we must look to our Lord and Savior Jesus Christ for help and consolation in this our hour of grief and sorrow."

Ragsdale came down to the steamer for Molokai carrying his Bible and his lawbooks, and wearing a gardenia *lei.* A crowd of hundreds was at the wharf to see him off, and a Hawaiian glee club sang him away from his friends and his family and his lively life forever.

In talent and professional experience, Ragsdale was a cut above most people at Kalawao. The Board of Health made him resident superintendent. "Governor" Ragsdale, he liked to be called; and he was good at his work, as good as anyone could be in the ramshackle world of the settlement. "I mean," he wrote, "to make the balance of my days here, useful to my friends in affliction, as well as to the public at large." His health "too precarious for manual labor," he lived about four and a half years, thinking up schemes to improve the local administration, quelling disaffection and promoting "industry among the natives," writing articles for the Hawaiian-language papers of Honolulu, and extending a grave gubernatorial welcome to the occasional authorized visitor who came on business to the settlement.

In the summer of 1876, a United States Navy doctor named G.

W. Woods, who interested himself in leprosy, came ashore at Kalaupapa off a warship, and was met by Damien and by Ragsdale, "presenting . . . his contracted claw-like gloved hand." Woods and Ragsdale ate together each evening, at separate tables. After dinner one evening, Damien visited them, leading the settlement band, a procession of boys with swinging lanterns and Hawaiian and American flags, who marched up to the Governor's cottage playing American military music. Late at night, the doctor and the priest sat while Ragsdale recited Scott or Byron or Tennyson for them, "often manifesting great emotion" at his own words, especially at an episode from "The Lay of the Last Minstrel." Woods grew to like Ragsdale. Most people did, white or Hawaiian. Damien had a great affection for him.

Unlike Peter Kaeo, Ragsdale had never bothered about treatment for his disease. "Ragsdale," wrote Kaeo, "told the Dr. that he new the Medicine could not cure him or any that was inflicted with the Leper, but that the Dr. was administering the medicine in order to check the disease from progressing, and Ragsdale was aware of the fact, but as he was to die sooner or later, he would not take it." In mid-1877, his health collapsed. By early November, Rudolph Meyer was warning the Board of Health that Ragsdale "may now be taken away at any time," and that the Board should be thinking of a successor. Two weeks later, Damien wrote to Honolulu: "Our beloved Bill Ragsdale is nearly at the term of his days." Please tell the president of the Board of Health, he continued in his homemade English, "y will grumble him—if he appoints a bad man for this place."

XIII

Ragsdale died on November 24. Damien was staggered to hear, a day or two later, that the man picked to succeed the Governor as resident superintendent was his contentious colleague Father André. Burgerman, so it turned out, had been negotiating with the

Board of Health; and Rudolph Meyer, who was handling arrangements, apparently favored the appointment.

Damien was taken aback even more to find that Burgerman had not mentioned these plans to his superiors. Now, at the last moment, he wanted Damien to find out for him what the bishop and the provincial thought of the idea of a Sacred Hearts priest as resident superintendent. If they would allow him to take the job and stay within the Congregation, well and good, so Burgerman said; for his own part, he really wanted to be released from his vows. He told Damien that he would say Mass on the coming Sunday for the "public usefulness"; but that he would do nothing more as a priest until he heard the decision of the ecclesiastical and religious authorities.

Damien had long since made up his mind that Father André was not a suitable man for the work he was doing—nor, in the end, a suitable member of the Congregation. "This priest," he wrote to the father-general in 1876, "is not in his place here on Molokai—not even in the Islands. His way of acting and talking have convinced me that he is attached neither to his post nor to the mission here nor even to the Congregation."

Damien's opinions seemed to be borne out, at least in part, by what Burgerman was proposing: first to change posts on his own initiative, then to leave the Congregation. On the other hand, Burgerman, in or out of the Sacred Hearts mission, wanted to be connected with the leprosy settlement. He had no goal, he told Damien, but to live and die there, helping sufferers bear the disease with resignation.

Damien had no confidence that a disobedient priest—virtually a renegade—would make a good superintendent. He told Meyer that if Burgerman was appointed he—Damien—would withdraw all his help from the settlement.

This was a strong statement, as strong as any that Burgerman had made. There was a reconsideration on all sides, with the upshot that Damien was offered the superintendent's post. He accepted it, obviously so that Burgerman should not get it; but he agreed to serve only on a temporary, unpaid basis, until someone else could be found. A salary was suggested. Damien turned it down; that was not the issue, he said; if he took money for the work, his mother would not recognize him as her child.

Damien's appointment did not last long. Meyer never thought it was a good idea; Damien himself, having taken it on only to avoid a worse situation, was of two minds about it. Unhappily, there was as well a disturbance of the old anarchic kind at the settlement in January, 1878. Damien, of course, was responsible for maintaining order; and he chose to have the ringleader arrested and sent back to Honolulu for punishment. Most unhappily of all, the Hawaiian in question was a Protestant clergyman. Meyer had cautioned Damien against religious discrimination, and Damien had agreed in principle; but this man, so he wrote to the Board of Health, was a "great rebel and disturber of peace," who used "infamous and rebellious" language against the Board of Health. When Damien had him arrested, he resisted by force, "several of his party with large rocks in hand." Damien was embarrassed "for his being a reverend gentle man etc but in such circumstance—no consideration."

Damien's superiors had never wanted any of their priests working for the government, even unpaid. Damien withdrew from his temporary superintendency after three months, at the end of February, 1878; and the responsibility passed to a part-Hawaiian named William Sumner, an amiable and conscientious man, but already far gone with disease. "The Govenor is failing fast," wrote the white man Clayton Strawn, Sumner's assistant, to the Board of Health; he would not be able to "ride about" much longer; he was "old and forgetful." The problem of authority remained. With the "priest on one side, the govenor on the other," there were too many bosses at the settlement, Strawn said. "It hurts the Govnors feeling to think that the natives go to father Dameon before comeing to him he says it makes him look small." Strawn himself was an active man; but Damien could never have approved of him. He bent regulations to suit himself; he was living in sin with two

women at once; he was rumored to have been a blackbirder, a
trader in the labor of Pacific islanders, the next thing to a slaver;
and certainly he had nothing but contempt for Hawaiians. The
administration of Kalawao stumbled along, with disorder never far
away.

XIV

Father André had not given up his strong wish to work at the
settlement. His great interest was the practice of medicine; he
labored hard at it, preparing and dispensing as many as four to five
thousand pills a week; and the Hawaiians seemed to like him as a
doctor, an unusual circumstance between *haole* and *kanaka*. In
May, 1878, a petition arrived at the offices of the Board of Health
in Honolulu, signed by a good many Hawaiians at Kalawao, asking
that Burgerman be appointed settlement physician.

The Board did not name him; but a month later, Burgerman was
at the settlement in any case, practicing medicine. He had left his
parish at Kaluaaha to come down the *pali*, and was living in Peter
Kaeo's old house on the way to Kalaupapa, across the peninsula
from Damien at Kalawao. Damien had put up a church for the
Kalaupapa people some years before, and Burgerman was saying
Mass there. Damien's superiors directed him to help support
Burgerman, and to climb the *pali* regularly and visit the districts
left unattended by Burgerman's descent.

This was a usurpation of sorts, certainly a partial displacement
of Damien. The situation was complicated by the fact that at least
some of the Hawaiians apparently preferred Burgerman's doctoring to Damien's attentions. As for Burgerman himself, even after
his arrival at the settlement he was still restless. He kept talking
about leaving the Congregation, complaining at one point that he
was "in slavery," asking the bishop for passage money away from
the islands. Damien wrote to his superiors at the end of 1878: "My
great pain all through this year comes from seeing my sole col-

league distancing himself more and more from the Congregation
and even from the mission, his superiors, and his companion."
Damien told Burgerman that, if he left the Congregation, he
might find himself without a church to preach in at Kalaupapa.
"This opinion enraged him. He answered me with a letter full of
injury—showing his determination to separate himself entirely
from the body of the Congregation. I went to see him last night,
and after a most animated conversation, he agreed not to do it."
So, month by month, balanced always on the disturbed edge of
departure, Burgerman stayed, and stayed within the Sacred
Hearts Congregation.

"Please," wrote Damien to his superiors, "keep secret what I
have told you . . . about my companion—taking into consideration
his Dutchman's character, and not pushing too hard, we will manage him, because he could still do much good here." Certainly
there was much good to be done at the settlement; and Damien
thought Burgerman was more popular among the Hawaiians than
Nathaniel Emerson, the newly appointed settlement physician.
The doctor, on his side, gave Burgerman—and Damien—medicine to dispense as they requested it. But by mid-1879 Emerson
was writing to the Board of Health: "They give too much medicine, give it indiscriminately, most always unwisely and not infrequently with visible injury—visible to my eyes—to the patient."
Emerson wanted a change in these arrangements. (Another thing,
said Emerson—he was going to buy up some land on the promontory being offered at an executor's sale. "I should dislike very
much to have this fall into the hands of the Catholic priests. They
are always trying to buy; it gives them power. In my opinion they
have quite enough already.")

Emerson, son of a Protestant missionary, spoke of the Catholic
priests as one. They saw themselves as two, and as two who found
it hard to get on together. They heard each other's confessions; but
more and more this became their only communication—a difficult
situation indeed. Their superiors recognized the "diametric opposition" of their characters, the common "hastiness" of their tem-

pers. There was also that subtler complication arising from Burgerman's medical enthusiasms and skills, leading a good many Hawaiians to prefer him to Damien, who was pained, so the provincial heard, to see them going for priestly offices to the other side of the promontory.

Whatever the Hawaiians thought of Burgerman, Dr. Emerson wanted him restrained (along with Damien) from practicing amateur medicine. And the superiors of the mission, having trouble getting him to agree to restraint, concluded—as Damien was no doubt pleased to have them conclude—that Burgerman was by no means a satisfactory member of the Congregation. Damien had been writing that a new missionary was needed at the settlement. Burgerman was not to be counted on: he wanted to be independent. Send me, wrote Damien, a good child of the Congregation, not a stubborn man. The bishop and the provincial, for their part, wanted Burgerman away from the islands altogether, but could not decide on the best tactics to use in getting him to leave. They had some grounds, so they believed, for fearing that if they used "severe measures," the ultimate scandal might occur—Burgerman might "unfrock himself and marry." Eventually, in July, 1880, a compromise measure was tried: Burgerman was directed to leave Molokai for Lahaina on Maui.

Following this, in the middle of the month, Dr. Emerson received a letter about Father André from Damien, "humbly" requesting the Board of Health not to allow Burgerman to stay at the settlement "because I such is the order of his ecclesiastical superiors. II He has threated me yesterday to shoot me in his house." Dr. Emerson wrote to the Board the same day, saying that Damien had visited Burgerman for "friendly conversation" with him, "previous to the supposed departure"; whereupon Burgerman "became very violent towards him and without provocation threatened to take his life ('blow out his brains'), at the same time hastily going into an adjoining room as if to procure the means of carrying out his threat." Damien "hastened from the house," and appealed to Emerson for protection.

Burgerman did not actually shoot. Indeed, whether he waved
a gun or not was problematical. Emerson had only Damien's word
for what happened; Burgerman told someone else a somewhat
different story. The day of the argument, a young part-Hawaiian
named Ambrose Hutchison was on his way to Burgerman's house.
Outside, Hutchison saw Damien, who told him not to go in—
"there is a devil in there"—and rode off on his horse. Hutchison
went in and found Burgerman sitting with a book in his lap, holding a long-stemmed meerschaum pipe. Hutchison asked what had
happened, and Burgerman pointed the pipe at him in its case,
holding it by the bowl end, and said, "Nothing, its only in the
blood." Hutchison, so he wrote, "understood this was the cause of
Father Damien's rushing out of the house for the Meerschaum
case look like a gun." Burgerman was a tempestuous man; he had
the capacity to upset Damien greatly; and Damien was more than
a little shortsighted. Myopia and agitation over harsh words might
well have combined to make the meerschaum case look like a
pistol.

Burgerman himself calmed down enough to leave for Maui.
There had been work enough for two priests at the settlement,
without question, but those two priests could not work together.
Gun or no gun, the promontory was not big enough for both of
them. Burgerman had come to Molokai expecting—wanting—to
share in Damien's work, and in his own way he was good at his
amateur doctor's work. But whatever he did, he never did what
was finally necessary: accommodate himself both to Damien and
to his superiors in the Congregation. So he had to go; and now that
he was gone, Damien was alone again at Kalawao.

X V

The unhappy affair of Damien and Burgerman had a curious and
unsettling undertone, concerning the health of the two priests.
One of the reasons why Burgerman had left his old post in Tahiti

asking for an assignment to Molokai was his own ill-defined but persistent medical problem. On Molokai, the disease, whatever it was, got worse; and by the time Burgerman came to present himself for the job of resident superintendent late in 1877, he was writing privately as if he thought his affliction was leprosy. "I have some enormous spots," he told Damien, "and almost no feeling in my left hand." When he spoke of his goal of "living and dying" with the "poor lepers," helping them to bear leprosy with resignation, he called it "our disease." Perhaps he did not mean this literally, and was speaking as Damien had done ever since his arrival at Kalawao, in addressing his congregation as "we lepers." But if Burgerman really did have leprosy, this would have explained a great deal about his impulsive unauthorized descent to the settlement, and his erratic urgency about staying there or leaving the islands altogether.

From the beginning of 1878 on, in any case, not only Burgerman himself but his superiors spoke as if he had leprosy. And, quite out of the blue, as if Damien had the disease too. "It is said," wrote the mission's new vice-provincial, Father Régis Moncany, to the father-general in February, "that both are leprous, but hiding their illness as much as possible." A few weeks later, the provincial, Father Favens, wrote of yet a third priest—not on Molokai—who was afraid that he had the disease, and added: "Father André says that Father Damien has the beginnings of it."

Damien, looking back years later, recalled from his earliest years at the settlement an itching or burning on his face and legs, and a feverish hotness about his feet. Some small dry spots appeared on his arms and back in 1876; they grew in size and became a more defined yellowish color in 1877 and 1878. He took sarsaparilla as a blood purifier, but this did not get rid of them; a lotion of "corrosive sublimate" would make them go away, but then they came back.

At the time, Damien evidently did not connect these symptoms with leprosy. At least, he did not say so, publicly or privately; though, telling a visiting "sanitary committee" of the legislature in early 1878 that his health was sound, he allowed the possibility, "as he sadly supposed, that the seeds of leprosy are implanted in his system." But then, early in 1879, Damien told the father-general in a letter: "My health is very good and every symptom of illness has disappeared." He rested on his old certainty. "The experience of six years shows me that it was not in vain that I put my health under the protection of the Sacred Hearts, so as to be preserved from this terrible contagion that surrounds me." Later in the same year, however, the vice-provincial, writing to the father-general about the embarrassment of the developing disagreements between Damien and Burgerman, remarked that "in any case there is no way to withdraw them from there, both of them quite leprous." Almost to the very day, Damien was writing to a doctor on one of the other islands: "My own health continues to be the same as before; perhaps I have the germs of leprosy in my system, I am not sure." In April, 1880, before Burgerman, leprous or not, left for Maui, the vice-provincial had written to the father-general with what he called "a good piece of news. Father Damien is not a leper! His illness, familiar to a skilled doctor, was only an eruption of the blood. It has disappeared entirely."

Those who saw Damien in that period of his life carried away a sense of physical strength and personal force, of a powerful man with nothing at all debilitated about him, and certainly nothing to suggest leprosy. The American naval doctor G. W. Woods, meeting Damien in the summer of 1876, saw his face as "smooth and rather thin, but not emaciated, and his features irradiated by an almost constant humorous smile, transiently ceasing to leave an earnest expression intensified by a fixed gaze of calm dark eyes. The chin slightly projected, with a deep sulcus below thick, widely parted lips, and the head, poised upon rather a long neck, was covered with black curly hair carelessly brushed or unbrushed." This was Damien in his mid-thirties. Woods, the doctor, summed him up as being "in the prime of life . . . and the perfection of youthful health and vigor."

Damien wrote one of his occasional letters home to Tremeloo

in 1880, sending a picture of himself. His health, he said, was excellent; he was still the same *"gros Joseph."*

XVI

Damien's superiors were no doubt pleased to think of him as being in good health; and they could hardly have been less than impressed with the work he was doing at Kalawao. Still, the man himself—in their eyes, at least—left something to be desired. No priest was perfect, any more than bishops and provincials were by their office made perfect: every member of the mission needed the prayers of his colleagues and the helpful guidance and instruction of his superiors. In the case of Damien, as with most priests (most men of any kind, for that matter), virtues and faults were inextricable one from the other. He had chosen to work at Kalawao because he was the man he was. Alone there for much of the time, unavoidably out of close touch with his superiors, he tended to do things in his own way; and this was not always pleasing to the bishop and the provincial. He was, in their opinion, too quick to make demands; and, having got what he wanted, too quick to put things to use as he saw fit. There was, for instance, the matter of some building material sent from Honolulu for a chapel to be constructed at a place called Pelekunu. Damien unloaded the lumber at Kalaupapa, demolished the almost new chapel there, rebuilt it with part of the debris and the new material intended for Pelekunu, then took what remained to Pelekunu, and asked for more still to do what he had been told to do there in the first place —all this without direct permission from Honolulu. He had "followed his head," said the vice-provincial in some irritation; and the bishop was "far from pleased." This was typical of Damien, as his superiors saw him—eager to do good, full of energy, full of plans, devoted to his work, but not always sensitively aware of the larger scheme of things in the mission.

In the midst of the arguments between Damien and Burgerman, the bishop described both priests, without distinction, as "over-animated and tempestuous"—certainly not to be thought of, either one, as material for, say, a provincial of the mission. A man's inherent failings might well be mitigated by education and training; but Damien lacked these in all their polish, hurried as his preparation for the priesthood had been. "Without attacking his virtue and his zeal," wrote the vice-provincial in 1880, "he remains a priest missed by the mill of Louvain. Further, he has no common sense and is ill-bred." Damien would have been the first to agree with this, in its general drift, at least. He was no savant, no sophisticate, after all: just an earnest peasant hard at work in his own way for God.

XVII

The government of the Hawaiian kingdom, seeing Damien less for the imperfect priest he was in his superiors' eyes than for what he had managed to accomplish at the leprosy settlement, gave him a decoration. In September, 1881, Liliuokalani, sister of the reigning Hawaiian monarch, Kalakaua, visited Kalawao. At that moment, she was Princess Regent, since Kalakaua was away on a trip around the world; in his absence, Liliuokalani was making a royal tour of all the islands. She came ashore at Kalaupapa with her retinue; was welcomed by her eight hundred diseased subjects dressed in their best; made her way through the settlement escorted by horseback riders clad in red and black; heard the singing of the Kalawao choir; tried to speak to them all; and was overcome. On her return to Honolulu, she had documents prepared in the name of her brother the king, making Damien a Knight Commander of the Royal Order of Kalakaua.

At the same time, the veteran bishop of the Sacred Hearts mission, Louis Maigret, aged and withdrawing from active work, was decorated too. His successor, Coadjutor Bishop Hermann Koeckemann, took Damien's jeweled medal and ribbon to him at the settlement.

Damien met his new superior at the steamer landing at Kaunakakai, on the south side of Molokai. They rode to Rudolph Meyer's house at Kalae, then to the top of the *pali*, and went down on foot, with Damien, "strong as a Turk," in Koeckemann's words, carrying the bishop's bags. Horseback riders met them at the foot of the trail, and escorted them to the settlement with banners and music. The presentation ceremony went off well and emotionally, with good feeling everywhere; even the Protestants attended.

The new Knight Commander of the Royal Order of Kalakaua wore his decoration just once, on the day it was awarded. Later, on Hawaiian national holidays, he might wear the ribbon. Personally, he did not take such things any more seriously than he had to do for the sake of protocol; to Pamphile he wrote in an amused way: "Sir Knight will have to be in the confessional from two to nine o'clock!" He knew that the mission might benefit from the publicity; but even that had its other side. "Much fanfare in the papers about the priest of Kalawao—that causes jealousy among some people here." He could only have meant the extreme Protestants.

As Damien had learned, the Honolulu newspapers were again bestowing their own blessing on his works. The *Hawaiian Gazette*, one voice of sound, respectable, *haole* opinion at Honolulu, was pleased with the decoration, the more so since Liliuokalani, not herself a Catholic, had risen in awarding it "above all petty cliques —giving honors for merit, no matter what the religious belief of the recipient may be. . . . If there is one thing the nineteenth century can be proud of, it is this liberality of thought, this rising above bigotry, that most contemptible offspring of what ought to be the most ennobling feature of the human intellect. We are proud to see, then, that the Princess Regent is swayed by no such motives, but that she, a staunch Protestant, can see motives worthy of reward in those who are doctrinally opposed to her in religion."

So Damien, as Knight Commander, was part of the spirit of the age. He was also, in the words of the *Pacific Commercial Advertiser*, part of the true spirit of Christianity in its fervent beginnings. "He resuscitates the saintly heroism of the bloody arenas of the ages of old; nay, he does even more. Would it not be a great favor to be thrown a prey to a wild beast rather than be condemned to live in the poisonous atmosphere of a leper settlement?"

Not so much because he was in the distant and difficult country of saints and martyrs, as because he found himself in the unfamiliar and contentious country of the press, Damien asked for the blessing of his bishop "on your unworthy child of Kalawao."

XVIII

Among the spectators who watched Damien receive his jeweled medal and the eulogy of the Hawaiian monarchy was a new colleague, Father Albert Montiton, a Frenchman, who had been at the settlement less than three weeks. Montiton's feelings about the ceremony must have been mixed, because he came to Kalawao convinced that Damien was not a good man: that he was, to be specific, sexually immoral—that he had "lived evilly" with a woman. Montiton had heard this said on the island of Hawaii, where he had most recently been stationed; and evidently the vice-provincial of the mission at Honolulu had heard something to the same effect. As soon as Montiton arrived at Kalawao, he taxed Damien with the sin, talking to him about it three days in a row. Damien, greatly hurt to have his "reputation put under suspicion," restrained himself, simply asking that Montiton should be an eyewitness to his conduct rather than a witness at a distance.

This was hardly a good beginning to what would necessarily be a close association. Damien tried to make optimistic sounds about cooperation. "Father Albert and I pull on the same rope, and I hope this will continue." But Montiton had not let go of his suspicions, and at the first opportunity he demonstrated this. In December, 1881, Damien spent some weeks at Kalaupapa, where Montiton was stationed, doing carpentry work; and Montiton came to live in Damien's house at Kalawao and serve the congregation there. For five years, two Hawaiian women, one of them over fifty years old, had been cooking for Damien and looking after orphan children for him: "true sisters of charity," Damien called them. Before a week was out, Montiton had turned this arrangement upside down, forbidding the women to enter Damien's house at all. He gave the cooking job to the husband of one of the women, went on to get rid of another of Damien's helpers as well, and checked constantly to see that no females came into the kitchen. Damien reported all this to Bishop Koeckemann, adding a little bemusedly that the prohibition against women was not total: Montiton, an enthusiastic musician, held singing practice with women in his room. Damien did not criticize him for this, so he said; he just wondered what it all meant. Whatever the meaning, it was enough to try Damien's patience. He recognized in himself a tendency to be too sensitive if he was pushed hard; but certainly he felt an excessive push from Montiton. "Everything would go well," wrote Damien somewhat wearily, "if he would get off his high horse with those unreasonable demands."

In the wake of this unpleasantness, Damien asked the bishop to define authority at Kalawao. He had always wanted responsibility for the whole settlement. Koeckemann's view was that, since Damien and Montiton apparently could not get on well, it would be best for them to work "in concert" in "separate places," meaning, in effect, that Kalawao and Kalaupapa should be considered separate districts, each with an independent priest. Damien did not like that idea nearly as well as Montiton did; and he asked again, without getting a more satisfactory answer from Koeckemann, where final jurisdiction should lie.

In the early months of 1882, the two priests managed to disagree about everything, most conspicuously over a marriage that Damien had performed. A fairly fine point of doctrine was involved. Montiton thought it was somewhat irregular, and he wrote to Koeckemann, who sided with him against Damien. Just then, Damien happened to be at Kalaupapa again, doing more building for Montiton; and the closeness was more than usually irritating. "I am having trouble keeping my temper," wrote Damien to the bishop.

All in all, Montiton was putting Damien through a bad period. Damien was in his tenth year at the settlement; he had seen and done more than most men were ever called upon to experience; he had learned how to tolerate the intolerable; he had found ways to live in a world of leprosy. In short, he thought he knew best how to do things at Kalawao—and now here was Montiton invading his territory, upsetting his arrangements, ordering him around, virtually telling him how to be a priest. It was hard for Damien to tolerate. He kept applying himself to the task, and doubting at the same time that he could manage it. "I renew to you, Monsignor," he wrote to Bishop Koeckemann in May, 1882, "my great desire to live in harmony with my colleague, which, however, is no easy thing."

Another matter was nagging at Damien—his health. He was older: in his years at the settlement he had passed from his thirties to his forties. He was still powerfully strong—strong as a Turk, Koeckemann had said, watching him carry heavy bags down the *pali* trail; but his body, that great and indispensable asset, was beginning to give him trouble. At about the time Montiton arrived at the settlement, Damien started to feel pains in his feet; and in 1882, with Montiton disputing everything from Damien's domestic arrangements to his competence in his pastorate, the pain spread along his left leg: severe sciatic nerve trouble.

Damien was, in short, emotionally and physically vexed beyond endurance, near to feeling beleaguered. Abruptly, Montiton and his meddling, and his own pains, became too much for him. In the same letter as his expressed wish to live fraternally with Montiton and his gloom at the difficulty of it all, there was another sentence, one that raised the momentous question of "withdrawing from the island of Molokai."

In the summer of 1882, Damien came still closer to desperation. He had, as usual, been doing simple medical work among the

Hawaiians—for its own sake, but also because it gave him a way to monitor the morals of the people he treated. He had been paying particular attention to patients in the settlement hospital, because under a lax administration there a great deal of concubinage had sprung up, illicit unions that "turned the priest's voice to ridicule," "disorder" that was "frightful." In what he was doing, Damien could see nothing but good; but Montiton, for his own reasons, objected and wrote to the bishop. Perhaps once again Montiton thought Damien was putting himself in the way of evil too directly, almost courting immorality. By this time, Damien had all but run out of strategies for coping with Montiton's management of his affairs. He could do nothing but explain himself, and put himself in the hands of his superiors. "If my conduct, badly viewed by Father Albert here, displeases you," he wrote Koeckemann, "I will willingly leave Molokai." And having set those words down on paper, he found himself unable to stop. Montiton, he said in so many words, was making his life intolerable. "If you do not work to soften Father Albert's insupportable temper, you will soon see me, even without obedience."

These assertions, raising the question of the limits of obedience, were—for a priest writing to his superior—uncomfortably close to an ultimatum, of the kind that André Burgerman used to deliver. A few days later, Damien wrote again to Koeckemann in a more accommodating mood, but still looking for surcease. "Is it true," he asked—a leading question—"that our fathers do not often visit the lepers' hospital" (he meant the receiving hospital at Honolulu) "and would it be agreeable to your Highness that, being more used to lepers, I come to Honolulu from time to time to take care of it specially? You know my good will."

No answer was forthcoming from the bishop, and 1882 ended with both priests still at the settlement. Over the New Year, Damien spent a few days at Honolulu. He helped to serve Mass at the cathedral, and noted ruefully that, being "more accustomed to being at the side of the lepers than at the side of the bishop," he forgot part of the ritual, and had to be guided by signs from a helpful colleague. Still, things went off "passably well." Montiton wrote him a New Year's message from the settlement, counseling him to devote less time in future to the service of the Board of Health and more to the spiritual and material good of the mission. In particular, Montiton wanted Damien on his return to replace the catch on the door of the tabernacle at the church in Kalaupapa. It was faulty, and sometimes Montiton had to force it open in front of the congregation, which embarrassed him. Damien had promised to do the work, but had not; and that was months ago, said Montiton.

So 1883 began and continued much as 1882 had ended, with disagreements and misunderstandings and contretemps. One was over the quality of a cemetery gate Damien made for Montiton. Another was over the distribution of charity goods to Hawaiians living in sin. Damien saw this liberality as true charity; Montiton disagreed. And always there was the question of the division of responsibility.

Damien's pains persisted, without forcing him to the outcries of the previous year. He continued to serve Kalawao, and to climb the *pali* with his afflicted leg, to tour the healthy districts, while Montiton stayed at Kalaupapa. The question of his leaving Molokai came up again at the end of the year, but the vice-provincial said he did not think the bishop would allow it; and Damien, in his Christmas letter to Koeckemann, managed to say that he and Montiton understood each other well now.

XIX

Damien did not have a monopoly of physical pain. Montiton, in his late fifties, was a sick man. His early life as a priest had been spent in the Tuamotu Archipelago in the South Pacific, where he had made a fine reputation for himself, and where—like André Burg-erman—he had contracted a disease thought to be elephantiasis. Again like Burgerman, he had come to the Hawaiian Islands with the idea of serving at the leprosy settlement. By the time he reached Honolulu in 1874, his condition was so obvious and so unsightly that some of the priests at the Sacred Hearts mission could scarcely tolerate his presence. (Father Hermann Koeckemann, not yet the bishop who later had to arbitrate between Damien and Montiton, said that if Montiton stayed at Honolulu, he himself wanted to be sent somewhere else.) Montiton was a problem. His illness; a special diet he had to have; his "system of evangelization, applicable in the Tuamotus," but not, apparently, in the Hawaiian Islands—all this made it difficult to dispose of him properly. In 1877 he was sent to Kona, on the west coast of the island of Hawaii, an extensive, lightly populated district, where he would be by himself (and, a tacit consideration, out of the way of other missionaries). But not even distance could muffle his complaints. "As for Father Albert," wrote the vice-provincial to the father-general in 1879, "nothing pleases him; everything has to be done over again, everyone is wrong, almost everyone complains about him, myself the first."

Montiton was transferred to Molokai in 1881 because his disease had taken a turn for the worse, appearing—again as in Burgerman's case—to be turning into something like leprosy. Furthermore, at the settlement, he would be conclusively out of the way of the Honolulu priests with their rather delicate sensibilities—a delicacy Damien had long since had to dispense with.

Then, in March, 1884, after two and a half vexing years with Damien, Montiton suddenly became much more ill. His skin condition flared up badly, and he received permission to go to Honolulu for treatment. The effect of his arrival on the numerous Sacred Hearts Fathers of the capital was comic and sad and embarrassing all at the same time. He stayed at the mission for several weeks, with everyone trying to avoid him—a difficult matter, "because he runs after everyone," as the new vice-provincial, Father Léonor Fouesnel, wrote. "He looks like a man who has been skinned; by doctor's orders he has to be greased and bandaged from head to foot twice a day; his ointment, a grease with a very disagreeable smell, does not stop him from being everywhere, touching everything, greasing everything. Monsignor has fled from him, the saintly Father Modeste has had to change places in church, for air, and he pursues me repeating every day that the mission must take care of him etc etc."

This was Molokai come to town in the flesh, and it was too strong a dose of disease for Honolulu. The physical presence alone of Montiton would hardly have dismayed Damien. But the way in which the skinned and greased priest, turning up everywhere in the capital, making incessant demands, was able to disconcert the entire mission, from the bishop and the saintly old provincial down, threw some light on the difficulties Damien must have had in dealing with Montiton at Kalawao. Father Albert—perhaps, indeed, because of the torment of his disease—was, in the words of one of the Honolulu Fathers, an *"énergumène"*: a man possessed, restless, cranky, perpetually in motion, seeking friction with his colleagues almost literally, physically, both for human contact and for a kind of surcease.

"I do not," Damien had written at the height of his difficulties with Montiton in 1882, "want to live at war with the colleagues the Congregation has given me at Molokai." Burgerman with his fierce waywardness and incipient violence, then Montiton the energumen: it was an open question whether anyone could have sustained his equanimity while living point-blank with either of them for months and years at a time.

It had to be said as well that Damien, entering his mid-forties, had left behind a great deal of his own youthful amiability, at least where his work was in question. Growing older and more set in his ways at Kalawao, he could be obstinate and unyielding: a father confirmed in authority among children, unwilling to see his control diluted by the fraternal presence of a colleague. When he was alone with Hawaiians, this might pass more or less unremarked; though his superiors were already drawing attention to it in their letters. With a colleague on the spot, it was bound to make itself felt—and especially with a colleague like Montiton. Taxed once by another member of the mission with being an energumen and begged to moderate himself, Father Albert had said, in beautifully apt proverbial self-diagnosis and prognosis: "The fox will die in his skin."

Montiton's actual skin condition was much improved by the offensive greasing; but then, still in Honolulu, he came down with pneumonia. Recovered at last in mid-1884, he went back to Kalawao, and to the life of divided responsibility and close propinquity he shared with Damien. The settlement, that natural prison, was unquestionably capable of inducing something like prison fever in the two priests, whose sentences there were at least to a degree self-imposed, but who were further imprisoned for life in bodies with aches and pains and ominous symptoms that augured both exacerbation and termination of the sentence. For his part, at that stage, Damien might almost have preferred solitary confinement.

XX

Alone or in the company of incompatible colleagues, Damien lived by the Rule of his Congregation, trying as best he could to conform himself to his vows. He also drew up for himself in 1879 what he called a "Personal Rule," intended to organize his life day by day, hour by hour, bringing together the most private and most public functions of his Christian life and his ministry:

> 5 a.m. Get up—go to the church as soon as possible. Morning prayer —adoration and meditation until 6:30. Mass. Instruction. Thanksgiving till quarter to eight. Then take care of one and another thing for the good of the faithful. 8 o'clock breakfast—followed by a little talk and other domestic business 9 o'clock—small hours—under the *waranda*. 9:30 spiritual reading followed by study or letter-writing till noon. 12 o'clock lunch. After lunch visit the sick and the Christians in general—so as to see every week all that goes on in each house in my district—If I can get back by 5 o'clock—say vespers and do housework. 6 o'clock. Dinner. at first dusk rosary breviary—and evening prayer. Between 8 and 10 o'clock bed.

At the time he set this schedule for himself, he was eating and sleeping in a new presbytery, bigger than the one-room shack of 1873: still small, twenty-four feet by fourteen, but designed in two stories with a kitchen below and an outside staircase leading up to his workroom and bedroom on the second floor. "Nothing could suit me better," he wrote when he finished it at the end of 1878. He liked carpentry work very well, and his set of tools was more than well used. He had planned and constructed his house between bouts of church building in the healthy districts, together with work on the enlargement of St. Philomena's church at Kalawao village and the wooden church at Kalaupapa, made necessary by the remorseless growth of the settlement and the even faster rate of growth of the Catholic congregations. By 1880 there were more than eight hundred leprosy victims on the promontory of Kalawao, living in thatch huts or wooden cottages amid trees and vegetable gardens; and more than half were Catholics.

Whether Damien's cooks prepared his meals, or whether he cooked for himself, as he did from time to time, he ate simply, even roughly, as he had done all his life. When Charles Warren Stoddard dined with him, supper was "a bit of meat, a dish of rice, fried eggs, and large bowls of coffee, with nuggets of sugar on sea-biscuits, that served as trays, and were afterward to be eaten." Off and on, Damien brewed himself a kind of beer, and would serve it to guests if he had no wine.

His visiting rounds kept him busy, going on foot to those who lived near the presbytery, or fitting his horse William into some "fragments of harness" and attaching him to a light four-wheeled buggy the Board of Health had given him for the trip across the promontory to the more distant huts. Stoddard, seated beside him, remarked that Damien was "hardly a systematic driver"—most of the time he steered across house lots. Damien actually did have a system: it was to save time by going in a straight line. (One of the Protestant clergymen complained that Damien used to drive across the Protestant cemetery.) William the horse was long-suffering; he was old, and he liked his rest; but Damien worked him hard. And when, breaking his routine at the settlement, Damien climbed the *pali* once a month and borrowed a horse from Rudolph Meyer to do his rounds, he was likely to bring it back almost ridden into the ground—to Meyer's considerable annoyance. Damien remained what he had always been, a vigorous, demanding, even driven man—in his own way an energumen.

Many of the tasks that he found himself involved in were not listed in his Personal Rule. The Board of Health relied upon him to help, with or without benefit of an official title, in the general running of the settlement. Meyer, living over the *pali*, came down perhaps once a month; for much of the time Kalawao had no resident physician; and the resident superintendents were a mixed lot. The hospital had to keep up its work; there was a small store, a slaughterhouse, the landing place at Kalaupapa—each with its problems of administration, each with improvements to be considered and carried out. At one time or another, Damien had a part in the laying of water pipes, the construction of a new road from Kalawao village to Kalaupapa, the blasting of rocks at the landing place to make better access for boats. If huts were blown down by the high winds of winter, he rebuilt them. He made coffins and dug graves, if there was no one else to do it. And, both in the huts and at the hospital, he practiced his amateur brand of medicine. He cleaned and bandaged sores, prescribed pills and simple drugs, and—once, at least—amputated a gangrenous foot, though none too neatly, according to a visiting doctor who saw the result shortly afterward.

As for the moral improvement of the people of Kalawao, Damien had the most pressing of responsibilities. The resident superintendent was in charge of law and order, but Damien was never satisfied with the level of enforcement. He could always find breaches of the moral law: concubinage at the hospital, adultery —even prostitution—in the huts. The drinkers kept operating their secret stills; and often enough their silent secret turned noisy, with "women . . . roariously drunk staggering about the village of Kalawao naked," as Ambrose Hutchison recalled. Drinkers and dancers of the *hula* used to meet at a place known as *ka pā pupule,* the crazy pen, or the village of fools, just outside Kalawao. Damien was known to invade the dance house, hefting the walking stick he carried, to break up the dances, scattering the performers and overturning the drinking calabashes. Some of those who approved of what he was doing said he waved the stick for emphasis; those who were aggrieved said he belabored them. Ambrose Hutchison, a good Catholic on the side of right, was clear on what happened. "The hilarious feasters abruptly break up making quick get away from the place thru the back door to escape his big stick, for he would not hesitate to lay it on good and hard on the poor hapless person who happened to come within reach of his cane."

Attempting to tame the eternal animal was unhappy work. It was more pleasant to build churches, and to build the Church. By 1876, Damien was able to start religious associations among his people, one for men, one for women, one for children. In 1879, he instituted perpetual adoration, the ritual that distinguished the observances of the Congregation of the Sacred Hearts. All over the world, wherever there were Sacred Hearts missions, the faithful knelt in turn at the altar, day and night; and Damien wanted no less than this for Kalawao. His congregation had special difficulties, "because of the infirmities of the members of the adoration. If they cannot come to do their half-hour of adoration in the church, I am often edified to see them in adoration at the prescribed time—on their bed of pain in their miserable huts."

One of the harshest of leprosy's cruelties was that it attacked children as well as adults. By the end of the 1870s, there had been a number of boys and girls sent to the settlement with no one to look after them—effectively orphaned. Another handful of children, born at the settlement of unions licit or illicit, had no guardians: their parents had died, or simply did not want them. Of all fates, theirs was perhaps the worst. They might be taken by the unscrupulous and turned into drudges or—worse—child prostitutes; and when they were exhausted, or when their disease was far advanced, they might be simply abandoned, thrown out of the hut, left to look after themselves as best they could. Damien got permission from the Board of Health to take orphans under his wing; and with some charity money he built dormitories and kitchens near his presbytery, first for boys, then for girls. By 1883, he had forty-four orphans in his care. He did all he could to encourage the boys to farm, the girls to sew and cook, and all to marry decently when they were of age.

Every Sunday at the settlement, the faithful, young and old, turned out for Mass, the women neat and modest in beribboned straw hats and *holokū*, long-sleeved, neck-to-ankle fitted gowns; the men in calico shirts and white trousers; all wearing flower *lei*. Hawaiians were in favor of brightness; and the interior of St. Philomena's and the church at Kalaupapa were painted in all colors. There was an idiosyncratic mixture of the cheerful and the decrepit. Charles Warren Stoddard, a Catholic convert of some sophistication and taste, had his criticisms of the décor: "The stations were tilted . . . the holy water font was a tin cup; some rosaries were scattered about . . . the chalice was small, the altar decorations cheap and tawdry; the candles tilted all ways." But whoever saw a Sunday service at St. Philomena's was impressed —Stoddard too—by the fervor of the prayers, the beauty of the voices of Hawaiians singing, and the total seriousness with which the communicants brought their doomed bodies to the sacramental table to partake of the wine and the bread, the blood and body of their Savior. On such days, with the sun shining outside, a gentle trade wind blowing, and the surf adding its soothing bass notes as counterpoint to the Mozart mass being sung by the church choir, it was possible to think of Kalawao as a community.

And if this was possible, Damien, being what he was, had made it so. Ambrose Hutchison watched him at work for years, "a vigorous, forceful, impellant man with a generous heart in the prime of life and a jack of all trades, carpenter, mason, baker, farmer, Medico and nurse, no lazy bone in the make up of his manhood, busy from morning till nightfall." Charles Warren Stoddard, in no doubt of the role Damien played, drew a self-conscious word picture of the priest to make the point. The clear reference was to St. Francis of Assisi, lover of animals and birds and all things living, roller in filth, welcomer of Sister Death. Stoddard meant another, more human point to be taken as well, about priest and flock, father and children, provider and provided-for, about Damien as the embodiment of love and charity, consumed in his congregation. "He brought from his cottage into the churchyard a handful of corn, and, scattering a little of it on the ground, he gave a peculiar cry. In a moment his fowls flocked from all quarters; they seemed to descend out of the air in clouds; they lit upon his arms, and fed out of his hands; they fought for footing upon his shoulders and even upon his head; they covered him with caresses and with feathers."

XXI

If leprosy had to be lived with—and it did—Kalawao was as pleasant a place as most: all open space and freshness and beauty in good weather, all fruitfulness in its trees and gardens. The Board of Health was fond of pointing out that the promontory, as a place of isolation, was better by far than the grim stone asylums that walled in the leprosy victims of Europe. And in the opinion of the seafaring doctor G. W. Woods, who made it his business to look at every leprosy settlement he could find, there was no better place of its kind in the world.

An oddity, of whatever significance, was that Hawaiians at Kalawao rarely if ever chose to kill themselves: two only in the thirty-five years of the settlement's existence up to 1900. (Both poured kerosene over themselves and set it afire, perhaps seeking a final cauterization and purification of their decaying flesh.) Another oddity, this one most difficult for *haole* to comprehend, was that the *kōkua*, the Hawaiian helpers, remained part of the settlement, year after year, decade after decade. By the early 1880s—and this

Damien at twenty-three, just before he left Europe. *Sacred Hearts Archives, Louvain*

Damien in 1873, the year he went to Molokai. *Sacred Hearts Archives, Rome*

The priest of Kalawao, with some children of the settlement. *Sacred Hearts Archives, Rome*

Walter Murray Gibson. *Archives of Hawaii*

King David Kalakaua. *Archives of Hawaii*

Bishop Hermann Koeckmann.
Sacred Hearts Archives, Rome

Father Léonor Fouesnel.
Sacred Hearts Archives, Rome

Father André Burgerman.
Sacred Hearts Archives, Rome

Father Albert Montiton.
Sacred Hearts Archives, Rome

The Reverend Doctor Charles McEwen
Hyde. *Hawaiian Mission Children's Society*

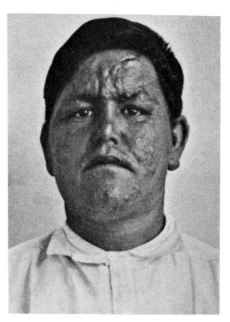

Eduard Arning. *Private collection*

Keanu. *Private collection*

Joseph Dutton, late in life. *Sacred Hearts Archives, Rome*

Robert Louis Stevenson, with King Kalakaua. *Archives of Hawaii*

Three views of the settlement by Edward Clifford *(above, and facing page)*.
Damien Museum, Tremeloo

Damien in December 1888, painted by Edward Clifford.
Sacred Hearts Archives, Louvain

Father Pamphile De Veuster. *Sacred Hearts Archives, Rome*

Damien with boys of the settlement, 1889. *Sacred Hearts Archives, Rome*

Damien several weeks before his death, photographed by William Brigham.
Sacred Hearts Archives, Rome

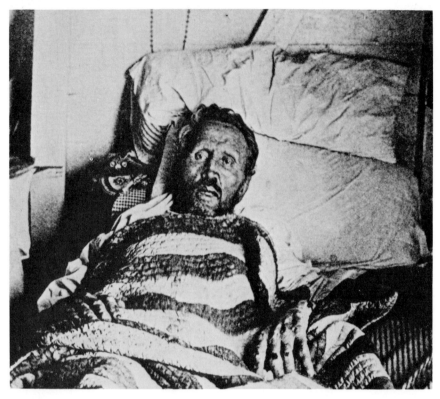

Damien on his deathbed, photographed by the settlement physician, Sidney Bourne Swift. *Sacred Hearts Archives, Rome*

was the ultimate puzzle—a certain number of them were seeking to be classified as sufferers, so as to be put on the free list for Board of Health rations and supplies. Some tried to simulate the marks of the disease. Others, out of friendship turned pathological, seemed actually to be willing to contract leprosy, to put themselves in the way of it, for the sake of a life of ease among friends until deformity and death should overtake them.

The Board of Health sought to explain this, at least in part, by claiming that Hawaiians at Kalawao were better provided for than Hawaiians anywhere else in the kingdom, with little or no work on their own part. Still, there must have been more to it than a scheme to get free board and lodging. Arthur Mouritz, the settlement doctor, may have been hinting at deeper truths when he said that a *haole* lay down sick determined to get better, but that a sick Hawaiian lay down resigned to dying. Mouritz could not account for this, and neither could anyone else; but perhaps by the late nineteenth century a good many Hawaiians had concluded that their life as a people was already over, and that their lives as individuals did not matter any more. If that was true, then Kalawao, the natural prison, offered them a strange kind of freedom from most of the pains of the *haole* world, which had brought down upon them the disease called Western civilization; and leprosy in turn offered them, finally, freedom from life.

This, in the end, was what it all came to at Kalawao. In the midst of life, the settlement was in death. Around the hospital, cows and sheep and pigs and dogs and chickens scavenged among the kitchen leavings and the repulsive off-scourings of the wards. The green grass that grew so high, and the vegetables in the gardens, and the pleasant papaya trees, all took root in a soil that was finally graveyard earth.

The simplest things, the liveliest and most harmless of pastimes and entertainments, were touched with horror. The musicians for whom Damien made flutes out of old coal-oil cans played with only two or three fingers. Boys running in friendly competitive races toiled along on stumps of feet. Damien said of one young runner that he had failed to toe the mark; and it was true, the boy had no toes. At Kalawao, all jokes were black. And all self-perceptions were warped: women straightening their hats in the mirror to go to Mass could look at themselves, and see in their faces not so much the record of all their life as the clinical course of the disease. St. Philomena's had holes in its floor for those who coughed and had to spit. The communion wafer was held to tongues in remnants of mouths. One church organist, lacking most of a left hand, tied a piece of wood to the arm to sound the low notes on the keyboard. At another time, two boys played the organ together, four-handed, but still not much more than ten-fingered. The choir sang and sang, heartbreakingly well; and voice after voice was lost as throats were drained of strength and life was exhausted.

Of all the elements that made Kalawao—however limpingly— a community, the most familiar and most often repeated was the funeral. It was all but omnipresent. The funeral society was one of the earliest successful Christian organizations at the settlement: a coffin association whose members would contribute to raise the two dollars which was the price of a rough board casket. On a funeral day, flags were flown, and the members would assemble in their black clothes with the colored scarf of the club at the throat, and follow the coffin to the graveyard to the sound of music and the beating of drums. Every few days, never less often than two or three times a week, someone died. The coffin makers working at the hospital gate labored endlessly.

This was one way, perhaps the only way, to come to terms with life and death at Kalawao: through the decencies and sociabilities of the coffin associations, and through the sacraments of the church. Outside this frail community, the ugliness was brutal. The day after Ambrose Hutchison arrived at Kalawao in 1879, as a diseased boy in his teens, he saw a man dumping a barrowload of what appeared to be old rags, but which was in fact a dying leprosy victim. This was not uncommon, indeed usual enough, even then, fourteen years after the settlement was founded, six years after

Damien began his work. Men strewed human bodies on the ground; pigs snouted among them. The brute lived still, the eternal animal. Some of Damien's own orphans, rescued from squalor and servitude and sin, and educated for the moral best, drew obscenities on the walls of their dormitories, and crept out at night to the dance house to drink and watch the *hula*. There was no end to it all, short of death.

"Disrespect paid to the moral law"—this was the festering sore that drained off much of Damien's energy. "How this can be bettered is my dayly study." Always he began his daily study for betterment with his own life, and returned constantly to it. In 1880, Damien rewrote his Personal Rule, keeping to the terms of his hourly schedule, but adding a number of stringent admonitions to himself:

> The memory of your past infidelities must move you at each present moment to acts of humility and contrition, with the renewing of firm vows for the future. Be severe toward yourself, indulgent toward others. Have a scrupulous exactitude for everything regarding God; that is to say, in prayer, meditation, the holy service, the administration of the sacraments. Unite your heart with God; and especially, in the midst of temptation, protest ceaselessly that you would die instantly rather than consent to the least venial sin. May passion lead you to whisper these words continually: *"Cupio dissolvi et esse cum Christo."* I wish to be dissolved and to be with Christ. To stave off consent to sin, remember the invisible judgment of God, who watches and knows all the actions of your free will. Be good, vigilant; remember always your three vows, by which you are dead to the things of the world. All that you have is only for you to use, not your personal property. Death to the pleasures of the flesh: purity makes you like an angel; impurity makes a devil out of a priest; no sensuality, no looking for ease. Death to all the caprices of your own will: as with the corpse, let your superiors do what they think best with you. . . .
>
> Remember always the immutability of God, and imitate it by a patience in the face of all tests. Remember always that God is eternal, and work courageously in order one day to be united with him forever.

XXII

To be a priest, and especially the priest of Kalawao, was to live and move, physically and spiritually, in the territory between life and death, trying by teaching and example to show others the way to make the passage. Damien's parishioners were farther along the path than he was: they knew the inevitability of their death, the manner of it, and with some certainty its nearness. Their priest knew none of this for himself. His body had always been, and still was—despite the now constant pain in his legs—almost furiously alive. He was, then, the living father of a family alive and yet dead, dead yet alive. This ambiguity, productive of a spiritual tension that he somehow managed to translate into physical energy, was as much as anything the reason for Damien's staying at Kalawao. He had chosen to make his whole life a mortification of the flesh, by surrounding himself with the mortified flesh of others. In his chosen land of exile, awaiting the dissolution of his body, he was trying to come to his own understanding of life and death.

He had long since reconciled himself to the certainty that he would never see his own family again in this world. He said so, more than once; and his use of language showed it. He was spending his days ceaselessly with Hawaiians, tending their bodies, ministering to their souls, speaking a father's words to them in their own tongue. When he spoke to a Westerner, which was not often, Hawaiian words crept into his speech. In his forgetfulness of the outside world, he was likely to mix French and English together. And, as early as the late 1870s, he had even begun to lose command of Flemish, his native language, the language of his family. Writing home to Tremeloo, he more and more spelled words incorrectly, remembering only their sound and putting that on paper. It became hard for him; such letters got shorter and less frequent.

His one constant reference point in Europe was his brother. He still wrote to Pamphile, still making observations, sometimes with a little sting, about the missionary vocation. Once he repeated his joke about being in a hospital and wishing the same for his brother.

Another time, he remarked upon the speed with which mail was arriving from Europe in the age of transatlantic and transpacific steamers and the American transcontinental railroad; just think, he said to Pamphile, it only takes a month from Belgium to the Hawaiian Islands; you could be here as fast as any package.

His sister Pauline, about whom he had been worried before he left Kohala, in fact died not long after he reached Kalawao. His father, the old farmer, died the next year, in 1874. To his mother, now a widow growing old, he wrote once more (when the wife of one of Damien's farming brothers died) about earth as a land of exile, heaven as the land of happiness. "Sometimes I envy my poor sick Christians, when I give them the last sacraments and bury them."

This was almost in the vein of his old besetting "black thoughts." Yet there was a difference. His "melancholy" was no longer "insupportable." He was at a point in his expectation of life from which he could, with some sense of balance, look back to beginnings and at the same time contemplate endings. One of his parents was dead; all his sisters too. He himself was entering middle age. If he did not know when his own death would come, he was more than ready for it to happen at Kalawao. In short, he had found a place to live and die. His house was built close to the cemetery, and he had a close identification with the spot. "The other day," he wrote to Pamphile in 1880, "I could not help being annoyed because someone had started to dig a grave close to the big cross, right at the spot that I had reserved for myself a long time ago!! By insisting, I kept my place vacant. As the cemetery, the church and the presbytery form a single park, I am the sole night-watchman of this fine garden of the dead—all my spiritual children—I find my pleasure in going there to say my rosary and to meditate on the eternal happiness which a great number of them already enjoy, on the eternal unhappiness of some who would not obey me. . . . I swear to you, my brother, that the cemetery and the dying-ward are my finest books of meditation, both to nourish my own heart and to prepare my instructions."

Out of meditation came action; out of the contemplation of
death came a life of superabundant exertion and formidable endurance. He remarked in 1880 that virtually none of the Catholics
of 1873 were still alive. He had seen death turn over the population
of the settlement completely, and the continuation of leprosy replenish it; and he was still at Kalawao, working as he had always
worked. He had chosen to go there, then chosen to stay; and he
had stayed; and he would stay.

XXIII

"Good man of religion, good priest, excessively devoted to the
lepers," wrote Father Léonor Fouesnel, the new vice-provincial of
the mission at Honolulu, characterizing Damien for the father-
general at the end of 1883. "I say excessively, because he does not
know how to *sapere ad sobrietatem*, to have sober wisdom, and
sometimes indiscreet zeal leads him to say, to write, and even to
do things which ecclesiastical authority can only criticize; as in
marrying men or women who in leaving for the leprosy settlement have left the other party behind. That comes from not informing himself correctly; but his blind zeal does not permit him
to correct himself. He is loved and esteemed just the same, because it is well known that it is his thoughtlessness alone which
leads him astray, and not a lack of good will." Father Léonor had
been only once to Kalawao, for a few days, many years before.

In 1884, Damien would have been twenty years a priest, and
eleven years the pastor of Kalawao. Inevitably, the years that took
his old parishioners away and brought him new ones marked him
as well; but surprisingly little. When he went to Kalawao in 1873,
he had a photograph taken. The camera found him, in his thirty-
fourth year, physically solid as always, serious but self-composed;
his face was quite unlined. For several months in 1875–1876 he
cultivated a beard, noted the absence of gray, and then shaved it
off. Appearing to G. W. Woods in 1876 as "the very perfection of

youthful vigor," and describing himself to his family four years later as the same *"dikken Jef," "gros Joseph,"* he seemed almost to deny the passage of time. Early in 1883, in his forty-fourth year, he wrote to Pamphile about visiting Honolulu briefly, and noticing how age was catching up with most of his colleagues. "As for me, I am still almost the same, except for my beard which is beginning to turn a little grey."

"Here I am," he went on, omitting the least mention of those enigmatic spots on his skin or the pains in his legs and feet, "already 10 years in the service of the plague-stricken—without having contracted the disease. The papers this week cite my name to prove that there is no need for alarm at seeing lepers in our small towns, that there is no danger of contracting the disease by living near them etc. These gentlemen judge only from what they see on the outside—without understanding that God has a special care for those who devote themselves in his name to the service of the unfortunate.

"As for me, since coming to the leprosy settlement, I have confided to Our Lord, his Holy Mother, and Saint Joseph the matter of my health. It is up to them to preserve me from this terrible sickness, which they have done so far. And even as for physical things, I often repeat in the midst of the dangers that surround me—*'In te Domine speravi non confundar in eternam'* —I have put my hope in Thee, Lord, and I will not be wounded in eternity." And he added, in Hawaiian, *"pau ia!"*—enough of this.

CHAPTER FOUR

A
PECULIAR
GOLGOTHA

I

The Hawaiian royal family of Damien's time at Kalawao took more than a formal interest in the question of leprosy. King David Kalakaua had come to the throne in 1874 determined to see the chronic depopulation of his realm reversed. "The increase of the people" was his slogan; and, leprosy being the great decreaser, Kalakaua made an official visit to the settlement not long after his accession. Touring the world in 1881, he asked in Japan about treatments used there. And, good Western-educated Hawaiian nationalist that he was, he tried personally, at home in Honolulu, to put native medical tradition to work, more or less as the *kahuna* did, practicing what he called "physchological medicine" on one leprosy sufferer with results that seemed to him encouraging.

Kalakaua's sister Liliuokalani, having arranged for Damien to be decorated after her visit to Kalawao in 1881, went to the settlement again in 1884 with the king's wife, Queen Kapiolani. Later, Kapiolani corresponded at length with Damien about charity, and about the best way to distribute royal gifts. (Damien went to great pains to see that each man, woman, and child at the settlement got a gift bundle addressed individually.) The queen also lent her name and her active patronage to the establishment of a home in Honolulu for girls born free of the disease at the settlement.

Leprosy was a royal question because it was a national question. Inevitably, it was political as well. Kalakaua's premier from 1882 to 1887 was a consummate politician, an accumulator and juggler of offices, part visionary, part opportunist, part statesman, part demagogue, named Walter Murray Gibson—"Minister of Everything," his opponents called him—an American, a Southerner of obscure origins, who had made his way up in the public life of the kingdom as the natural enemy of the white Protestant business and moral élite, and as the somewhat ambiguous champion of the native Hawaiians. Gibson was never reluctant to use tax money for the combined purposes of the social good of the Hawaiians and his own political advancement. It had been his "respectful suggestion" as editor of the *Nūhou* in 1873 that the then king, Lunalilo, ought to visit Kalawao, and that a priest was needed there. Leprosy later became one of Gibson's favorite areas of political operation: there was the chance to take the part of the Hawaiian, make speeches about what he was doing, and win votes for himself among the *kanaka*.

In 1865–1866, the first years of Kalawao's existence, the Board of Health, with a total appropriation of thirty thousand dollars, allowed sixteen thousand dollars for leprosy—more than half its budget. This was as much as the kingdom seemed able to afford just then; and yet it was nothing like enough, as the squalor and hopelessness of Kalawao in the early days showed. By the time Damien went to the settlement in 1873, the budget for leprosy had more than doubled. By 1875–1876, it had risen again, to more than fifty thousand dollars for the biennium. During Gibson's regime, from 1882 to 1887, the biennial figure was one hundred thousand dollars.

This great increase came about because the kingdom had found a new and lucrative source of wealth. The sugar industry of the islands had taken firm hold. A commercial treaty with the United States in the mid-seventies guaranteed the crop a market; *haole* plantation owners were amassing fortunes; and the government was taking its share of the wealth in taxes. The Board of Health generally got something like 10 percent of government revenues, and devoted between one-half and two-thirds of its appropriation to leprosy. This kind of allocation—5 percent or more of a nation's resources to treat a single disease—had no equal in the world, as Gibson was always pleased to point out.

And yet the combination of national necessity and governmental generosity by no means brought luxury to the leprosy settlement. Food supplies, after the first unplanned and dismal years, were generally adequate; perhaps even better than in the population at large. But clothes were budgeted for a long time at only six dollars a year for each person, which in Kalawao's changeable climate was not enough; and at the beginning of the 1880s, the drug budget amounted to no more than one cent per month per person. In 1872, each leprosy sufferer cost the government only 10 cents a day; in 1886, under Gibson the benefactor, still no more than 21 1/13 cents per day.

However high the government appropriation was set and reset, the kingdom could not keep up with the disease. There were now usually between seven and eight hundred people confined at Kalawao (a figure that represented something like 2 percent of the native Hawaiian and part-Hawaiian population). And, as Damien observed, the only reason there were not more was that the government could not afford to have the islands combed regularly for suspects.

There was also, in this regard, the recurrent suspicion that Walter Murray Gibson was not "sincere" about leprosy—that he was not a convinced and rigorous segregationist. Segregation, especially among the white Protestants of Honolulu, was an article of faith. But for all Gibson's oratory on the floor of the legislature, his editorializing in the newspapers he owned and ran from time to time, his endless soliciting of professional medical opinion, his publishing of elaborate "sanitary regulations" for Hawaiians—for all this, Gibson's political enemies thought they could see him manipulating the issue for votes.

Certainly, Gibson had taken to heart the Hawaiians' deep aversion to the idea of isolation. He said repeatedly that Kalawao need not be the only place for restraining leprosy sufferers. He suggested instead local centers of detention, perhaps one—or more than one—on each island. Ultimately, he supported strongly a branch hospital in Honolulu, on the waterfront at a place called Kakaako. Gibson, a considerable word spinner, could make Kakaako sound like a patient's paradise: a place of neat, spotless rooms adorned with "pleasing pictures and knick-knacks," and gardens a riot of color with hibiscus and geraniums, where little boys flew kites or played marbles, little girls dressed their dolls, and women sewed and stitched quilts, all to the accompaniment of song, so that "lovers of music can go to our lepers of Kakaako and have their ears gratified with a pleasant concert of melodies."

Others did not see Kakaako in quite the same mellow light. The hospital was built close to the water, between a "salt marsh" and an "offensive foreshore"; in a severe storm with onshore winds, the yard was likely to be flooded to a considerable depth. The place was overcrowded, beyond the possibility of good hygiene. And segregation there was a mockery. Visitors' permits were given out on a "very *liberal* scale." The fence was easily climbed in either direction; there was traffic between the men's and women's wards. Outside, "at the gate of the hospital, a crowd assembles daily; and seats have been provided on both sides of the fence, where patients and friends are in close communication. Stalls for the sale of various luxuries, tobacco, &c., have been frequently erected, and many articles are passed in and out without difficulty." While Gibson and his Board of Health kept on asserting that Kakaako was fulfilling its function superbly, his enemies—and they were many, enough eventually to bring him down by revolution—claimed that the place was not being used as a way station for Kalawao, but as a substitute. This might be more congenial to Hawaiians, but it was regarded by many *haole* as a bane, and a fearsome source of potential contagion at the heart of the political and commercial capital of the kingdom. Gibson, in that light, appeared to be playing off leprosy against liberty, all for the Hawaiian vote.

If Gibson had made leprosy political, then the Catholic Church was in politics. Damien, a Sacred Hearts Father, was the singular priest of Kalawao; and the branch hospital at Kakaako was run, after November, 1883, by Sisters of Charity of the Third Order of St. Francis, from the Convent of St. Anthony in Syracuse, New York, recruited by Father Léonor Fouesnel with the blessing of the Gibson administration. The extremists among the Protestants of Honolulu did not like this new accession of charitable power to the Catholics, any more than they had liked Damien's original emergence as the indisputable exemplar of Christian generosity.

Neither did most *haole* Protestants like Gibson. And if for the moment they did not have political power, they had great economic power: the power of the plantations and their revenues, the power of lucrative business in Honolulu. Gibson's powers of office rested on his control of the Hawaiian vote; but the taxes of planters and businessmen paid for the running of the kingdom, including the leprosy programs of the Board of Health. So things political were more than a little precariously balanced, and the Catholic mission and its works were in the balance along with everything else.

Gibson, in his private life a somewhat disturbed seeker after religious truth, was flirting with Catholicism. The public and political expression of this interest was a willingness—most unusual in the history of Hawaiian politics—to make generous appropriations for Catholic schools, and a readiness to have the Hawaiian monarchy and the Vatican mutually bestow honorific titles upon deserving people. There was Damien's medal to begin with. Then Father Léonor Fouesnel, having arranged for the Franciscan Sisters of Charity to come to the islands, was made an officer of the Royal Order of the Crown of Hawaii. And the mother superior of the Sisters, Marianne Kopp, Gibson's special favorite, for whom he had a liking that amounted almost to elderly infatuation, was decorated as well, with the Royal Order of Kapiolani. On the other side, Gibson himself, King Kalakaua, and Governor of Oahu John Dominis (husband of Kalakaua's sister Liliuokalani), became, without fanfare—a precaution against Protestant agitation—members of the Order of Pope Pius IX. In all this, there was a certain amount

of political expediency. Gibson might have been ready to embrace
the Church. But Kalakaua and Dominis were no Catholics, even
by inclination: both, in fact, were Episcopalians, and Freemasons
as well.

Amid it all, the superiors of the Sacred Hearts mission had to
tread carefully. They regarded themselves always as very much in
enemy territory, with Protestant hostility always possible and
often actual. To be sure, Gibson in power was better than Protestants in power; and the bishop and the provincial could see the
usefulness of his professed friendship. But they were never whole-
hearted in their acceptance of the sincerity and integrity of the
Minister of Everything—"the old fox," as Bishop Koeckemann
called him—and they understood very well that, however much
Gibson might have wanted the support and friendship of the Catholics, he feared still more the displeasure of his "numerous and
powerful adversaries." So the Catholic superiors watched and
waited, with each year in the 1880s appearing to them more perilous than the last.

II

This was leprosy as politics; there was also, of course, leprosy as
leprosy. The disease persisted, remorselessly. The easy optimism
of the Board of Health about the speed with which the scourge
would be put down had evaporated with the 1860s—that is to say,
with experience. The rigorous enforcement of the segregation
laws under King Lunalilo in 1873, intended to bring the epidemic
to a halt, showed only that no end was in sight. And nothing that
happened in the reign of Lunalilo's successor, Kalakaua, suggested
even remotely that the leprosy settlement might one day no
longer be needed, that Damien's vocation might one day have no
imperative usefulness in the Hawaiian Islands. Leprosy continued
to be, as the Board of Health said, "the most burdensome tax that
Hawaii has to bear with." Kalawao earned the epithet of "an

almost bottomless pit" into which the money "appropriated by the Board of Health is cast." The disease, in the Board's words, was "everywhere among us, members of the police, the soldiers, the band boys, pastors of churches, teachers, students, are all among the sufferers." Throughout the 1870s, into the '80s—and on into the '90s—the Hawaiian Islands remained "full of leprosy."

The kingdom's physicians had every chance to become well acquainted with the disease, and they learned a great deal about it; but most of what they learned merely added to their puzzlement. Leprosy continued to strike Hawaiians far more frequently than *haole*, and Hawaiian men rather than Hawaiian women— something like two to one. Between the mid-1860s and the mid-1880s, the life expectancy of a diagnosed sufferer seemed to lengthen considerably, from between three and five years to between ten and fifteen years. But perhaps this was only because in the early years of the segregation laws only the most severe and advanced cases were recognized and isolated, and they died off quickly. As the disease became more familiar to the inspecting eye, the signs could be picked up sooner, the segregation made sooner, and the period of survival "lengthened," though in an administrative sense only.

Beyond such simple assertions, nothing seemed really sure. Indeed, one of the perplexing things about leprosy was the apparent randomness of its incidence. In the matter of the transmission of the disease, some sufferers could trace it back to a personal contact; some could not. This was particularly true of the handful of "respectable" *haole* who came down with leprosy. One *haole* couple, for instance, a Honolulu merchant and his wife, evidently quite healthy, had three children who caught leprosy one after the other. Among Hawaiians, there were well-authenticated stories of women, attractive and with no sign of the disease, who married, lost a husband to leprosy, married again, and lost this husband in the same way. One *kōkua* woman at Kalawao married five times; all five husbands died with leprosy. Then there were cases of another kind, severe enough to lead to segregation at Kalawao, which seemed to burn themselves out there. Ambrose Hutchison, for example, was exiled as a youth in 1879, but survived to become assistant superintendent in 1885 (and an admirer of Damien's work); he lived on—and on—into the 1930s, fifty-three years and six months at the settlement, sole remnant of several of Kalawao's truncated generations.

Whoever tried to go beyond noting the symptoms and stages of leprosy, to get at its causes, to understand how and why and where individual cases of the disease originated, and how it became epidemic, was hampered as always by noncooperation. Hawaiians—and for that matter *haole*—who suspected that they had the disease still tried to evade the authorities. Until the end of the nineteenth century, a *haole* could often buy his way out of the hands of the examining physician, and leave the islands. (One government doctor even suggested an official fund to pay the fares of diseased white men, on the grounds that this would spare them the horror of life and death among Hawaiians at Kalawao, and spare the government expense.) Hawaiians, with nowhere to go in the outside world, continued to hide for months or years in remote valleys, caves, and lava tubes; or—more riskily—to take to the canefields when the government physician and the sheriff, the instruments of examination and exile, made their rounds.

In the absence of sound clinical evidence, all theories about the origin and transmission of leprosy remained no more than theories. One body of opinion could attach itself to another for reasons which had not much to do with the rules of strict medical investigation. Thus, George Fitch, a government physician of the 1880s, was able to develop a theory of leprosy as a fourth stage of syphilis. "Syphilis," he argued, "was introduced here about one hundred years ago. Sixty years afterward leprosy appeared, or as soon as syphilis had a chance to fairly permeate the community, which among a people as licentious as these, was shortly accomplished. A person with syphilis presents a most favorable field for leprosy to work upon. . . . I defy anyone to produce a single case of leprosy in which Syphilis inherited or acquired has not been antecedent."

The white man, the *haole*, according to Fitch, had acquired a kind of hereditary immunity to leprosy as a result of centuries of exposure in Europe; and so, in the Hawaiian Islands, even those bad *haole* who gave way to "licentiousness" and contracted syphilis were largely protected from the fourth stage of its consequences, leprosy.

Fitch had next to no support for his ideas in the medical profession itself, even from doctors such as Nathaniel Emerson, who would have agreed with his reading of the medical and social record on syphilis among Hawaiians. But among good Christians Fitch's ideas acquired a sort of moral persuasiveness. To the rigorous Christian mind, Hawaiians were immoral because sexually promiscuous. Promiscuity among the *kanaka* seemed impossible to stamp out. It was a form of contagion, epidemic in its incidence, awful in its consequences. So was leprosy. The Christian mind readily linked one with the other, and Christians talked in the same breath of the contagion of the soul and of the body, of moral and physical leprosy.

Damien himself, with as much practical experience of the disease among Hawaiians as anyone, was a believer in this connection between promiscuity, syphilis, and leprosy. He did not see it as an exclusive connection. In perhaps one-tenth of the cases, Damien thought, a faulty vaccination for smallpox, or inhalation of the "foul air" surrounding a leprosy sufferer, or physical contact of a nonsexual kind could bring on leprosy. But in nine-tenths of the cases syphilis was there, hereditary or acquired. Untreated—or inadequately treated by Hawaiian *kahuna*—it became leprosy. "It is admitted fact," Damien wrote, "that the great majority, if not the total number of all pure natives, have the syphilitic blood, very well developed in their system. This poisonous root has shot into different ramifications, and as we are now, at least at the third generation, it developed it self in some instance in the way of what we called leprosy."

Damien's exceptional vocation led him to find ways to tolerate physical closeness to diseased Hawaiians, despite their physical repulsiveness, and despite the moral leprosy that he took to be part of their condition. Most white Protestants could not bring themselves to do what Damien did. Indeed, they were moving as a group in another direction, to almost total moral self-isolation from the contagion of Hawaiian culture. Increasingly, during Kalakaua's reign, as the 1870s became the 1880s, respectable *haole* Protestant opinion was coming to regard Hawaiian culture as corrupt and diseased, not only in its syphilitic and leprous manifestations, but in its very nature, at its very source.

Whether or not they could bring themselves—as representatives of the West, of course, not as individuals—to accept responsibility for having introduced syphilis and leprosy to the islands in the first place, they insisted that the root of the Hawaiians' disastrous condition was indigenous. This root they identified as the endless and endlessly renewed sexuality of the culture. The Hawaiian view of life was permeated by the generative principle. Sex was the expression, the ultimate incarnation, of the beauty and power of the forces of existence, something to be celebrated—privately, publicly, ritually. This perception was essentially what had reduced Damien himself in his days at Kohala to "black thoughts" of "insupportable melancholy." So with the convinced *haole* Protestants of Honolulu. Even where disease was not directly concerned, they discovered among the Hawaiians the presence of another deadly infection: sex.

When King Kalakaua, having returned from his tour of the world, held a greatly belated but elaborate coronation ceremony for himself in 1883, his royal *hula* dancers publicly extolled the vastness of his inherent *mana:* his procreative powers and his sexual potency. The English-language *Hawaiian Gazette* was deeply shocked: "No *cleanly wantonness* this, but a deliberate attempt to exalt and glorify that which every pure mind must hold as the type of what is to be kept out of sight, and out of mind as the representative of all that is animal and gross, the very apotheosis of grossness."

Only one word could convey the awfulness of it all—phallic

worship at the royal level, the monstrous incarnation of brutish-
ness—and that word was "leprosy." In the highest and most elaborate public expression of Hawaiian culture, the coronation ceremonies of King Kalakaua, the Protestants saw only revolting
sickness. They conceived of themselves as being thrust "face to
face" with a "leprous visage."

III

For the Reverend Doctor Charles McEwen Hyde, this "leprous
visage" was very real. Arriving at Honolulu in 1877 to take up the
directorship of a theological institute for the training of young
Hawaiians in the Protestant ministry, he was appalled. "Accustomed as I was to the purity of a New England home, there
yawned before me, in Hawaiian social and family life, an abysmal
depth of heathen degradation, unutterable in its loathesomeness.
Obscenity takes the place, among Hawaiians and other heathen
nations, of the profaneness that pollutes our Christian civilization.
Hawaiian home life, apart from Christian home life, is abominably
filthy." Experience did not change Hyde's mind. Those words
were written for publication after thirteen years in the Hawaiian
Islands; they represented his considered judgment.

In such matters, Hyde could see no essential difference between
the Hawaiian commoner and the Hawaiian monarch. King Kalakaua, in cultivating Hawaiian tradition, was cultivating obscenity;
and the royal household was a sink of iniquity. Hyde stopped just
short of calling the palace a "commercial brothel"—he actually
used the words, but then qualified them by saying that he did not
think the exchange of sexual favors there involved money.

So much for Hawaiian culture's leprous visage. As for literal
leprosy, Hyde looked for and saw it everywhere among the Hawaiians who surrounded him: reddish spots on the faces of students
at his theological institute; ghastly matter oozing through the
clothes of a patient in a doctor's office; a clot of blood on the

ground at the wharf where the condemned embarked for Molokai. Hyde had to ask himself a crucial question: "Could I safely hold intercourse with such a set?" There was only one way to find out. "I investigated the question for myself." His exhaustive inquiries showed that doctors contradicted each other on whether leprosy was hereditary or contagious, and whether it represented a late stage of syphilis. But "by all that I saw and heard and read, I was soon convinced of this one fact, that leprosy is one of the results of licentiousness." And, of course, it was overwhelmingly a disease of Hawaiians rather than *haole*. The connections were clear. Hyde was one of those who could hardly help thinking that the Hawaiians deserved their fate. When even the best of them—his theological students—came down with the disease, there was not much to be said in favor of the rest of the population.

And yet Hyde felt himself constrained to do his best for them, to meet foulness face to face. No one was more active than he in arranging benefits for Hawaiians who would accept gifts from Protestants. Hyde prided himself especially on being active in charity toward the victims of leprosy; and he made it a point to include in his pastoral visits the branch hospital at Kakaako.

So, if Hyde was no Damien—and there was only one Damien —he was by no means negligent of leprosy, not blind to what it might demand of a Christian minister. And yet, unable to pass by on the other side, having in fact come to the middle of the road, he would not cross all the way over as Damien had done. Indeed, Hyde was capable of halting his pastoral visits to Kakaako when a doctor friend of his—George Fitch, the strong believer in the connection between leprosy and syphilis—was removed from the staff. And he was capable of ceasing to help raise money for the Kapiolani Home for Girls when Walter Murray Gibson expressed an interest in the project. "If you take hold of it," Hyde told Gibson, "I shall drop it." Hyde, like a good many other *haole* Protestants, saw Gibson as "making of this national calamity a lever to hoist himself to place and power," and Hyde would have none of it: he would "keep aloof."

This was Hyde's practice of the politics of leprosy: a kind of public moral isolation. What he never revealed in public was that for one terrible moment he was all but convinced that the objects of his own charity had infected him: that he, who knew the unholiness of dirt and kept himself clean so as to make certain of keeping himself godly, had leprosy. "I have been warned," he wrote home in confidence to New England in 1884, "of the risks of working for such a people. For economy's sake we have our washing done at one of the Chinese laundries. Six weeks ago in putting on my stockings fresh from the wash, with a new pair of shoes fresh from Boston, I noticed an irritation which I attributed to the tightness of new shoes. The next week a rash came out. That disappeared leaving some pimples on the ankles, which I took to be flea bites, such as I had before. These disappeared but left a discolored spot. Last week in shaving I found that my skin was easily cut by the razor and that the blotches were spreading." Hyde put himself at once in the care of his family physician, who "cannot tell how it will result."

For a man who had convinced himself of the connection between leprosy and licentiousness, this was a horrifying situation, even though licentiousness, however much it was on Hyde's mind, could only have touched his body at second hand. And for a man who saw Hawaiians failing to live up to his version of the moral cure of souls and becoming diseased in consequence, to be infected by the same disease would have been catastrophic. For Hyde, or anyone like him, to have died in the service of Hawaiians, and of their affliction, would have been to fly in the face of respectability and all that was holy in it.

Hyde did not die of leprosy. The blotches and skin irritations and ominous razor cuts which had so disconcerted him turned out to be, blessedly, a false alarm; and he was able to go back to his good works in good conscience.

I V

The Christian view, and especially the Protestant view—the comprehensive moral diagnosis of Hawaiian culture—began and ended with what Dr. Nathaniel Emerson called the "ultimate, frigid fact that leprosy is contagious." There were certain ruthless corollaries. If the Hawaiian race was ever to be "rescued from the slough into which it is sinking, the fatal lethargy that stupefies them must be dispelled, the instinct of self-preservation must be awakened, and it must be written upon their hearts, as with the point of a diamond, that to voluntarily contaminate oneself with leprosy is a crime." Segregation, "complete, thorough, and absolute," was the only safeguard. Frigid facts, diamond-hard insistences, absolute judgments about crime and punishment: this was the moral diagnosis in all its rigor. And yet it offered no cure for leprosy.

Indeed, the medical treatments for leprosy applied in the context of this moral diagnosis were wildly heterogeneous, hopeful perhaps, but feeble—palliatives at best. There were various kinds of patent medicines in bottles, pills, poultices, dietary recommendations (farinaceous foods, cod-liver oil, measured doses of strychnine), and an extraordinary number of things, soothing and stinging, to rub on the skin: beeswax and lard; salicylic acid followed by a solution of arsenite of potash; a mixture of tobacco juice and papaya juice; the lotion of corrosive sublimate that Damien used on his problematical yellowish spots in 1876; a blend of dog manure and molasses. These were *haole* decoctions. The Hawaiian *kahuna* had their own applications: wild ginger, turmeric, mountain apple, and on, and on, another endless list. The line between practical folk medicine and folk magic ran erratically back and forth between the two cultures.

The best thinking in the *haole* medical profession insisted, of course, that magic would not do: that it was foolish to "expect to find an arcanum, an oil or extract with very nearly supernatural qualities, as has only too long been done in connection with this

most intractable disease." Neither was it sufficient, or even war-
rantable, simply to call leprosy incurable, and to "remove the
afflicted out of sight," as the implacable—and dismissive—moral
diagnosticians were concerned to do. "This is a remnant of medieval barbarism which every professional man ought to oppose," on
a scientific basis, but on moral grounds as well, "in our relation to
a race which has had our civilization forced upon it, and which is
accustomed to look up to us for help and support." Conscientious
representatives of a superior civilization, practitioners of its advanced medicine, "ought never, for a moment, to accept the saying of the incurability of leprosy as true; but ought to go on fighting
against it. Perhaps we have been on the wrong track of treatment,
and there is yet a solution of the problem to be found." In particular, "the recent experiences concerning the germ nature of disease may be the means of showing us the path of rational treatment; and they must and do give a new impulse and new
encouragement to us to persevere in trying and experimenting."

This was clearly the voice of modern nineteenth-century scientific medical thought, as rigorous in its own way as the voice of
moral diagnosis. The speaker was a highly talented and hard-
working young German bacteriologist, Eduard Christian Arning,
a student of the well-known Albert Neisser, who had in turn studied the techniques and findings of Gerhard Armauer Hansen, discoverer of *Bacillus leprae.* Arning's reference to the germ theory
of disease, and the impetus it gave to experimentation, was made
early in 1884; and remarkably enough, he spoke from Honolulu, a
center of leprosy, but hardly, in world terms, a center of scientific
research.

Arning had come to the Hawaiian Islands in November, 1883, at
the invitation and the expense of the Board of Health and its
president Walter Murray Gibson. In the matter of leprosy, as with
most other affairs of politics, Gibson took the broad view. He did
not see the islands as isolated from the rest of the world. If there
was something to be learned from outside about control of the
disease, then the Hawaiian kingdom ought to have access to the

new learning. If the kingdom could sponsor research leading to
the eradication of leprosy, then the Board of Health should make
the arrangements, and reap the simultaneous rewards of local
well-being and world glory.Gibson saw the appointment of Arning
as another way for the Minister of Everything to do good, and to
be seen doing good. "Let Hawaii," he wrote, "continue to maintain her honorable and enlightened position in Oceanica by her
advanced philanthropic enterprise."

Arning was quick to discredit one part of the moral diagnosis of
leprosy: the idea that it sprang from syphilis. "I avow that this
hypothesis, which, if true, would entirely overthrow our hitherto
accepted ideas not only of leprosy, but still more so of syphilis,
seems to me to be so extraordinary and self-condemning that it
would scarcely necessitate my entering on the subject . . . but, on
the other hand, the theory has been most energetically brought
before the public and found believers, so that I consider it my duty
to support with the full force of my opinion the endeavors of the
other members of the medical profession who have already some
time ago refuted this idea.

"The theory," Arning went on, "is, perhaps, not quite as harmless as many would believe, as it has led, and may still further lead,
the public to consider leprosy as one outcome of licentiousness,
which term certain classes of society unhappily seem to use as a
synonym of syphilis, and to look upon the unfortunate lepers as the
victims of their own or their parents' transgressions." Dryly, Arning pointed out that if leprosy was an extension, a fourth stage, of
syphilis, then surely the thing to do was to halt syphilis before it
turned into leprosy—to have syphilis settlements instead of leprosy settlements. "Singularly enough," this logic seemed never to
have struck the moral diagnosticians. But then, in truth, leprosy
was not really an extension of syphilis. "I wish it to be understood
that neither clinically nor pathologically does the leprosy of these
Islands present any peculiar feature or combination of symptoms
which any physician accustomed to see and treat syphilis would
recognize as belonging to the latter." For another thing, again

connected with the moral diagnosis of Hawaiians, Arning simply did not find syphilis everywhere in the islands, as others seemed to do; and he suggested that "an inquiry on this subject, issued by the Board of Health, would . . . very likely lead to a correction of the general opinion in this matter."

With this much misconception out of the way, Arning proceeded to explain what he was doing, and what he would be doing, by way of experimentation in the Hawaiian Islands. He had already found the bacillus of leprosy in the bodies of victims of the disease, in the living by "excision of tubercles," in the dead through post-mortem examination. The bacillus in the Hawaiian Islands was the same as elsewhere in the world—the *Bacillus leprae* of Hansen. Now, said Arning, he would go on "firstly, to gain knowledge of the paths the germ follows in the organism, and the changes it brings about in the tissues of the body; then to gather information as to the life history of the germ itself; and last but not least, to see to what extent the presence of the bacillus can be used as a practical test for leprosy."

He proposed to devote several months to "cultivation experiments—i.e. to try and grow the Bacillus leprae on specially prepared substances outside of the human body. This work is of the most tedious and delicate nature, and always associated with many discouraging failures; but, nevertheless, it has to be undertaken, forming an essential part of the modern methods of investigating disease."

Arning also proposed to carry out "inoculation experiments," trying to implant the disease in living tissue, a technique "of late perseveringly tried by quite a number of authorities, so far without result as regards general infection." He had, he reported early in 1884, "procured a monkey for these experiments."

Another subject for experimentation soon presented itself—this time a human being. Dr. George Fitch had already made the suggestion that, in the spirit of science, "condemned criminals should be given the choice of inoculation with the blood and matter from leprous patients or execution as preferred by them."

In 1884, a Hawaiian named Keanu committed murder, bludgeon-
ing to death the husband of his lover. He was tried for the crime,
convicted, and sentenced to be hanged. Arning applied to the
Privy Council for permission to "perform some inoculation experiments" on Keanu. The Privy Council agreed; Keanu agreed; his
sentence was commuted to life imprisonment. On September 30,
1884, Arning cut a leproma about the size of a hen's egg from the
neck of a diseased girl, made an incision in Keanu's right forearm,
and sutured the leproma into position.

Keanu was a man in his forties, vigorous, powerfully built. Arning, noting this, pointed out that physical strength did not necessarily exempt a man from leprosy. The leprosy bacillus apparently
required "a certain disposition of the human soil to strike and
thrive." What that disposition might be, "we are at present unable
to define. It is evidently a disposition which may co-exist with
apparent good health, as many examples of strong robust men,
developing leprosy, show us." Arning thought there might be
some hereditary factor involved. He did not believe there was
such a thing as congenital leprosy, that a person could be born
with the disease; "but I do believe that a certain weakness to resist
its attacks may be transmitted."

For the four weeks following the implantation of the leproma,
Arning saw Keanu every day, "and after that once a week for
several months, a microscopic examination of the inoculation spot
being made every time." While a scar was forming on Keanu's
stitched-up arm, Arning went about the rest of his research at
Kakaako hospital and Kalawao settlement, gathering specimens of
leprous tissue from every part of the bodies of patients, examining
them microscopically, trying in hundreds of ways, unsuccessfully,
to culture them. Once, doing a post-mortem on a diseased
cadaver, he neglected to cover a cut on his own finger, and
watched for weeks afterward while his arm swelled up and then
subsided to normality.

V

Arning, waiting for the vigorous body of a murderer to tell him what he wanted to know, found leprosy in the vigorous body of a priest. Between early 1884 and early 1885, it became clear that Damien was another of those "strong, robust men" in whom good health coexisted with the disposition to develop leprosy.

In the early 1880s, Damien had begun to be bothered by pain in his left leg. Then, about the end of 1882 or the beginning of 1883, the outside of his left foot lost feeling, and became unresponsive to the touch. He could draw a line along the flesh where pain gave way to insensibility. By the early part of 1884, the condition was bad enough to give him pause about climbing the *pali*. At some point during the next several months, he was examined by a doctor, very likely Eduard Arning, and the result was ominous. By mid-September, Bishop Koeckemann was writing that he had been told, on medical authority, that Damien had leprosy.

The news was kept secret within the mission. In October, Charles Warren Stoddard visited Kalawao and spent several days in Damien's company. Two doctors knowledgeable about leprosy were there at the same time: George Fitch, the Board of Health physician, making an official visit, and Arthur Mouritz, about to take up the post of resident physician. Stoddard heard nothing from them about Damien's condition, and nothing from Damien either, except for one oblique reference. Damien gave Stoddard a photograph of himself, not a very recent one: it showed Damien clean-shaven and without glasses, whereas the Damien that Stoddard saw was bearded and wore wire-rimmed spectacles all the time. Damien remarked of the photograph that it "looks like a leper," and Stoddard noted in his diary: "And so it does."

Eduard Arning prescribed some medicine for Damien. "I have taken the arcenica pill as by your advise," Damien wrote to him at the end of October, "but on account of the redness—appearing at my afflicted foot—y thought best to suspend there use a few weeks—I have resumed again—as they do not alter at all my good health, and intend to continue." Arning had also made some new medical equipment available to Kalawao. "I am anxious," wrote Damien, "to apply electricity every day, as soon as our machine has been put in order."

Damien was by no means ready at that point to give himself up passively to leprosy. "Dr. Mouritz—y hope will assist me in trying to stop—the progress of this incurable disease," he wrote to Arning, ". . . and with the help of the Allmight. your serv . . . may be use full for many years to our people." Damien was not, in fact, ready to concede until the last moment that his disease really was leprosy, despite the scarcely veiled remark he had made to Stoddard early in October. Apologizing to Arning for "not having fulfiled my promis to send you a description of my own case," he went on: "I thought it is better to wait a little and see the progress of the disease—and if new indices appear to corroborate the verdict of true genuine leprosy. than it will be use full for science to take a detailed statement of all the circumstances."

The indices appeared in due course. Late in November, Arning probed Damien's foot and leg with an electrically-charged platinum needle, and found "the typical analgesia, with atrophy of the skin on the outer side of the left foot, accompanied by a swelling of the superficial peroneal nerve." Arning "did not conceal" from Damien his diagnosis, "which amounted to leprosy." Then, at the turn of 1885, Damien, in the course of a short visit to the mission at Honolulu, scalded his foot. Father Léonor Fouesnel telephoned for his own physician, Dr. George Trousseau, and Trousseau, not liking what he saw, telephoned Arning in turn, to have the finding confirmed.

Arning made one of his occasional visits to Kalawao in the spring of 1885. Early in May, he and Arthur Mouritz examined Damien thoroughly at the hospital dispensary, for leprosy, as well as for any "evidence of other diseases." There was no trace of other disease. In its own way, this was most important. It meant that, however Damien had contracted leprosy, it had not been by first contracting syphilis. That in turn meant that the moral diagnosis could not scientifically be applied to him. It was good to have this information, to be attested to if necessary, in view of the "syphilis-leprosy" theory, which, as Mouritz said, was then "hypnotizing a certain part of the popular mind," and which he thought "might be invoked" in Damien's case.

As for leprosy itself, it was clearly there. No "striking changes" had occurred since Damien had last been examined, but the identifying marks had become visible on his forehead. Over the next few months, up to the fall of 1885, "a small leprous tubercle manifested itself on the lobe of the right ear," and the steady invasion of Damien's face began: "infiltration of the integument over the forehead and cheeks," "diminution and loss of eyebrows."

It was a year since Mouritz had first set eyes on Damien. The doctor had come ashore at Kalawao to take up his job as resident physician in the fall of 1884, and, like everyone else who saw Damien in those years, had been struck by his presence.

He was active and vigorous, of good physique, upright in his carriage, measured 5 feet and 8 inches in height, weighed 204 pounds, his chest was 41 inches in circumference, his hands and feet were shapely, although his fingers were stubbed and calloused from toil. . . . His features were regular, his face fleshy, round, and of good dimensions; the color of his eyes brown, his hair black and abundant; his forehead of average breadth and height. He had a clear ringing voice, possessed a powerful barytone, and was a good singer. . . . The view of his full face gave the onlooker the idea of force, harshness and sternness, due in part to the squareness of his chin and lower jaw. His profile was handsome, was softer and more in harmony with the entire cast of his features than the view his full face presented. . . . Having a wealth of hair, he roamed about bareheaded, resulting in his face becoming bronzed by exposure to the wind and sun's rays.

Now Damien, in all his strength, had leprosy. Leaving Europe for the islands in 1863, he had asked Our Lady of Montaigu for the privilege of twelve years in the missionary vineyards. Since then, he had been more than twenty years in the field; but in the special vineyard of Kalawao, it was twelve years and some months when the harvester of souls became part of death's certain harvest.

VI

To a man such as Eduard Arning, Damien's leprosy was of clinical
interest only: another case, of undetermined origin. The bacteriologist was more interested in seeing if leprosy would declare itself
in the powerful frame of his experimental subject, Keanu. And
while he waited for this to happen, if it was ever to happen, Arning
pored endlessly over the bodies of those in whom the disease was
far advanced, photographing them for the sake of science; making
casts of their deformed hands and feet; pressing the wet, white
plaster down over their collapsing faces, to preserve disintegrat-
ing features in unchanging identity after leprosy had robbed them
of the human look they were born with and grew into. Arning was
only one step ahead of the disease. Leprosy in its severest form
took away the senses one by one—taste and smell and touch and
sight—leaving the victim at last only his hearing, so that he could
do not much more than listen to his own breathing, until death
pressed that out of him too.

VII

Damien's leprosy was known to his priestly family in the islands;
it was apparent to his family of Hawaiian parishioners at the settlement; how long it could be kept out of the newspapers was ques-
tionable. Somehow his first family, the De Veusters, would have
to be told. But for the moment Damien could not bring himself
to break the news to his aging mother.

He wrote home to Tremeloo in February, 1885, after Arning and
his platinum needle had confirmed the diagnosis, but before the
marks on his forehead made the disease obvious to anyone who
looked at him. The letter was addressed to his mother, his brothers, and his relatives. He spoke, in French, about why he was not
writing in Flemish: "because without having forgotten our beautiful mother tongue, the expressions no longer come to mind." That

in itself, he said, was one of the reasons why he did not write home often. Then, too, he said—rehearsing once more the passage he had made more than twenty years before from one family to another—"with the advance of age my ideas become more concentrated in the occupations of the Holy Ministry."

His own health, he said, was passably good, thanks to God. He was almost the same as usual; sometimes he let his beard grow; it was turning white. He talked about being caught in the rain one day, and having to cross "two torrents" to get home, and being bothered with a cold since then. And he spoke of another accident, of having scalded his foot with boiling water. For two weeks it was hard for him to say Mass; he had to preach sitting down. For a month, indeed, he could scarcely walk; and he used his carriage to get about. "Thus amid my sick people I play the sick man myself." But in a little while, he said, he would be cured: the injury was healing, the inflammation beginning to disappear, and new skin was forming. He made it sound like nothing very much, hardly anything at all; but then he spoke of trying to "bear his cross with joy—like Our Lord Jesus Christ," which would have been, for nothing but a scalded foot, an overblown comparison, especially coming from a man who all his life had exposed his body to extraordinary stress without complaint.

He spoke of health and sickness, aging and death, referring ostensibly to his congregation, but in words that chose themselves because his own body was now fatefully involved. The phrase he used for his parishioners was *"mes membres malades"*—"my sick members"—but the word *"membres"* had also the meaning of "limbs": Damien was concerned, beneath the surface of the language, about "my sick limbs." He had, he said, already filled a cemetery with the dead. "Soon we will have to push the coffins down so as to bury others." And the word he used to describe the pushing down—*"enfoncer"*—was the same word he used to describe how he had accidentally plunged his foot into the boiling water.

He talked about death in the De Veuster family—Eugénie,

Pauline, his father, all in heaven—and how he himself, for the glory of God and the salvation of souls, hoped to stay on at his post "until death." A doctor had advised him to go home for his health, and breathe the air of his native land; but then what would happen to his parishioners? He would stay with them, happy, content, "doing some little good." For that reason, he said, his family should not look forward too much to seeing him again in "this low world." He made his mother a joking invitation, writing a few words in Flemish for her: she should come to the settlement and spend her old age with him. She could help him cook—good coffee and plenty of eggs at Kalawao. And his brother Léonce, who had stayed at home on the farm—he would do well to set aside one of his many children to take Damien's place when he was gone. He finished by urging—again in Flemish—daily prayers for the reunion of the family in heaven.

Nowhere in the long, musing letter did he use the word "leprosy" about himself. He spoke instead about time and eternity; about the work of a priest; and about separations and reunions, exacted and promised by the procession of the generations in a family broken apart and brought together anew under the stringent demands and manifold blessings of the Sacred Hearts.

To Pamphile, Damien wrote separately, partly in English, partly in French; and again, at least to begin with, he used veiled words about his condition. Pamphile, still the scholar, never the missionary, had for some reason been asking about the Hawaiian language. Damien could instruct him in that, as Pamphile had instructed him long ago in Latin. Hawaiian, said Damien, was "the clearest and most agreable language ever y have studied." He spoke of his work, and of how he needed help: "Being trouble with a kind of nerf disease in my left foot traveling become difficult for me." In the settlement, with its seven or eight hundred leprosy cases, as soon as the dead were buried the government sent fresh sufferers. All were incurable. And here Damien linked his own case—his difficulty in traveling—with death by leprosy: "The only way out of here is by the cemetery road."

Damien had not wanted to frighten his mother with the terrible name of his incurable disease. But Pamphile could be told; indeed, finally, there were special fraternal reasons that made it essential to tell him. Illness and priestly accomplishment were linked in the brothers' lives. Pamphile's typhus in 1863 had made the careers of the two Father De Veusters what they were, Pamphile's in the religious academy, Damien's at Kalawao. Late in 1884, Pamphile had written about a new illness of his own, something that seemed serious; and now Damien, early in 1885, answered in kind—and more than in kind. He was concerned, he said, to hear that Pamphile was ill, "and as you seem to be hinting that it could turn into consumption, which I hope God will not allow, I can no longer hide from you that I also am threatened with a disease still more terrible than consumption. Here I am, soon to be twelve years among the lepers—leprosy is a contagious disease. I do not think I have reason to complain of the visible protection that God has given me, the Holy Virgin and St. Joseph also count for something, because really I am still today strong and robust as you saw me when I left in 1863, with the exception of my left foot which three years ago lost almost all feeling. It is a secret poison which threatens to poison the whole body." In every sense, Damien's leprosy was a matter between the two brothers. "Do not gossip about it too much," he wrote, "but let us pray for one another." And, having once more outdistanced Pamphile, this time on the road to the cemetery, he signed himself, "your younger brother, J. Damien De Veuster."

Within the religious family, the priesthood and sisterhood of the Sacred Hearts, Damien felt more secure and certain of his place than ever. He was able to write to others who had taken vows like his that his leprosy was "anticipated from my first arrival into this leper asylum . . . and *voluntarely* accepted before hand, and y hope that, helped by the prayers of many, our Lord will grant me the necessary graces—to carry my cross—behind him on our peculiar *Golgota* of Kalawao."

Writing to the father-general, he recalled a letter he had sent to the mother house in Paris several years before, suspecting "even then" that "the first germs of the disease were in my body. That was the natural and recognized consequence of a long sojourn among the lepers. Do not be too afflicted that one of your children should be decorated not only with the royal Cross of Kalakaua but also with the heavier and less honorable cross of leprosy. Our Lord has willed that I be stigmatized with it."

He was at yet another clearly marked stage in his passage from life to death. A quarter-century before, taking his vows at the mother house of the Congregation, he had lain beneath the burial pall and caught a glimpse of eternity. Going ashore in 1873 at Kalawao, his chosen land of exile, he recalled the ceremony. And now, in 1885, writing to Bishop Koeckemann, he returned to that same part of the Rule of the Congregation, which had begun by making itself the ruling image of his life, and had then persisted, to become his ruling passion. "It is the memory of having lain beneath the mortuary drape twenty-five years ago—the day of my vows—that led me to brave the danger of contracting this terrible disease in doing my duty here and trying to die more and more to myself . . . the more the disease advances, I find myself content and happy at Kalawao."

VIII

Damien, first among the Sacred Hearts priests in the Hawaiian Islands to put himself consciously and continuously in the way of leprosy, had finally caught the disease. The question was to what degree he himself was responsible: to what extent he brought his fate upon himself, not alone by going to Kalawao, but by what he did with himself there. A priest could—must—always speak of resignation to God's will. A physician might take account of human behavior in other terms, and Dr. Arthur Mouritz did. "I have never seen," he wrote, "any other priest, doctor, or other contact, assume the same careless and indifferent attitude towards infec-

tion with leprosy as Fr. Damien did, save and except Dr. Fitch."
(George Fitch, believing that leprosy derived solely from syphilis,
did not believe in its contagiousness in and of itself.) "Fr. Damien
took no precautions whatever. In the kindness of his nature, he
never forbade lepers entering his house; they had access to it any
time, night or day. I named his house 'Kalawao Family House and
Lepers' Rest,' free beds, free board for the needy; this designation
I believe could not be improved upon, it exactly fitted the daily
prevailing conditions." Another man who knew Damien at Kalawao, John Wilmington, himself suffering from leprosy, observed
the same sort of thing: that Damien was careless about what he did
and what he touched, his attitude being that "the body decayed
rapidly no matter what, and that only the soul counts."

No doubt what Mouritz and Wilmington said was true, but the
question was, when did it become true? Mouritz did not arrive at
the settlement to stay until late in 1884, by which time Damien
was on the brink of authoritative diagnosis of his disease. From
then on, there could have been no reason for the priest to shun
contact with the diseased of the settlement. Wilmington, for his
part, did not come to Kalawao until 1888, by which time Damien's
condition was very bad, his body decaying rapidly no matter what.
So in the sojourn of both Mouritz and Wilmington, Damien was
already, in medical fact, one of the people of Kalawao.

Certainly, when Damien landed at the settlement in 1873, he
was cautious about contact, sleeping under his pandanus tree
rather than sharing a hut, keeping the diseased out of his house
once it was built. Just the same, Mouritz later remarked disapprov-
ingly upon the site Damien had chosen for his house—close in the
lee of the graveyard of St. Philomena's. The cemetery was rocky
ground; graves were hard to dig; coffins were piled two, three, and
four deep. The bodies decomposed slowly; the surrounding air was
filled with "foetid and foul vapors"; "the odor around Damien's
home was similar to a charnel house."

But then Damien was hardly the most fastidious of men. He was
born and raised a peasant, and remained one when he became a

priest. Bad smells were nothing new to him. Sweat and hard work
and often-worn clothes and dirt on the hands were also intimately
familiar, perhaps even necessary to him as part of his sense of
himself. He was a haphazard housekeeper, as he once remarked
to Pamphile with a kind of perverse pride; and he was a haphazard
groomer of himself, not the sort of man to make a ritual of washing
his hands before he ate. Then again, the settlement at large was
no place to keep clean, if for no other reason than that the water
supply was never comprehensive, always erratic, sometimes
downright inadequate. Damien was everywhere, working hard all
the time. There was not always a tap or even a calabash of water
to be found where he found himself. If the whole of Kalawao
promontory was, in a loose sense, a hospital, there was no possible
way of maintaining hospital hygiene everywhere.

The crux of the matter was that Damien was Kalawao's priest.
Because he was the kind of man he was, he was the kind of priest
he was. And, as man and priest, he could put up with Kalawao and
serve its people. With parishioners like his Hawaiians, touch was
all-important. With a priest like Damien, in whom belief was un-
affectedly incarnate, faith was made physical. To mortify the body,
to die to himself, to risk physical leprosy in order to cure moral
leprosy—this was to be a good priest. If it meant touching the
untouchable, then that was what had to be done. The touch of the
priest was the indispensable connection between parishioner and
church, sinner and salvation.

And so at some point—a point that only he would ever be able
to identify, and that he never communicated except by way of his
unrecorded daily acts—he made his decision to touch without
reserve the people of Kalawao, his family in Christ. It must have
been early in his ministry there, very likely a matter only of
months. Certainly by the time G. W. Woods saw him in 1876 he
was eating *poi* from the common calabash, sharing his pipe with
Hawaiians, dressing sores confidently, and playing unselfcon-
sciously with diseased children.

Somewhere along the way—in the confines of the confessional, in the touch of hand on body during the administering of extreme unction, or perhaps in the sharing of a meal, or in an embrace of greeting or farewell—leprosy passed from parishioner to priest. If it went unremarked at first, an imperceptible transformation of Damien's flesh and blood, still it made him what he, from the beginning, said out of priestly charity that he was: one of his congregation, "we lepers."

IX

So much for what was clear about Damien's case, and what must necessarily remain obscure. In the fact that a priest had caught leprosy there was something at once ghastly and moving—a mingling of what Robert Louis Stevenson called horror and moral beauty. When Damien professed himself to be happy and content, and said he would go on working in the hope of being useful for many years, this was something that in one sense had to be said: there seemed little else for someone in his position to say. But, in another sense, his priestly resignation and personal resilience seemed exceptional and admirable, even heroic—particularly in view of the fact that another Sacred Hearts Father was diagnosed as having leprosy at the same time as Damien, by the same doctors, and was all but broken by the news.

Father Grégoire Archambaux, a man in his mid-sixties, had been in the field on Maui since 1852, most of the time at the port town of Lahaina. He was volatile, sensitive, "far from robust," as one of his colleagues said, subject all his life to debilitating attacks of asthma. Like a good many of the Maui priests, who did occasional double duty on Molokai, Archambaux had visited Kalawao. The first time was in 1876. His natural sympathies were lively and openly expressed; and his earliest sight of the ravages of the disease affected and appalled him simultaneously. "In different degrees they are all leprous. One of them tried to hide his face with his hand. Do not be afraid, my child, I said to him, and he took his hand away. Oh frightful sores! Oh horrible emptiness! It was no longer a face! Unfortunate youth! And emotion seized me." Going with Damien on his rounds, Archambaux got violent headaches; and in church he burst into tears.

Father Grégoire was at the settlement only to preach a retreat. The Hawaiians asked him to stay on. He could not; his own parishioners at Lahaina needed him. But at least he "did not hesitate to tell them in a loud voice: if by misfortune your young, robust, zealous and charitable priest should be stolen away from you by death, no, no, you would not be abandoned." The people of Kalawao, said Archambaux, had "too much of a claim on our compassion and our love" for that. If his legs would carry him, "you will see me come back to live among you."

In October, 1884, he came back as a priest, but as a priest with leprosy. The month before, worried about his health, he had gone to Honolulu for a medical examination by Eduard Arning; and the electric needle had shown his body to be partly insensitive, his face almost completely so. Arning thought Archambaux had probably had the disease for as long as ten years. The sores would soon start to appear. He should be isolated as soon as possible.

Archambaux arrived at Kalawao distressed and bewildered. Damien, himself newly diagnosed, looked after him. "I intend," he wrote to Arning, "to give him a lotion of Bi. chl. Hydr.—to keep his skin clean—as y have done for my self. Would it be good to give him the arcenic pill y am take my self?"

To Damien's eye, at least, Archambaux's general health seemed unimpaired; but he began to have desperate attacks of asthma, and he came to believe that if he stayed at the settlement he would suffocate long before he died of leprosy—if indeed he did have leprosy, which he could not altogether bring himself to accept. In the blackness of his thoughts, he came to speak wildly of his superiors as "murderers" for having condemned him to Kalawao. He petitioned urgently for release, on the grounds of his asthma; and at the turn of 1885, when he had been at the settlement only a few months, Walter Murray Gibson wrote to Arthur Mouritz, authorizing Archambaux's departure for Lahaina.

This was certainly a bending of the segregation laws, of the kind that the rigorous political and moral opponents of Gibson liked to use in evidence against him. It was an even more sensitive case because Gibson's enemies were Protestants, and the beneficiary of the bending was a Catholic priest. More serious still, the integrity of the Sacred Hearts mission was put in question by the medical condition of Archambaux's colleague at Lahaina, Father André Burgerman, Damien's old uneasy, unconformable companion of several years before at Kalawao. Burgerman, according to Father Léonor Fouesnel, was still much as he had been: still erratic in his relations with his superiors, still running "like a madman from one end of the district to another, giving much more care to bodies than to souls, working hard, especially physically, spending an insane amount on buildings." All this activity, all this contact with Hawaiians, was the work of a man who himself very likely suffered from leprosy. Not that he had been declared as such, because he had never been examined by doctors for the disease. But, Fouesnel wrote, "he says so himself"; and Burgerman took pride in his medical knowledge.

So, with Archambaux and Burgerman at Lahaina, the mission seemed to have two leprous priests in the open field, an extraordinary situation. Fouesnel, writing to the father-general about it, was surprisingly brief and offhand. Lahaina, he said, was full of leprosy; the two could do as they pleased in the district.

Whatever the disposition of these two cases, the prospect of leprosy spreading within the mission was appalling. Burgerman probably diseased, and now Damien and Archambaux reliably diagnosed within weeks of each other—"This news has staggered us," wrote Fouesnel. He himself knew something about leprosy. Four days a week, he went to Kakaako hospital to preach, hear confession, and serve communion; and, like Damien, he was aware of the difficulty of administering the holy wafer without touching the tongue of the communicant. "What a scourge this disease is," wrote Fouesnel. "May God preserve the mission from being destroyed in this way." The provincial council of the mission at Honolulu took protective steps of its own. Priests ought not to

distance themselves from the sick, or shun the victims of leprosy:
Damien's vocation asserted this, triumphantly and tragically. And
yet, by no means every Hawaiian victim of the disease was segregated at Kalawao. Potential contagion was everywhere, as the sad
case of Archambaux showed. Fouesnel and his fellow council
members agreed that priests whose work brought them into contact with the disease must wear gloves; wash with carbolic acid
after contact; and breathe "camphorated vinegar" in the confessional.

X

Archambaux had come and gone quickly. His departure left
Damien closeted alone once more with Father Albert Montiton,
the "energumen," installed again after his return from Honolulu
in his church at Kalaupapa. Always something of a problem for the
mission, Montiton was now more so than ever, because to all ap-
pearances his skin disease had cleared up; he was cured; and in the
thinking of the mission's superiors, a healthy priest really ought
not to be left at the settlement. There were posts vacant in the
field, several of them—the mission was chronically short of workers—but Bishop Koeckemann hesitated to turn the energumen
loose on the islands at large. Montiton, after all, said the bishop,
"has never been able to make peace with his superiors, his colleagues, or with the faithful, or with outsiders." Koeckemann remarked that he would shed no tears if the father-general allowed
Montiton to go back to his old field of work in the Tuamotu Archipelago.

Montiton would have found this agreeable enough. He began to
talk generally in those terms, then to make up his mind firmly to
the idea. But when a possible replacement for him at Kalawao was
considered, a new problem arose. Damien heard indirectly that
Bishop Koeckemann was thinking of returning Father André
Burgerman to the settlement. Damien would not have been able

to stand this, and said so: he could not bring himself to be either the penitent or the confessor of Burgerman.

But if Montiton left, and Burgerman did not come, Damien would be alone, and he found that idea intolerable too. He had managed before to survive spiritually for long periods without a confessor—indeed, he had been in this unsatisfactory case most of his priestly life, from Puna to Kalawao. It had been difficult enough when he was healthy. Now he was ill, mortally so, and his need of a companion was desperate. He told the bishop that he hoped Montiton would not be allowed to leave so easily. His argument was urgent: a confessor was necessary to him; separation from Montiton would cause him great pain. Writing to Koeckemann only a few weeks after the letter to his mother in which, out of calculated kindness, he had made a light affair, a near-nothing, of his accident with the scalding water, he said: "I am disabled, prob-ably for life. My terrible foot, which you saw at Honolulu, is far from being cured; though the wound has formed a scar the inflam-mation and the swelling of the large nerve on top of the toe continues." He had had to give up all thought of climbing the *pali*. "I walk dragging my leg—to go to the hospital and back, which is less than five minutes—is a fatigue that makes me cry all night." Beyond that, there were some final questions to be faced. "If I am really attacked by this terrible disease it has to be clearly recog-nized that death is coming near little by little—without occupying myself too much with my body—I have especially to concern myself with my soul." For that, Montiton would serve. Damien, in fact, was now willing to think well of him, despite their chronic disagreements. "Oh well, Father Albert has really been a good guide for me; his direction has done me some good—and I would be happy to have him as a confessor until I am on my deathbed."

Montiton would not stay, for Damien or anyone else. He did not take kindly to Damien's petition to the bishop to keep him at the settlement; in fact, he called it "intrigue," and loosed some verbal "thunderclaps" at Damien. In mid-March, 1885, he packed his bags and left for Honolulu to arrange passage back to the South

Seas; and once he was conclusively away from the Hawaiian Islands, he wrote to the father-general that a single priest was sufficient for Molokai, and that in any case Damien liked to be alone.

On Damien's side, at least, this was not true. The fact that he
could no longer climb the *pali* and serve the healthy districts
tormented him. At the settlement itself, Montiton's departure
doubled his work, at a time when a five-minute walk fatigued him.
And in the absence of a regular confessor, he was forced back upon
the imperfect arrangement of the early days: a visit every two or
three months from a Maui priest who would preach in the healthy
districts and then come down the *pali*.

Never, so Damien wrote to Pamphile in November, 1885, eight
months after Montiton's departure, had he been so alone, so isolated. He chided Pamphile for adding to his loneliness by not
writing, and then wondered about the reason. "I often think of you
—and I am surprised at every mail not to find a letter from you.
I start to say to myself—why, is Father Pamphile dead? Has last
year's illness taken him off, or what?"

Unable to heal himself, able only to speculate about his brother's
illness, worried about the sickness of his own spirit, Damien kept
up his preaching and his visits to the diseased at Kalawao and
Kalaupapa. "I usually go from one church to the other in a carriage," he told Pamphile. "On Sunday I usually celebrate 2 Masses.
I preach four times, and give communion twice. I have my two
little pharmacies—and always my little bottles of medicine in my
pocket on my house visits, and I try in this way to imitate my
patron saint. Sometimes, by doing good to the body of our unhappy sick one arrives little by little at the soul."

As for his own soul, Damien—alone, contrary to the Rule of the
Congregation—was reduced to making a solitary confession. "I
resign myself to Divine Providence, and find my consolation in the
only companion who does not leave me—that is to say, our Divine
Savior in the Holy Eucharist—it is at the foot of the altar that I
often confess myself and seek relief from spiritual pain. Before
Him and before the statue of our Holy Mother I sometimes whis-
per, asking for the conservation of my health."

Toward the end of 1885, Damien asked tentatively to be allowed a room at Kakaako branch hospital in Honolulu, where he could spend a few days at a time when his conscience demanded confession. But the vice-provincial, Father Fouesnel, expressly forbade Damien to visit the capital. Damien had made the trip only a handful of times in the past, before his disease was diagnosed, and then only when he could combine some useful business for the settlement with an overdue confession. Now he was told, as a matter of religious obedience, that he was not to think of this contact with the outside world again. With the receipt of Fouesnel's edict, a sort of blackness laid itself over Damien in his loneliness. He took to speaking of Kalawao as a "tomb."

XI

If Damien found it hard to let go of the idea of a visit to Honolulu, his superiors, on their side, found it hard to condone such thinking. They had to consider the work of the mission as a whole, and that meant considering at the same time the politics of religion. For a priest, a well-known priest, whose leprosy was confirmed, to leave the settlement and appear at the capital— this was to court political trouble. Not only the bishop and the vice-provincial saw the situation in this light: Walter Murray Gibson did too. And since his was the unsteady political regime which might suffer, he opposed any visit by Damien. Fouesnel wrote again to Damien in February, 1886, once more forbidding him to come to Honolulu. Fouesnel gave the order the weight of a ruling by the mission's provincial council, adding his own view that if Damien made the trip it would be an embarrassment to the whole mission, proof that Damien was—strong words from the vice-provincial—excessively "egoist," "without delicacy or charity." Damien was wounded. This "absolute refusal, expressed in the voice of a policeman rather than a religious superior, and in the name of the bishop and the prime minister, as if the mission would be quarantined if ever I showed myself at

Honolulu, gave me, I admit frankly, more pain than everything I have had to suffer since my childhood."

It was not, he insisted, that he wanted to go to Honolulu to stay. A few days sequestered at the mission, or at Kakaako if necessary, to be confessed, and to try whatever treatment was available there —that was as much as he asked.

He kept after the idea. Dr. Arthur Mouritz supported him, writing in June, 1886, to Bishop Koeckemann to say that he—Mouritz —had suggested the trip to Honolulu in the first place. Damien's outlook, said Mouritz, was unfavorable as he was then situated. His leprosy was making rapid progress; and his life was so cheerless and arduous that a little relaxation and some nursing would be beneficial. Rudolph Meyer, too, made some inquiries on Damien's behalf, without getting any clear permission. Meyer himself could see the advantages of a visit; but, as he soon found out, Gibson did not want Damien in Honolulu, and Fouesnel was still not in favor of it. If Damien went, Meyer said, it would be on his own responsibility.

This was the problem: Damien, as a member of the Congregation of the Sacred Hearts, was under a vow of obedience to his religious superiors. On July 2, he wrote to Bishop Koeckemann saying that until Koeckemann got the provincial to revoke his "severe order," no visit would be possible. Over the next few days, some messages were passed back and forth between Kalawao and Honolulu; Damien came to believe that he saw a kind of opening in the wall of prohibitions; and he left the settlement for Honolulu, arriving there on July 10.

Without question, he had forced the issue upon his reluctant superiors. This troubled him. He was worried, so one of the Catholic nursing sisters at Kakaako heard him say, that he might be at Honolulu "fraudulently"; and he spoke later of having made the trip "almost contrary to obedience." But evidently his superiors admitted the legitimacy of his needs, at least tacitly. There was no remonstrance, no chastisement; Damien was not considered to have overstepped his vows.

Gibson, on his side, made no public move against Damien; in fact the premier and King Kalakaua visited Damien at Kakaako. Gibson, however, wrote in his diary: "He is a confirmed leper—was advised not to come—but was determined to visit the Sisters. I begin to doubt the genuineness of his religious vocation." To have some conversation with the Franciscan Sisters was certainly one thing Damien had in mind. He wanted to try to convince their mother superior, Marianne Kopp, to send a contingent to the settlement. Gibson, with his involved pious affection for Mother Marianne, watched developments with mixed emotions. "At Convent this morning," he wrote in his diary on July 12. "S. M. [Sister Marianne] and Sisters touched by the misfortune of the 'noble priest'—are deeply moved. I doubt not the charity of S. M.'s noble heart." Damien himself Gibson could not come to like unreservedly. But then anyone who made a claim on Mother Marianne would meet with Gibson's displeasure. "I sent Father Damien some wine & many other things for his use and comfort. S. M. rewarded me with tender thanks. I called on Father D——and still I have some misgivings—he talks too much." Two days later, Gibson was recording in a pleased way that "S.M. told me she was completely wearied out with Father Damien's talk—will be content when he returns to Molokai." Without any question, a life at Kalawao was one of strain; and equally without question, one result of a prolonged sojourn there might be a certain insensitivity to the subtle permissions and prohibitions of religious sociability at the capital. Probably Damien, having been without the refreshment of conversation for months, indeed for years overall, and likely to be denied it altogether in the future, wanted to get as many words said, as many impressions registered as possible, in the few days he allowed himself at Honolulu.

Damien left again for the settlement on July 16. Gibson went back with him on the steamer, to spend a day politicking among the voters of Kalawao. The premier got what he considered an "unsatisfactory reception," prompted, he felt, "by the Opposition from Honolulu."

XII

One other thing in Damien's mind when he went to Honolulu was that he would be able to try a new treatment being used on leprosy patients at Kakaako. An elaborate regimen involving diet, medication, and hot baths, it was the specialty of a Japanese doctor named Masanao Goto. King Kalakaua had learned about the Goto method during his visit to Japan in 1881. Two years later, a white man named Gilbert Waller, struck with leprosy, was allowed to leave the islands and go to Tokyo to be treated, rather than be sent to Kalawao to die. He carried a letter of introduction from Walter Murray Gibson to the Goto family, physicians for generations. By 1885, Waller was back on the American mainland, believing himself convalescent, and certain that the Goto method could cure. The "knowledge and experience" possessed by the Gotos, wrote Waller to Gibson, was "the result of the study of Japanese and Chinese Physicians for over a thousand years," and there were hundreds of cases to prove their competency. He urged the Board of Health to try it out.

Gibson, waiting impatiently for the laborious scientific experimenter Eduard Arning to bring forth his proofs from Keanu, the murderer, and his other, nonhuman, laboratory subjects, was more than ready to give a well-recommended practical healer the chance to demonstrate his skills. Toward the end of 1885, Masanao Goto arrived to work on contract with the Board of Health at Kakaako. At least one *haole* influential at Honolulu, Charles McEwen Hyde, was upset by this incursion of the Oriental into what had been a Western preserve of well-intentioned medicine. But Damien, who had the strongest of personal interests in the efficacy of treatment, was optimistic in advance about Goto's work. Having, as he said, fairly much lost faith in European physicians, he presented himself at Kakaako, and took with enthusiasm to Goto's daily round of medicaments and baths: as he described it, two immersions daily in hot water containing a "certain quantity" of Japanese medicine; "a grain of little pills" after each meal, and one hour later "an ounce of a certain decoction or tisane made from Japanese tree bark."

Damien, bringing his enthusiasm back to Kalawao, planned to introduce the Goto treatment there. He wrote immediately to the Board of Health, asking for "50 boxes of Kai Gio Kioso Yoku Yaku —bath medicine, 50 boxes of Sei Kets-uren pills, 50 packages of Decoction Hichiyon bark, 10 pound of Bicarb Sodium." And two weeks later, he submitted to Gibson a long letter which he called, in English, "a few propositions which I make after a careful study of the japonaise treatment." It was actually nothing less than a plan for a Goto "complex," accompanied by a set of drawings for a "regular hospital," on the "beautiful sloping plain directly east of my house"; with a boiler room, two bathhouses, a dining room, a cookhouse, six dormitories, and a manager's house with a dispensary.

This was the quintessential Damien, seized as always with an enthusiasm for service among the victims of leprosy, seeing a way to convert enthusiasm into a plan of action, ready to take the task of implementation upon himself. Something new was added as well: an indication that at this late date he was beginning to become aware that the leprosy settlement was not the whole world —or, rather, that he might be able to accomplish more at Kalawao by involving the outside world more. Damien conceded that Gibson might think his plans expensive; but he argued that after a time the Goto treatment, "by bringing a good number of light cases so far that they may be discharged," would actually diminish the current expenses of the Board of Health. The point, he wrote, winding up his proposal, was to make the Goto complex a first-rate institution. It would be to the honor of His Majesty the King, who suggested it; and to the honor of the Board of Health, for supplying the necessary. Damien had never said anything like that before— perhaps just once, when he politely and formally thanked the Hawaiian monarchy for his decoration in 1881. What had happened since then was that the priest, following his visit to Honolulu in July and his conversations with Gibson and Kalakaua

—after sufficient exposure not only to leprosy but to the politics of leprosy—was learning the rudiments of the art of public relations: how to talk to politicians.

Damien's Goto hospital complex, in all its elaborate usefulness, was never built. Gibson ruled it out as too expensive. But Damien managed, with considerable effort over several months, to get the Goto treatment started, bathhouses, boiler room and all, on a modest scale. He bought empty bread boxes from the settlement store to be used as tubs. Kalawao was short of fuel; he had his Hawaiians go out and cut *kukui* trees for wood; and he asked Rudolph Meyer to order a ton of coal. One way and another, the boilers were stoked, the water kept hot, and the bathers encouraged—against the Hawaiian propensity to lose interest in long-term treatment—to turn up day after day for their time in the tubs.

Damien thought he began to see a general improvement in health at the settlement, even a drop in the death rate. As for himself, he was sanguine. After about three months of the Goto treatment, he was writing: "My right hand appears now to be out of danger of becoming crippled. . . . My system is generally better and with the aid of God—and the treatment I follow—I will pull through." In December, 1886, he spoke of yet further improvement. "Six months ago—I was crippled and feeble—saying Mass with difficulty . . . today . . . I feel strong and robust again." Thanks to "God and the Holy Virgin," of course, but thanks also to the Goto treatment. It was a virtual testimonial letter. And he went on to describe his activities at Christmas, beginning with his medicinal bath at five in the morning on December 24, and continuing with an uninterrupted round of religious exercises until ten in the morning on Christmas Day. This was not the regimen of an enfeebled man.

Damien's occasional confessor, Father Columban Beissel of Maui, saw him every few months, and found him looking and feeling better under the Goto treatment, at least to begin with. But Dr. Arthur Mouritz, not an uncritical admirer of Dr. Goto and his works, watched the effect of the treatment on Damien well into 1887, and concluded that over the long run it was, if anything, harmful. It did not halt the progress of the disease; and Damien, as usual zealous to excess in anything he took up, tended to overdo the hot baths, Mouritz thought. He was losing a great deal of weight, and some of his strength as well. Mouritz saw him one day after his session at the bathhouse, tottering along, his clothes hanging off him like bags.

XIII

The news that Damien had caught leprosy became public knowledge in the United States early in 1886, and in Europe as well. It was picked up by newspapers in Belgium, and Damien's mother heard it in an embellished form: that her son was already hideously diseased, the flesh falling off his bones. Anne-Catherine De Veuster was eighty-three years old; the shock was great; it killed her. She died well and piously, clutching to her heart a picture of the Holy Virgin and a photograph of Damien.

Within a month or two, the news of her passing reached Kalawao. Damien took it calmly enough. He did not see it as a matter for great grief. He had long since resigned himself to never seeing his mother again on earth; he was sure now, he said, that her holy spirit had gone to its true home.

Later in 1886, stories began to crop up here and there in the European press to the effect that Damien himself had died. Copies made their way to the islands; Bishop Koeckemann sent one of them to Damien in December. Writing to Europe, Damien could say only what was the case: that disease was shortening his journey to heaven, but that he was not yet dead.

Alive, he still needed a confessor. Father Columban Beissel could come to see him once every few months, but Damien needed a colleague who would live at the settlement. In July, 1886, just after Damien had got back from his trip to Honolulu, a letter

arrived from Pamphile, proposing to Bishop Koeckemann that he
should come out and help his brother. Damien had lately begun
to blow hot and cold on that idea: rather a change from the insist-
ence of his earlier years that Pamphile somehow owed him his
presence. Now he wrote to his older brother that God had arranged for Pamphile to stay at home. It would be best for them
both to let religious and ecclesiastical authority decide whether
Damien would one day have the pleasure of working with "a
brother to whom I am indebted, after God, for having been chosen
to go on a distant mission." But he put Pamphile's case to the
bishop just the same. Koeckemann in turn wrote to Pamphile that
all such decisions were in the hands of the father-general alone;
and then Koeckemann wrote to Paris saying that he would rather
have a good simple man of religion, less learned, than an old
scholar like Pamphile. That was as far as the matter went.

So Damien was still alone. At the end of 1886, he wrote to the
secretary of the father-general: "Being deprived of the compan-
ionship of my colleagues of our dear Congregation is more painful
to bear than leprosy."

XIV

Pamphile was not the only one to make an offer of help. For the
next several years, letters came in quantity, to Damien personally,
to his superiors, and to the Board of Health, from all kinds of
people: a lady claiming, inaccurately, to be the "only woman"
ready to offer her life to the victims of leprosy; a young man "fond
of boys"; any number of others. It was hard to distinguish, through
the mails, what might constitute a genuine vocation from what
might be no more than a dubious long-distance leprophilia. Damien's bishop developed a stock response. It was to suggest that
the inquirers submit to a novitiate in the Congregation of the
Sacred Hearts; or, in the case of women, in the appropriate reli-

gious sisterhood. After that, they could ask to be sent to work in the Hawaiian Islands. Very few of the letter writers were heard from again.

Ira Barnes Dutton arranged things differently. He wrote no letter, but simply appeared in Honolulu one day late in July, 1886, and asked to be allowed to go to work at Kalawao. Walter Murray Gibson interviewed him: "He says he wants to do the will of the 'Blessed Lord' by waiting on lepers. . . . He may be genuine—but a good deal of cant in him." Cant or no cant, Dutton got his wish from the Board of Health: an authorization for Kalawao. He went ashore at the settlement on July 29.

Damien saw no cant in Dutton. He took to him immediately. "Ira B. Dutton is truly an exemplary self devoting man," he wrote to Gibson. "He will be our right hand . . . he would be at once my secretary—and cashier—the Bishop not wishing me to handle any money etc. He is a true brother to me."

Arthur Mouritz was at the settlement the day Dutton arrived. The two lunched together, and Mouritz "scanned him carefully." "He wore a blue denim shirt, which fitted his well-knit, slim, lithe, muscular figure. He stood about five feet seven inches tall; had dark brown hair and grayish blue eyes; a low voice, placid features, and a pleasant smile. He was reserved and thoughtful, had nothing to say about the reason for seeking seclusion and work at Molokai, and turning his back on the world."

Dutton was forty-three, three years younger than Damien. He had fought in the Civil War, on the Northern side, and had spent the first two years of the peace working among the Union dead, collecting bodies and seeing to their burial in national cemeteries. He married badly; separated from his wife; began to drink heavily and continued for a long time—about a barrel of whiskey a year, he estimated; finally got a divorce; and on his fortieth birthday, in 1883, entered the Catholic Church as a convert, and decided to devote the rest of his life to penance. He spent two years in a Trappist monastery without taking vows; then left, without much in mind; and, quite by accident, found what he had been unknowingly looking for, in an old Catholic newspaper—a "brief item" about Damien.

"It was a new subject and attracted me wonderfully," Dutton recalled long afterward. "After weighing it for a while I became convinced that it would suit my wants—for labor, for a penitential life, and for seclusion as well as complete separation from scenes of all past experiences. . . . Yet I was not thinking to hide, exactly; it was a good deal the idea of 'beginning again.' But the real motive was to do some good for my neighbor and at the same time make it my penitentiary in doing penance for my sins and errors. The only question was, could I get in there and be useful?" Dutton heard about Charles Warren Stoddard, who not long after his visit to Molokai had taken a teaching post at Notre Dame University. "At once, then, I decided to go and see him about (1) how to get to Molokai, and (2) once there, if I could be sure of finding plenty of work. I went; I saw him; and, as expected, I was satisfied as to both questions; so, I set off at once."

Damien called Dutton, unofficially, Brother Joseph; and put him to work at once. Dutton never stopped. He was a totally devoted laborer, extraordinarily industrious, and always calm: preternaturally so. No one ever heard him raise his voice or saw him lose his temper. He did all he could, and asked for nothing in return; or perhaps only one thing. "Speaking to him about his works of charity," wrote Rudolph Meyer, "he at least three times assured me that his sole object of living was to do all the good he could to these people and to please the Almighty God, & that he constantly prayed and hoped his labors would be acceptable to God and that he could not conceive a greater happiness or blessing if the Almighty God would reward his services by inflicting upon him this (to me) dreadful scourge of Leprosy to enable him to die a Martyr."

Damien built Dutton a one-room house close to his own, near St. Philomena's church and the cemetery. The place suited Dutton, just as it suited Damien. "The principal graveyard back of my cabin," wrote Dutton in 1887, long enough after his arrival for him to know that he would stay, "has about two thousand graves and nearly one thousand are buried elsewhere. . . . Take it all in all, this is a fine locality for meditation, surrounded by the best symbol of eternity, the boundless ocean."

XV

Another man impressed by Damien's sacrifice was the Reverend Hugh B. Chapman of St. Luke's Church, Camberwell, in London. As soon as he heard through the press that Damien had caught leprosy, Chapman set to work raising money for Kalawao. The vicar of St. Luke's was an energetic man, and a liberal-minded Christian as well. He had the strong feeling that a Christian response to the example of a life like Damien's ought not to be sectarian. An Anglican himself, he wanted his charitable fund to be supported by Protestants and Catholics alike; and he arranged for the patronage of the leading Catholic prelate of England, Cardinal Henry Edward Manning, Archbishop of Westminster.

This raised a small storm in the mind of one convinced Protestant in London, who attacked Chapman in print for endeavoring to "create sympathy for an idolatrous priest of that abominable religion." In this man's view, all that Damien had done was to make his Hawaiian converts "twofold more children of hell than he is himself." Chapman answered tersely: "Your letter is a very wicked one, though I excuse it on the grounds of its utter folly. Go and do thou likewise." His opponent replied that Scripture did not require him to. "Lepers" were to be kept apart. The Bible said so. Leprosy was "a prominent mark of God's displeasure." To go and do likewise, then, would be "utterly at a variance alike with any man's moral or religious obligation." Even if there was a duty to "do good unto all men," in no case was it enjoined by God "that our lives should be sacrificed, as all men were born for His glory. Life is given to us to preserve to that end."

This argument raised echoes of the discussion that had taken place in Honolulu in 1873: the responsibilities of the Christian; sectarianism and the nature of charity; the rights and wrongs of embracing the "leper"—in short, whether to touch or not to touch. Chapman wrote at the end of it all that a life such as Damien's "makes one's own appear very easy and selfish, and I consider it an honour to lay the slightest offering at the feet of the man who is brave enough to lead it." Late in 1886, he sent Damien a check for £975; and three times in the next three years he raised and sent more money, a total of £2,625, an amount equal to several months of Board of Health appropriations for Kalawao.

Chapman was by no means the first to raise charity money for Damien. There had been those well-disposed Honolulu business-men who got up a subscription for him in 1873; his first house had been paid for by charity; small sums of money came from Europe from time to time; the Sacred Hearts Sisters in Honolulu collected gifts for him; and of course Queen Kapiolani had arranged in 1884 for gifts to be sent to Kalawao.

Still, there was clearly something new and different about Chap-man's fund-raising in London in 1886. For one thing, it was highly public: even the *Times* gave Chapman generous space. For an-other, the sums of money involved were much bigger than before, no doubt because the knowledge of Damien's disease opened up the consciences of those who led "very easy and selfish lives" to be more readily and deeply pricked.

There was one more thing. Damien was being portrayed as a figure of unmatchable heroic self-sacrifice; and this was an evalua-tion with which only the most unreasonable of sectarian Protes-tants would be expected to disagree. But then, out of the need to make total moral contrasts, the heroic self-sacrifice of Damien was held to have been made necessary by the dreadful delinquencies of others in the Hawaiian kingdom. In the "romance of sacrifice," the presence of a hero required the presence of a villain. And it was not enough for leprosy itself to be the villain; there had to be a human villain. Better still, many villains.

In the foreground, the horrible beauty of a single diseased

figure; in the background, the horrible ugliness of comfortable negligence—it made an instructive picture, good food for edifying thought, useful for the encouragement of charity at a distance. Out of all this came the conclusion that if Damien needed charity money to carry on his work, then obviously the government of the Hawaiian kingdom must have been shirking its responsibilities.

The government—meaning Walter Murray Gibson—responded with a kind of aggrieved aggressiveness. Gibson would have held that, under his leadership as premier and as president of the Board of Health, the kingdom was doing everything possible in the matter of leprosy, and more. Look at the appointment of Eduard Arning; look at the hiring of Masanao Goto; look at the biennial legislative appropriation of $100,000. Gibson had always made a point of holding all this worthiness up to approving view: it was part of his political stock-in-trade. As he said, he wanted Hawaii to be known as pre-eminent in Oceania for philanthropy. Yet now, on the other side of the world, in England, Gibson was being made the villain so that people would give more money to Damien the hero. It was too much.

Gibson took to the columns of his editorial mouthpiece in Honolulu, the daily *Pacific Commercial Advertiser*. He was defensive and aggressive at the same time, pitting the record of the government and its money against that of the priest and his money. A good many people, said the *Advertiser*, would be surprised at Damien's published assertion that the sufferers of Kalawao needed charity money to buy clothes. Yet there was "no mistaking" Damien's meaning. What he said

formulated a serious charge of neglect against the Board of Health. . . . It concerns the honor and humanity of the nation. No one ever suggested that the appropriation for the care of lepers should be curtailed. The money asked for by Ministers was freely voted, and its expenditure is entirely at the discretion of the Board of Health. Were it not that Father Damien makes the statement we could not for an instant credit the truth of such an imputation; and, to be candid about it, we are still in doubt regarding this matter. . . . The public, however, want to know all about this Father Damien fund expenditure, and the necessity therefor. Let us have all the facts without reserve or diminution, and then a correct judgment may be formed regarding them.

Leprosy had become political again, and in a more complicated way than ever before. Until this moment, in the spring of 1887, Gibson and the Sacred Hearts had been able to keep up a sort of working agreement. Now Damien and his disease and the embarrassing charity of foreigners seemed about to bring down the delicate alliance.

And at the worst possible moment. Whether or not Gibson was really delinquent about leprosy—and his enemies would not have quarreled with the size of the legislative appropriation, only with the maladministration of the segregation program—the government was in trouble on many fronts. There was a huge rise in the national debt; an unhealthy alliance between Gibson, King Kalakaua, and the millionaire businessman Claus Spreckels, who seemed able to buy his way to unlimited power and privilege in the kingdom; and a juicy scandal about the awarding of an opium-selling monopoly, which involved the taking of bribes, and which reached into the palace itself. It was possible, and becoming more likely every day in 1887, that the Gibson regime would fall. And if it did, the Minister of Everything, the Catholics' only friend in power, would be gone.

XVI

Bishop Koeckemann and Father Fouesnel could not regard this situation with any equanimity. In fact, it upset them greatly. In their agitation they looked for someone to blame, and chose Damien. He, or what he had done, or what had been done in his name, had become an embarrassment to the government; and this in turn unsettled the Sacred Hearts mission. By the beginning of 1887, Damien, marked by leprosy, confined at Kalawao, and irreversibly on the way to death, was being lauded as a hero in the outside world and yet condemned at the same time by his superiors at Honolulu as an incorrigible troublemaker.

In the early years of his ministry, Damien's relations with his superiors had been cordial enough. Bishop Maigret had liked him, and spoke well of him; and if the old provincial, Father Modeste Favens, and his vice-provincial, Father Régis Moncany, had had to chide him once or twice for his impetuosity, the criticism was never turned into anything like an indictment. When, in Maigret's old age, Koeckemann became the active leader of the mission, and Fouesnel became vice-provincial following Moncany, Damien fared less well. The unhappy affair of André Burgerman dated from the earlier regime; but it was Koeckemann and Fouesnel who first sent Albert Montiton to Kalawao and then allowed him to leave. And, as it turned out, in the opinion of Damien's new ecclesiastical and religious superiors there was not much to choose between those three priests of Molokai, the two who came and went, the one who stayed—there was official talk of stubbornness, self-centeredness, unmanageability equally distributed. By 1883, Damien was writing in distress that he did not realize he had fallen so low in the esteem of his superiors.

In the complicated situation that developed over Damien, there were still other complications. One sprang from the fact that there were disagreements within the mission over the quality of the new leadership. Father Fouesnel in particular was disliked by a good number of the priests and brothers who had to answer to him as vice-provincial and later as provincial. Even Koeckemann, who was Fouesnel's friend, and who depended on him greatly, recognized a number of defects in him: Fouesnel was perhaps too indulgent of himself; he enjoyed his food and drink too much; he rode about Honolulu in an elaborate carriage; he did not take part wholeheartedly in the communal life of the mission. And at the same time, where others were concerned, he was too harsh, in words and in action, unwilling to "sweeten any pills." Koeckemann tried always, he said, to dilute the harshness, to put a little water in Fouesnel's wine. Koeckemann himself, as bishop, was

perhaps a little too much water and not enough wine: a worthy
man, but not a particularly strong one, not able to muster any sort
of well-timed decisiveness, not a commander of confidence—in
short, not a leader for difficult times likely to be made more difficult by Fouesnel.

Koeckemann and Fouesnel were able to agree that a great part
of their public difficulties sprang from the fact that Damien kept
getting his name in the papers. Publicity for priests was certainly
a thorny question. Damien in his early years had self-consciously
shied away from it; but then, simply by going to Kalawao, he—
God's athlete—had done something which condemned him to
wide notice. He was singleminded about the settlement—that was
his world—and his life there was hard. His work was almost exclusively the subject of whatever letters he wrote; and from time to
time, because of the wide interest in what he was doing, parts of
his letters got into print. He did not write letters specifically for
publication; and in his early years at Kalawao he always professed
surprise, even amazement, to find that his private correspondence
had been given to editors to print.

Among those who upset him in this way was Pamphile, not long
after Damien landed at Kalawao; and Damien scolded him for it.
That particular published letter, which appeared in a journal
unexceptionable from the Congregation's point of view, its own
Annales des Sacrés Coeurs, annoyed Fouesnel (then still pastor of
the church at Wailuku whose blessing Damien had attended on
the eve of his departure for Kalawao). As Fouesnel read it,
Damien, out of a kind of vanity, seemed to be alleging that he was
abandoned on Molokai; whereas, said Fouesnel, the mission had
always looked after that post, and Damien had not been refused
anything since he went there. Granted that there was some "poetry" in the letter, still it was enough to shock the bishop; and one
of the other priests had "sermonized" Damien about it, to "make
him give up the idea of writing down everything that comes into
his small-brained head."

Those were strong words. Perhaps Fouesnel was already developing a special animus against Damien. Certainly, ten years later, writing to Damien as provincial to priest, or about him to others, Fouesnel dipped his pen in the strongest and sourest wine imaginable. His was the prohibition against travel to Honolulu in 1886 that Damien found "policeman"-like; and when Chapman's charity money began to find its way to Kalawao and the news of it was reported in the Honolulu papers, Fouesnel, intent on restraining Damien, found it impossible to restrain himself.

Fouesnel, evidently, was not against publicity for the mission on principle—just what he regarded as excessive attention to Damien. "It is," he wrote once, "absolutely as if we had nothing here but Molokai and its lepers." Bishop Koeckemann held the same view; and he expounded it at length in his letters to Damien in 1887. "As I have a sort of passion for justice to be done to everyone, even to my enemies and the enemies of good," he wrote early in the year, "I see with displeasure that the newspapers which admire you exaggerate and put things in a false light, without taking account of what the government and others do—the mission also has its share." A few weeks later, Koeckemann came back to the subject: "Allow me to add some prosaic reflections to so much poetry about the lepers of Molokai. . . . From what I can see in the papers, the world is under the impression that you are at the head of *your* lepers, their procurer, their doctor, their nurse, their grave-digger, etc., as if the government counted for nothing. That might rightly offend the king, Mr. Gibson, etc. . . . As for the Catholic mission, and its ecclesiastical and religious authorities, it must stand aside, and take criticism, indirect and sometimes direct, so that the hero can shine more brilliantly. I do not see how the glory of God and the honor of religion gain by that. *Suum cuique dare justitia est:* to give each his due is justice. The strict truth will yield you enough glory. Don't allow holes to be made in the bag that holds your incontestable merits."

Damien could hardly help being taken aback by all this: first the publicity itself, then the attacks on him for having unwittingly generated it. He himself would have said that he had encouraged charity, not courted publicity. He did not want renown. If renown came nonetheless, he wanted God's cause to benefit. And if in fact he did deserve the sympathy of the world, as even Koeckemann conceded, and the world sent him gifts to be dispensed at the settlement, why should his superiors criticize him? "From strangers, gold and incense; from my superiors myrrh." Damien could not understand it.

Koeckemann took Damien's figure of speech as an affront to episcopal dignity and authority. "After gold and incense, myrrh has not been to your taste, and you have spat it in my face with an ancient deposit of gall in your heart. Let us hope that there is no more left. For my part, I have never ceased to admire your heroism and to publicize it on every suitable occasion. If I have counted too much on your humility, I am sorry. For my own personal merit I am always too much honored, but for the glory of God, good order and the good of souls it is not desirable that the bishop should be singled out as hindering the good. That pains me."

Fouesnel also talked about gold, incense, and myrrh, lecturing Damien on his Christian duties. Damien should not think of having his own way all the time; he must be ready for opposition. "And if you wish to imitate our Divine Savior, in voluntarily receiving gold, and sweetly breathing the incense which is lavished on you, you must uncomplainingly take the myrrh and receive it, to temper a little the *human feeling* of receiving the two other things."

At the same time, Koeckemann and Fouesnel were writing in agitation to the father-general about their difficulties with this unmanageable priest. Damien, said Koeckemann, devoted himself so exclusively to the settlement that he seemed to think the "government, the mission, the Sisters should concentrate all their efforts on the lepers too, and be at his orders." In his impatience, Damien had written "to the four winds, exaggerating the material misery of the lepers, making insinuations if not open criticisms against the mission, against the government, and even against the

Sisters." And then from all sides compliments came back to him, so many "that he seems in danger of losing the balance of his head, which has always been hard enough."

Fouesnel's language in his letters to Paris was even more sourly impassioned. The charity money from Chapman, he told the father-general, was raised on the strength of "falsehoods" written by Damien, who claimed that he was "consoler, provider, nurse, shrouder and burier of the lepers, and he is no such thing." Damien was imperious, capricious, and vain. He "merits great praise for the sacrifice he has made of his life and liberty," but *"unfortunately,* this praise has come to him, he has swallowed it, he has become intoxicated and now he is becoming dangerous."

Walter Murray Gibson was also writing about Damien, not only defending the Board of Health in the Honolulu press, but confiding to his diary that he was "very much annoyed with Father Damien. He has written abroad representing the lepers as neglected by the Government. . . . Bishop Hermann is very much dissatisfied, and says Father D. has obtained money on false pretences—and now his Father D. disregards me and the Board of Health, and undertakes to manage the leper settlement without consulting me in the least."

Gibson, the politician, the old fox, thought he could see a way out of everybody's troubles. All money that came to Damien should be handed over to Bishop Koeckemann; it would be spent by the mission in consultation with the Board of Health; and the Board would officially acknowledge all gifts. It was a suggestion which might have worked, and which certainly would have given Gibson more control over the situation. It came, however, too late: positions were already being taken, harsh words being exchanged in all directions. Damien, so his superiors said, was a man who found it hard to retrace his steps. They themselves, though they did not say so, might have found it hard to retract some of their remarks about Damien. When Chapman's money first began to arrive, Damien had written from Kalawao, asking how it should be handled, especially since the gifts were directed to him, to be used as he saw fit. A bank account had been set up; the money could be disbursed. But eventually Fouesnel, in his mounting bad temper against Damien, said he wanted nothing at all to do with the money. Beyond directing Damien to make a will leaving everything to the bishop, Fouesnel washed his hands of Chapman's charity.

One extremely harsh letter of Fouesnel's must have crossed on its way to Paris a letter to Damien from Father Janvier Weiler of the mother house of the Sacred Hearts. Weiler's letter also concerned publicity; and it could not have been more different from the letters Damien was getting from his local superiors. "If you could send me some photographs of the leper settlement, such as: a general view, the church, hospital, lepers, etc., I would be very grateful," wrote Weiler, "and with your permission I would send them to the *Missions Catholiques,* which speaks too rarely about our missions and about Molokai in particular. If the Jesuits had a Molokai, the news would never dry up, and alms would keep pace."

In reality, no more than a handful of letters by Damien were ever published during his lifetime, in whole or in part. It was his situation itself that stirred up such interest, especially after he caught leprosy. If Damien himself had never written a word, Chapman would still have been able to raise a great deal of charity money for him—thus embarrassing Gibson, and in turn embarrassing Koeckemann and Fouesnel. So when Fouesnel ordered Damien to submit everything he wrote for reading at Honolulu before it was sent overseas, this was not really getting at the problem. And, in any case, as Damien pointed out, he had always sent his letters unsealed to his superiors for mailing; they were supposed to read them; so that if Fouesnel objected to some of the things he saw in print over Damien's name, and wanted to blame Damien, then he should at least blame himself as well.

Fouesnel, to be plain, was out of his depth. Koeckemann was too. They had been led into a world of affairs too complex for them. It was true, at the same time, that Damien's own attitude toward publicity was undergoing a subtle change. He was more than cautious in those troubled years about what he said in private letters, often stipulating that he did not want to see himself in print; but he was ready enough to recommend the book Charles Warren Stoddard had published about the settlement; and he could hardly help being impressed by the amount of money Hugh Chapman was able to raise for him. As long ago as 1880, he had written to Pamphile about charity and publicity: "During the first years of my ministry, I often received considerable alms through our Procurator in Paris, but not having played the part of a public beggar, the charity of our benefactors over the sea seems to have lost sight of the poor lepers of Molokai." Now he was a public beggar, one of the most notable public beggars in the world, without at all having meant to become one. It had somehow happened to him. Painful things had happened simultaneously: he seemed to have lost irremediably the approbation of his superiors. But the settlement needed the money that was coming in; and it would be pointless to forfeit that as well. Regardless of what his superiors thought of him, he could not afford to give up his work, or the means to do that work as well as possible. Charity, publicity, and criticism; gold, incense, and myrrh—all were likely to continue in large supply at Kalawao.

XVII

While all this was going on, Walter Murray Gibson's political enemies were preparing to get rid of him. It took revolution, minor and bloodless but conclusive: some mass meetings by reform-minded *haole* at Honolulu; a certain amount of public parading by armed *haole* militiamen; some pointed demands. Kalakaua was to be constitutionally muzzled; Gibson must resign; a new cabinet must be formed of men who had the confidence of the business community. June 30, 1887, was the critical day. Within two weeks, Gibson, half-seriously threatened with hanging and more than half-seriously tried for embezzlement, but acquitted, was gone from the kingdom, to a brief exile in San Francisco, where he died, of tuberculosis, in January, 1888. He ended his life a Catholic convert; and his body was brought back to the islands for a Catholic funeral and burial. Among the living, the Protestants were in power. What that might do to the Sacred Hearts mission, to Kalawao, to Damien's work, was problematical.

XVIII

For leprosy directly, the revolution of 1887 meant extensive changes in the personnel of the Board of Health, and a tightening-up of the administration of the segregation laws. Gibson, as president of the Board, was gone. Fred Hayselden, who had been secretary, went out of office and under the threat of the hangman's noose with Gibson, who happened to be his father-in-law. The broom of reform swept clean: Arthur Mouritz, who was a Gibson appointee, lost his job as resident physician at Kalawao. At Kakaako, Masanao Goto, the Japanese doctor, did not find the reform government congenial to work for; and eventually he resigned.

Beginning in the fall of 1887, the Board's new president was Nathaniel B. Emerson, conscientious physician, friend in his own way of the Hawaiian, missionary son, and good Protestant. In his first report to the legislature—the new postrevolutionary reform legislature, a distinctly *haole* body—Emerson took sharp aim at the departed Gibson and his works, or rather his lack of works. "The laxity that has for many years prevailed in regard to the execution of the law requiring the segregation of lepers has acted very disastrously, both in distributing the germs of the disease broadcast throughout the land, and in nurturing a feeling of opposition to the law itself, which at times has threatened to take the form of violence." There was to be more of that over the next few years, particularly on the island of Kauai, where an examining physician was killed, and a diseased Hawaiian took to the hills with his family and shot a pursuing sheriff dead. Emerson was prepared in advance for such eventualities. He discounted them in favor of the sort of "great regard for humanity" which "obliges one to look far ahead and contemplate the inevitable consequences of faltering in the unpleasant duty of segregation." Within "certain bounds," the interests of the nation must be considered as paramount over those of the individual; and "these demand that not a single life . . . be squandered in obedience to a false sentimentality."

XIX

Emerson happened to be speaking in this last instance of *kōkua*, Hawaiian helpers at the settlement; but he might just as well have been talking about Sacred Hearts priests, at least the two of them at Lahaina thought to be suffering from leprosy: André Burgerman and Grégoire Archambaux. Even before the revolution, Léonor Fouesnel was giving the matter some anxious thought. "How long will the authorities allow Father Grégoire and Father André to stay out of isolation? I do not know; but I am convinced that if Mr. Gibson was removed, they would immediately be sent off with the others."

Fouesnel was thinking, in turn, not only of the law and its possible effects on the mission's workings, but of Damien's position at Kalawao. If Fouesnel and Bishop Koeckemann had been lately bedeviled in their relations with Damien by national politics, Damien was eternally bedeviled in his relations with them by his lack of a regular confessor. He had been without one ever since Albert Montiton left the settlement early in 1885, abandoning Damien to the infrequent visits of Father Columban Beissel from Maui. It was a bad arrangement; everyone recognized that; and without much question, it contributed to the ill-feeling between Kalawao and Honolulu. Just before the storm over Chapman's charity money broke, Damien had written to Koeckemann, asking to be put down as a member of a religious association under the name of J. Damien De Veuster, "leprous sinner who confesses so rarely." Between arguments over money, publicity, and authority, Koeckemann and Fouesnel considered the problem of Damien's isolation; and came up, time and time again, with no solution. It was hard on Damien to have to live as he did; but it was just as hard on Father Beissel to have to risk seasickness between Maui and Molokai, and then risk his neck on the *pali* trail: he needed "a terrible courage and a health of iron" to keep it up, said Fouesnel. The mission was so "terribly short" of workers that there was no one to be spared for Molokai. And when a new priest, assigned in advance to Kalawao, arrived in the islands late in 1887, he turned out to have a "repugnance" even for the thought of the work; and the bishop could not make him go there.

The politics of leprosy offered a solution: the rigor of the post-revolutionary Board of Health, combined with the palpability of Grégoire Archambaux's disease. In the fall of 1887, Archambaux got a letter from the Board, directing him to report to Honolulu for a "definitive" medical examination. He knew what that meant, and so did his superiors. He decided that, rather than subject himself to a disagreeable inspection at the hands of the Board's physicians, he would go straight to the settlement. "We count on your great charity," wrote Fouesnel to Damien in November, "to take good care of Father Grégoire." On the same day Fouesnel wrote to the father-general: "The bishop, to get around the hard and headstrong character of Father Damien, is sending today Father Grégoire's nomination as priest of Kalaupapa . . . making him independent of the priest of Kalawao."

At least, as Fouesnel observed, this finally gave Damien a confessor. But for how long was uncertain. Koeckemann thought that incarceration at Kalawao would kill the sensitive Archambaux before leprosy did; and Archambaux was sure of it. His "ardent" imagination began to work. Writing a note to a colleague at Christmas, 1887, he spoke of himself as in a sense already dead. "As for me, in the moral state in which I find myself, I am led to leave to the living the trouble of wishing themselves a long and happy life." His weekly letters to Fouesnel became "cries of despair"; he came to need far more wine each day than his superiors thought proper; his asthma returned, and with it the black imaginings of his earlier enforced stay at the settlement—the fixed idea that his superiors had sent him there to be rid of him.

For a second time, the asthma that threatened to kill him was his means of escape from Kalawao. In February, 1888, the Board of Health relented sufficiently to allow Archambaux to be brought on doctor's orders to Kakaako branch hospital. It was not too unpleasant there, he wrote to Damien; he had a little room; he was reconciled to being caged. He said his prayers, and read, and went to Mass at the Sisters' chapel on the hospital grounds. Obviously, a priest's cell at Kakaako on the Honolulu waterfront was much less of a cage to Archambaux than the open settlement had been. He no longer felt smothered, suffocated, dead before dying. His asthma went away—away to the other side of the world, he said, mournfully fanciful. "Perhaps it is gone . . . in the immense extent of the great ocean that surrounds us, across North America, the Atlantic, my homeland, your Belgium, Denmark, Sweden, and has drowned in the frightful labyrinth of the northern seas. . . . That is why I have never seen it again, *goodby to it for ever!* I can only be better off for it."

XX

In November, 1887, not long after the desolate Archambaux arrived at Kalawao for the second time, Damien wrote to Pamphile: "Although leprosy has a strong hold on my body and has disfigured me a little, I continue to be strong and robust." The terrible pains in his feet had disappeared; and—a great consolation to him—his hands were not yet contorted, so that he could still say Mass every day. He was able to work hard; and there was much to do. In the last months of Gibson's regime, the number of leprosy cases at Kalawao had fallen as low as about five hundred, with the old sufferers dying off and not being replaced by new ones—that Gibsonian laxity in segregation. But now Nathaniel Emerson's Board of Health was sending freshly diagnosed patients to the settlement by the shipload: many of them, in Damien's opinion, spiritual as well as physical "lepers." With no one actively able to help him but Dutton, Brother Joseph, his load was heavy. And, as he said, he felt time running out. Still, he wanted Pamphile to know that he shouldered the burden willingly, and that it was the less onerous because he shared fully the life of the people of Kalawao. "Thus the sacrifice of my health, which God has been pleased to accept, fructifying a little my ministry among the lepers, is after all quite light and even agreeable to me." He believed himself to be—or so he told Pamphile—"the happiest missionary in the world."

Damien perhaps found it necessary to write to his older brother in this vein. But at the same time, Arthur Mouritz, who up to the moment he lost his government appointment at the settlement early in 1888 saw more of Damien than anyone else, found him dejected, disconsolate to the point of melancholia. His body was being invaded more and more by the disease: "The skin of the abdomen, chest, and back, both extensor and flexor surfaces of the arms and legs showed tubercles, masses of infiltration, deep maculation in varying degrees of extent and severity. The mucous membrane of the nose, palate, roof of the mouth, pharynx, and larynx became involved; the skin of his cheeks, nose, lips, forehead, and chin became excessively swollen, deep copper-colored macules and deep infiltration alternately prevailing; his body became emaciated." By the fall of 1887, Mouritz said, Damien had begun to lose faith in the Goto treatment, and had essentially "given up all hope of getting any relief or stay of his leprosy." His physical weakness "became apparent to himself; the slightest exertion brought on a difficulty of breathing." And his temper, "which previously had been alternately cheerful and irritable, became preternaturally calm, and permanent gloom settled down upon him." Mouritz, the medical man, had observed "despair and anguish" as a common condition at Kalawao. With Damien, he noted two forms: "First—Melancholia Attonita, where he remained motionless and silent with his eyes fixed into space. Second —'Melancholia Religiosa,' strange to say, occasionally troubled him—THE DELUSION OF HIS BEING UNWORTHY OF HEAVEN." Mouritz thought Damien's face, "although dreadful and distressingly disfigured by masses of leproma and general leprous infiltration, showed unmistakable signs of grief and anguish."

If Damien had the delusion of being unworthy of heaven, it was perhaps because his superiors were leading him to believe it of himself. Koeckemann and Fouesnel continued to show a steady hostility toward Damien, unchanged throughout 1887 and into 1888. Charitable gifts kept arriving for him from Hugh Chapman and others; the world press continued to laud him; and the bishop and the provincial continued to blame him for what the world made of his heroism. Fouesnel, in particular, was unrelenting. His letters to Kalawao became even more severe, if that was possible. He told Damien in mid-1888 that, given the circumstances, the unsatisfactory relation between provincial and priest, he had "resolved to have nothing more to do with you, until new orders." He was writing now only because business forced him to; and, business taken care of, he went on to lecture Damien, who had been asking again for a colleague to live with him and confess him. "Be patient," said Fouesnel, "as soon as you are helpless, you will have someone." Haughtiness on Damien's part would be unavailing: it would bring him myrrh even from those who had been prodigal with gold and incense for him. "Make a meditation on humility before writing to your superiors."

Damien had not been inconsiderate of humility. He thought a great deal about praise and blame, about the world and God, about who the priest should be serving, about the imitation of Christ, and what the imitator's rewards and punishments might be. He was in the habit of keeping a notebook of meditations and resolutions made during his infrequent retreats. In his upstairs room he had

a little makeshift library of several score books, most of them
volumes for pious study; and he would copy passages in pencil,
adapting them to his situation, or perhaps follow a train of thought
suggested by his reading.

> Pray to achieve the spirit of humility [he told himself], so as to
> desire scorn. If one is scorned, may one rejoice in it. Let us not be
> touched by the praises of men; let us not be self-satisfied; let us be
> grateful to those who cause us pain or treat us with scorn, and pray
> to God for them. To accomplish this, beyond grace there is needed
> a great self-abnegation and a continual mortification; by these one
> finds oneself transformed into Christ crucified. Saint John of the Cross
> always prayed: "Lord, may I be scorned for love of You!" Let us make
> frequent meditations on the scorn which Christ suffered before Pilate
> —the face covered with spittle—the crown of thorns—the reed—the
> cloak of scarlet—Barabbas is preferred, etc."

Damien found himself living amid tensions and contradictions.
The imitation of Christ had led him to Kalawao. Leprosy was a
continual mortification, a crown of thorns, a repulsive spittle on
the face, a slow crucifixion. It had brought him more praise from
the world than most men ever earned; and he tried to render all
that to God in mind, word, and deed. But from his superiors came
accusations of haughtiness. They were as much as putting him on
trial, jeering at him, spitting in his face. In imitation of Christ, he
would try to suffer anything; but endurance was hard—harder, he
said, than the bearing of his leprosy—when his superiors might
well have seemed to him to be acting in imitation of Pilate.

For Damien the victim of leprosy, there was no way to leave
Kalawao. For Damien the priest, there was no way out of his
dilemma with his superiors—except if he could somehow free
himself from their control and yet remain at the settlement. He
never put any ideas along these lines on paper; but Mouritz
thought he had something planned. Certainly the period of his
great difficulties with Koeckemann and Fouesnel was the time of
his most systematic thinking about leprosy and its institutions: he
had done a long and comprehensive report for Gibson early in

1886, and later that year he put forward his scheme for the big and efficient Goto complex at Kalawao. In this connection, Mouritz found Damien "always pleased to discuss" one interesting subject. "He was imbued with certain lofty ideas and believed in the possibility of their future realization—the Leper Settlement to be a special diocese, Damien to be vicar-apostolic, with special powers direct from the Pope, and the work of the whole Settlement to be carried on under strict ecclesiastical lines, like a monastery." Rudolph Meyer, said Mouritz, "took delight in teasing Damien on the possibilities of this scheme turning out, and would often say, 'Father, how soon shall we see you with shaven poll and tonsure, assuming this will mark your new order.' Damien would laugh heartily and refuse to be drawn out."

If this was only escapist daydreaming, it was at least anchored in history. The lazar houses of medieval Europe were run along the lines Damien evidently sketched out for Mouritz and Meyer. And if Damien wanted to free himself from ecclesiastical shackles that had come to seem more painfully constricting than his disease, then he was not the first priest in the history of the Church to see exceptional measures as the only worthwhile response to an exceptional situation.

In a general context, not involving Damien specifically, Bishop Koeckemann was prepared to point out to the father-general that one fixed rule for the whole Sacred Hearts mission in the Hawaiian Islands was impossible, because each station in the field was so different from the next. "Various priests are in fact independent as to the spiritual—and temporal, except as they lack resources." Damien's resources were multiplying, thanks to charity; and this was certainly one element in Koeckemann's judgment that Damien went impossibly far in the direction of independence, "seeming to have gone into a separate order, above all religious and ecclesiastical authorities who might not approve and further his views." But then Koeckemann, in Damien's judgment—and Fouesnel, and anyone else who would not exert himself to the uttermost for the sake of Kalawao—did not go far enough. Very

few men in the history of the world had been able to bring themselves to go as far as Damien. His was a harsh kind of solitude to
endure, but ennobling at the same time: Christ also had been
alone and scorned at the point of death. And if there was melancholia, beyond that springing from the disease itself, in the
thought of submission to superiors who, though not necessarily
unworthy, could never be brought to see things as he did, then in
the vision of a better and freer way to serve the settlement there
was a liberating joy, enough to restore to Damien—however
briefly—the appetite for laughter in good heart.

XXI

In the meantime, there was work to be done. It would wait neither
upon the establishment of a chimerical independent episcopate
nor upon the re-establishment of harmony with his superiors. And
its peremptory demands would not allow, in a man such as
Damien, the continuance of a debilitating melancholia. His temper, in those troubled times, continued uncertain: Mouritz, the
clinical characterizer, called him "nervo-bilious." But from the
warring elements contending in his life, inside and outside his own
mind and body, Damien drew an endlessly revived capacity for
energetic action. Operating at the limit of his resources—beyond
normal limits, indeed—he managed somehow to keep resuscitat-
ing himself physically and emotionally, throwing himself again
and again into his work.

There was, in fact, more work than ever, because the settlement, in 1888, was bigger than ever. Rudolph Meyer, reporting to
the legislature in March, counted

> 5 churches, two of which are Protestant, two Catholic and one Mor-
> mon; 2 store houses, 2 pai-ai receiving houses, 1 store, 2 dormitories,
> of which one is for boys and the other for girls; about 12 hospital
> buildings, and 1 prison with two cells, and 1 receiving house at
> Kalaupapa for the newcomers when they first land . . . 1 commodious

and comfortably arranged dwelling house for a physician and 2 dispensaries, one at Kalawao and the other at Kalaupapa. All the rest of the buildings are cottages, occupied by the sick and their friends or relatives.

The total number of buildings of all sorts was 374. The total number of cattle was about a thousand head. And in the wake of reform, the number of leprosy sufferers at the settlement rose, for the first time, above a thousand.

In deciding what ought to be done in the way of work, Damien never stood much on ceremony, or paid much attention to jurisdictional lines. He was the priest of Kalawao; the settlement was his to care for. Dutton pictured him "as always ready to take up with great vigor anything that presented itself as his actual duty; and further, anything at all that he thought would be good whether it was actually his duty or not; anything that appeared to him to be good—good to do—was something for his immediate action, apparently considering it really his duty. He did not give much time to the study of expediency, of the cost nor of the dangers."

Dutton saw Damien on his rounds in the last years of his robustness, when he could still work hard, but when he had already begun to sense that time was short, that his life would be over before his work was completed. As the settlement grew, his cares grew, till his activities became endless, a kind of priestly perpetual motion. Damien, said Dutton, would "drive ahead at what he deemed the most important until something else seemed more so, when he would jump over into that; so that he left a track of unfinished jobs. The thought of the moment, as things first occurred to him, gave his 'cue' and 'off he was'—to use one of his very frequent expressions. 'Off I am, Brother Joseph,' he said to me daily, almost hourly, and this was often coupled with the request that I finish what he was doing. . . . 'Brother Joseph, you are going to finish these'—referring to the previous jobs, and would laughingly add, 'I am the carpenter, Brother Joseph the joiner.' "

Just the same, Dutton remarked, in all this running about, with

innumerable projects taken up hurriedly and carried on by the
help of others, Damien had "a way of making things turn out all
right, at least so that a thing would work, though very often it
would be far different from what he had first intended. Sometimes
the result would be amusing, but he would say, 'Well, we can use
it!' "

XXII

A project close to Damien's heart was the orphanage he had set
up at Kalawao village in the late 1870s. He wanted more for this
than the merely makeshift; he wanted the institution to work well;
and he knew that it was beyond him to run it properly. By the
middle 1880s, he had more than a hundred boys and girls to look
after. At the end of 1886, he began to build two new dormitories,
and in the early part of 1887 he added two eating halls, one for girls
and one for boys. Dutton could help him with the boys; for the
girls, it would be best to have the help of the Franciscan Sisters.
Already they were working among the healthy children of
diseased parents, born at the settlement and sent for education to
the Kapiolani Home in Honolulu. And they were working among
leprosy sufferers at Kakaako branch hospital. When Damien made
his difficult visit to Honolulu in mid-1886, he discussed the question
with Mother Marianne. She was ready enough to see what could
be done about sending Sisters to Kalawao; but then the project
became mixed up with all the other difficulties of those years:
Damien's strained relations with his superiors; the delicate political situation; the revolution of 1887 and the Protestant political
hegemony that followed. In the midst of all this delay, rumors
began to be heard that a group of Episcopalian Sisters, English-
women, were to be brought to the settlement. Damien's superiors,
connecting this—as they did so much else—with Damien's exposure to publicity in England, were furious. They regarded it as
another of his attempts to force the hand of the mission, and now

the hand of the Sisters as well: Damien, they said, was making martyrs out of pious women, compelling them to descend into an earthly hell.

This was hardly true. Mother Marianne herself and some of her Sisters were more than willing to go to the settlement; and when the time was right, they did. In 1888, the Board of Health decided to dismantle the branch leprosy hospital at Kakaako—a bad, Gibsonian invention, best got rid of, in their opinion. The inmates were to be sent to the settlement. Some of the larger buildings at Kakaako were to be broken up for shipment there as well, and reassembled at Kalaupapa, not far from the boat landing, to serve as the nucleus of a girls' home, under the control of the Board of Health and staffed by the Sisters.

Part of the funding for all this came from the philanthropy of Charles Reed Bishop, a *haole* banker and businessman of Honolulu. Bishop had married a female Hawaiian chief, Bernice Pauahi, the last of the Kamehameha dynasty; and since her death in 1884 he had been administrator of her vast estates. He was also the owner of Molokai Ranch, which Rudolph Meyer managed for him; and this was the source of his informed interest in the problem of leprosy. One of Bishop's friendly advisers in the dispensation of charity was Charles McEwen Hyde.

XXIII

Damien's superiors, criticizing his "independence," used to say that he had no friends in the Congregation. No one, they said, could live with him; and they instanced André Burgerman, Albert Montiton, and Grégoire Archambaux. To be fair in even the most grudging sense to Damien, it might have been added that very few people ever found it possible to live contentedly with either Burgerman or Montiton; and that as for Archambaux, it was Kalawao—leprosy itself, at bottom—that he could not endure, rather than Damien as a person.

Damien and his latest companion, Joseph Dutton, in turn had a minor dispute over jurisdiction, brought about partly by Dutton's anomalous position (authorized to be at Kalawao by the Board of Health, he was under Damien's direction, but not a member of the Sacred Hearts). The bishop and the provincial immediately categorized the argument as the "martyrdom" of Dutton at the hands of Damien. "Martyrdom" was a word surely excessive for the outcome of a short-lived verbal disagreement, and one they never used for Damien's leprosy itself. Dutton, in fact, managed to get along well with Damien in what were appallingly difficult times for the sick priest—and then this working amicability was used by Koeckemann and Fouesnel as further evidence that Damien preferred outsiders over his fellow members of the Sacred Hearts Congregation.

In this regard, however, Dutton was only a secondary figure. The principal accusation of that sort against Damien concerned not Dutton, a nominal lay brother, but another man who arrived to work at Kalawao in mid-1888, an ordained priest from outside the Congregation.

Father Louis-Lambert Conrardy was like Damien in a number of ways. He was the same age: in his later forties. He was a Belgian (a Walloon, a French-speaker, not a Fleming like Damien; nonetheless this, to Damien's superiors—the bishop a German and the provincial a Frenchman—was yet another evidence of Damien's lack of family feeling for the Sacred Hearts: if he could not be sole authority at Kalawao, he would opt for tribal exclusivity, even if it involved reinforcing his station from outside the Congregation). Just as Damien had done, Conrardy yearned for a priest's life in the distant and difficult country of hermits and martyrs. He had spent between two and three years in Hindustan, then fifteen years in Indian territory in Oregon, where once he was nearly scalped. He had been aware of the existence of Kalawao settlement for several years, and had developed a longing to go there. He began to write in earnest to the Hawaiian Islands in 1881. Damien, in his troubles, began to encourage him late in 1887. No matter how often or how urgently he requested his superiors to send him a regular confessor, they would not, or at least they did not. Now here was an ordained priest, a confessor, burning to come.

Negotiations over Conrardy were prolonged, tangled, and bad-tempered, as were most of the dealings between Damien and his superiors in those troubled years; and the tangle did not finally resolve itself until several years after Damien's death. To begin with, Bishop Koeckemann did not want any "stranger" priests within his diocese. The Hawaiian mission had had a bad experience with such a man some years earlier, when an itinerant Irish priest had ingratiated himself with King Kalakaua, who then tried to have him made bishop, vicar-apostolic of the islands. The Irishman soon discredited himself in a spectacular and tragic way: a college building he erected in Honolulu collapsed, killing a student. The priest departed hastily, leaving Koeckemann to be named bishop. This was as much as Koeckemann ever wanted to have to do with outsiders.

Accordingly, he would have preferred Conrardy to become a member of the Congregation, to take a novitiate and profess his vows in the regular way. Then, if he still wanted to, and if conditions were right, he could go to Kalawao and work with Damien. Conrardy, on his side, was urgent about going straight to Molokai. He regretted not having been there for years already, so he told Damien; he wanted wings to fly there. Damien saw that, given Koeckemann's opposition to outsiders and his evident doubts about Conrardy as a person, to allow Conrardy to be sent to Europe for a novitiate would be tantamount to never seeing him at Kalawao.

Damien put his case to Koeckemann strongly, as he put all his cases, which were really just parts of the same case: he was in an exceptional situation, and an exceptional solution to his problems should be permitted. Koeckemann eventually capitulated. Conrardy would be allowed to go direct to Kalawao, without passing through a novitiate. But then Koeckemann, writing to the father-general, complained that Damien had forced his hand; and the bishop went on to rehearse all his old complaints about the way in which events kept escaping ecclesiastical control—all the unmanageable consequences of Damien's existence which made the life of a bishop so hard and rendered his authority so inadequate. Damien, said Koeckemann, had "ordered" Conrardy to come to Kalawao as soon as possible. "That really puts me in an embarrassing position. If I oppose his views, he will denounce me to the four winds as an enemy of the good of the poor lepers. He sees only the leper settlement and himself; everything else must give way to his ideas. In his letters, he intends to tell the truth; but certainly he often presents it in a false light, suppressing some truths; the government, the mission, and the Congregation are directly or indirectly and unjustly blamed for casting shadows on the hero."

Within the mission at large, Koeckemann went on, there was trouble over Conrardy's imminent arrival. Once the interloper was at work with Damien, the world would be filled with the "glory of the Belgians" at the expense of the Congregation of the Sacred Hearts. "Some of the Fathers have already expressed to me their mortification on this subject." A Honolulu paper had just reprinted an extract from a California paper: a letter in which Damien asked for Conrardy "so as to have someone to take care of the lepers after he was gone, as if there was no one among us who wished to take his place, whereas several of our Fathers are ready to go there at the first signal." This was true enough. When Koeckemann wrote a circular letter to all his priests asking for volunteers for Kalawao, the great majority answered that they would go if called—"an inundation of letters," Léonor Fouesnel called it.

It was true enough as well that all that was required for the press to shower praises on a priest was for him to go to Kalawao. So Koeckemann at any point could have redeemed himself, his mission, and his Congregation from the criticism to which he was so sensitive by arranging to send Damien a colleague, some solid, reliable, and willing member of the Sacred Hearts. But Koeckemann did not, and he did not, and he did not: not after André Burgerman left the leprosy settlement in 1880; nor when Albert Montiton left in 1885; nor when Grégoire Archambaux left once, then twice, in 1885 and 1888. Over the years, Damien was alone at Kalawao more than half the time. He had come to expect inaction from Koeckemann and Fouesnel, and so he himself was active in his own behalf. Having all but given up hope for a confessor from within the Congregation, he agitated for a companion from outside. He got what he wanted, or rather what the exhaustion of alternatives forced him to want. Koeckemann had the mortification of seeing the Honolulu papers praise Conrardy as the "new hero" of Kalawao. Not till then, in point of fact, did the bishop think to write his circular letter asking for volunteers; and the answers, of course, came too late. Conrardy was already at Kalawao, making plans with Damien to ensure that he would be able to stay, and preparing to succeed Damien on his death, whenever that might occur.

Damien wrote to the chapter-general of the Congregation, meeting in Paris—or, more exactly, being sick at that moment, he had Conrardy write in his name—asking for consideration of the best means to hold Conrardy without making him go through a novitiate. Conrardy, so the letter said, was a good worker, used to rough conditions. Damien genuinely needed him; Conrardy's presence had already improved his situation. It was a strong, persuasive letter, written within the Rule of the Congregation; there was nothing disobedient about what Damien was arguing. This letter would have reached Paris at the same time as letters from Koeckemann and Fouesnel, bemoaning the imposition of Conrardy on the mission, denigrating Damien as an unsuitable religious director for the outsider-priest and, further, as almost an enemy of the Sacred Hearts. If the two Belgians stayed too long together, wrote Koeckemann, it was to be feared that "they would end by bringing shame on the mission, either by mutual praise, or by false reports."

With a kind of fatedness which seemed to attach itself to corre-

spondence from Kalawao, Conrardy's letters began to find their
way into the papers. He wrote to friends in the United States, and
they passed the letters on for publication. Conrardy's descriptions
of life at the settlement were everything that Koeckemann and
Fouesnel feared: not prudent, not "official"; not, perhaps, false in
what they said, but "misleading" in what they left out, all to the
detriment of the mission and the government. Once again, this
new embarrassment could have been avoided if the bishop and
the provincial had placed a man of their choice at Kalawao in
advance of Conrardy. But they had not; and so they had to bear
the knowledge that the Protestant-dominated Board of Health,
proud of its conscientiousness, was yet again distinctly irritated.

The secretary of the Board wrote directly to Conrardy, inviting
him to reconsider what he was reported as saying. "Leprosy is our
bane, the nations ulcer, and good taste at least demands that it
should not be needlessly exposed to the gaze of the world." It was
not possible by means of "popular articles" to convey to "mixed
multitudes of readers" a correct and truthful impression of Kalawao settlement. The Board's conclusion was that such articles
were "not calculated to benefit this country or the government
but to injure us unnecessarily and place us in a false light."

In a later-published letter, Conrardy in fact said, among other
things, that the Hawaiian government was doing all it could to
help the people of Kalawao. Beyond that, he did no more than
describe what he experienced. Like every newcomer to Kalawao,
he was all but felled by the horror of the place: the sight of little
children washing their clothes with ravaged hands; a smell that
seemed to him purgatorial. Damien's own sores were enough to
take away Conrardy's appetite; he got severe headaches. An asth-
matic like Archambaux before him, he worried that he might be
incapacitated, unable to work in Kalawao's humid climate. But he
survived the weather and his early repugnance; he got used to
eating meals with Damien; and he became able to consider his
future calmly. Closeness to leprosy, Conrardy said, was "enough
to put to flight a regiment of brave soldiers." He proposed to stay

even so, though he considered it inevitable that he would catch the disease. Precautions might be talked about, but not infallibly practiced. He was at risk every moment. "I believe there is no more possibility of remaining uncontaminated than for a man to live in a fire without being burnt."

Damien, in his fifteen years at the settlement, had seen the population of Kalawao turn over three times. "How many times," Conrardy asked himself, "will it be given to me to see it renew itself?"

XXIV

Conrardy was living with Damien at Kalawao when the Franciscan Sisters arrived to take up work at the Bishop Home in November, 1888. They were in need of a priest, to serve as their chaplain. It could not be Damien: he was diseased. It would not be Conrardy: the Sisters, in consultation with Koeckemann and Fouesnel, had concluded that he was unsuitable. So the bishop and the provincial had to arrange for a member of their mission in good health and good standing to take up residence at the settlement—something they had refused to do for Damien when he was alone, despite his years of pleading.

When, at the height of the upset over Conrardy, Koeckemann had asked all his missionaries if they would go to Kalawao, and had been inundated with offers, one priest at least had not made his response in that way. Father Wendelin Moellers did not consider such a situation a matter for offers and acceptances. His answer, he said, was in the truest sense already in his superiors' hands. It was contained in his vows; he was under obedience; if his superiors gave him an obedience to go, he would go. This was clearly a good, conscientious priest. He was chosen; and he went ashore at Kalaupapa with the Sisters.

With him came a colleague, Father Corneille Limburg, to help temporarily with the installation of the Sisters. Limburg, reporting on his visit in a letter to the father-general, remarked that there were then four priests at the settlement—something unprecedented. A fifth, Damien's former occasional confessor, Father Columban Beissel, was just then visiting the healthy districts over the *pali*; and Damien said he wished he could shout loud enough to bring Beissel down to Kalawao to be with them. Five priests on Molokai; and even after Beissel went back to Maui and Limburg to Oahu, three at the settlement. And the Sisters at the new Bishop Home at Kalaupapa. And, coincidentally, another lay helper, who, like Joseph Dutton, had arrived out of nowhere: an Irishman named James Sinnett, who came ashore in November, and went to work with Dutton, under the informal name of Brother James, at the boys' dormitory at Kalawao.

If Damien never did get his independent diocese—if indeed he had really meant to pursue the idea seriously—he at least got his reinforcements: the hard way, the strenuous way. But then that was the way of his life, the only way he ever knew at Kalawao.

XXV

Earlier in 1888, Damien had written to his old acquaintance, the American naval doctor, G. W. Woods, to tell him, among other things, that "a terrible storm visited us last Saturday, and on Sunday morning we found the steeple of our church on the ground." The wind shook Joseph Dutton awake; and he went from his little hut close by St. Philomena's to check the safety of the church. He was inside when the steeple fell. He went across to Damien's house, and found him in his upstairs bedroom, sound asleep. Surveying the damage next morning, Damien was dismayed. He had rebuilt St. Philomena's once before, in 1876; but, as he wrote to Woods, "being not so strong now, I fear not to be able to do so, myself, a similar difficult work. My disease is progressing, and my hands and feet are undergoing a transformation."

In fact, Damien managed to find the energy he needed. Not

long after the storm, a gift he had been waiting for arrived from the United States: two handsome tabernacles, one each for the churches at Kalawao and Kalaupapa. He wrote a letter of thanks, repeating the story of the fallen steeple, and added: "Fortunately, my hands, though quite sore, are not yet crippled—and if our Blessed Lord continues to keep up my health in the condition in which I am now, I hope to be able to finish these improvements."

When he had completed the installation of the tabernacle in St. Philomena's, he decided that it looked too big for the sanctuary, and went on to decide that the whole building ought to be altered and enlarged. He and Dutton had some discussions about what would be best. In the end, they set out, with the help of a *haole* stonemason who happened to be at Kalawao, to rebuild in rock.

Father Corneille Limburg saw the work going on in its late stages, toward the end of the year, and was astonished to find Damien in the thick of it, on top of the church, in fact, putting on the roof. Damien's leprosy looked far gone: "the face puffy; the ears, one of which already has broken skin, swollen and elongated; the eyes red and the voice hoarse." But, incredibly, he was still strong and active. "You should have seen the wild activity he was directing, giving his orders now to the masons, now to the carpenters, now to the laborers, all lepers. You would have said he was a man in his element and perfectly healthy. This tells you that Father Damien seems not to want to stop until he falls."

XXVI

While Damien was working on St. Philomena's, Father Grégoire Archambaux was dying in his little cell at Kakaako. He managed to live a few months longer than his "drowned" asthma. His leprosy was not the same as Damien's; he suffered atrocious physical pain without being marked by sores on his skin. He died in November, 1888, the first of the Sacred Hearts mission in the Hawaiian Islands to be taken by leprosy: a good man, a worthy priest in his day, but no hero of self-sacrifice—an ordinary mortal in the end, trapped late in life by an extraordinary and loathsome disease, barely able to resign himself to his fate, and quite unable to match the ravages of leprosy with some powerful positive response of his own. None of his colleagues judged him harshly for this: they saw themselves in him.

XXVII

Someone once asked Damien if he wanted to be cured, and his answer was no—not if the price was his departure from the settlement and the abandonment of his labors. From time to time, he spoke of leprosy as doing him the favor of shortening his road to heaven; and for this he thanked God and the Virgin Mary. But on the other hand, even if he might have preferred to be "called away to a better world," as he put it, the life of a "leper priest" had its own value. So, although he could not ask his friends to pray for the miracle of a complete cure, something of which he held himself to be unworthy, those who remembered him in prayer might properly ask for at least "a stay of the progress of the malady."

Damien believed, of course, in "the possibility of a miracle, such as reported in Holy Scripture." As to medical cures, or even treatments that worked well, Damien had become skeptical. He had ceased to think that there was such a thing as "a natural remedy to cure leprosy." "So many doctors and others advise me to do this and that, but all in vain—to overcome this incurable disease." The best thing, then, was to try to bear his leprosy without complaining, and suffer it to the soul's sanctification. Sickness, after all, was a "providential agent," intended to "detach the heart from all earthly affection," to prompt the desire of a Christian soul to be united—the sooner the better—with God.

Be patient, Léonor Fouesnel had told Damien in 1886; as soon as you are helpless, you will have someone to help you. He had his helpers now, no great thanks to Fouesnel; and those who saw him daily thought that helplessness could not be far away.

But he kept deceiving them, and himself. Not long after Conrardy came, Damien's eyes began to give him serious trouble. For the first time since he was ordained in 1864, he wrote, he could not say Mass. He recovered his sight; and his strength permitted him to continue with his work, installing the two new tabernacles, planning ahead for the renovation of St. Philomena's church. Then, one day in October, while he was offering Mass, he fell at the altar and could not go on. "I am getting old and weak," he wrote at about that time. "I know that my days are numbered, and do not expect to be in this miserable world for a long while." He spoke of how the disease had "gone down to my lungs," and of how he was looking forward to his happy death: "Very soon I hope all will be right—when the body is under the green coverlet."

The disease was beginning to work a fundamental change in Damien's physique; he could feel it, and he knew what it meant. He had talked about it as a general thing earlier in the year, before he had begun to experience it himself. Leprosy, he wrote to a well-wisher, began and continued for a time as a disease of the exterior of the body. Throughout this stage, a man might remain strong and active. But, said Damien, the day the interior is affected, "we become generally feeble; then, enveloped in covers for months or years, our sole expectation and sole hope is no more than deliverance from our miseries by a happy death."

A kind of fever laid him low in October, and kept him close to Kalawao village. For six weeks he was unable to visit Kalaupapa; and when in mid-November he drove to the boat landing in his buggy to meet the newly arrived Franciscan Sisters, he was still convalescent. But by the end of the month he was back at the strenuous work of roofing his church, in a fever of activity. If the leprosy in his body was shortening his road to heaven, and if his soul yearned to be with God, he was still not ready to compose himself for death.

XXVIII

The act of mortuary composition was initiated for him, in advance
of his death, by an Englishman named Edward Clifford, a conscientious Protestant layman philanthropically interested in leprosy,
comfortably off, and possessing some skill as an artist. One Sunday
morning in the spring of 1887, Clifford came across an account of
Damien in "the magazine of the Soho girls' club," and decided to
visit Kalawao. He made the trip the following year, after a preliminary and scarifying tour of the leprosy centers of India, a subconti-
nent with a huge and hopeless population of sufferers, most of
them untreated. Arriving after this at Honolulu in December,
1888, Clifford took the little steamer *Mokoli'i* on its regular Monday sailing to Molokai, with the rest of its miscellaneous deck-
passenger list and thirteen victims of leprosy bound for Kalawao.
The *Mokoli'i* left Honolulu at sunset. Clifford spent the early hours
of the evening on deck, stretched out uncomfortably on a mattress
"invaded from the lower end by two pairs of legs—a Chinese pair
and a Hawaiian pair"; and when some of the Hawaiian passengers
started to sing to the music of a guitar, Clifford gave up trying to
sleep. "I relinquished my couch, and, retiring to another part of
the vessel, gave myself up to the enjoyment of the moonlit precipices and ravines of Molokai, which we began to coast about midnight. Very solemn and rather terrible they looked."

At dawn, the *Mokoli'i* was off Kalaupapa, but there was such a
heavy surf, with spray shooting up fifty feet from the rocks, that
the ship's boat could not go in. Kalawao was no better. "Finally it
was decided to put off a boat for a rocky point about a mile and
a half distant from the town. Climbing down this point we saw
about twenty lepers, and 'There is Father Damien!' said our
purser; and, slowly moving along the hillside I saw a dark figure
with a large straw hat. He came rather painfully down, and sat
near the water-side, and we exchanged friendly signals across the
waves while my baggage was being got out of the hold." The boat
went swinging in through the surf; Clifford jumped ashore; and

Damien "caught me by the hand, and a hearty welcome shone from his kindly face as he helped me up the rock."

Clifford had accepted the outstretched hand of Damien, but he did not want a diseased Hawaiian hand on his belongings. He carried his own bag a mile and a half to Kalawao village. The walk was tiring, "up and down hill, through a broad stream, and then along a beach of boulders shaded by great precipices"; but "the pleasure of discovering that Damien was a finer man than I had even expected made it delightful." About halfway, Clifford stopped to refresh himself in the foam of the waves; and he was impressed by the "quiet way" in which Damien "sat down and read and prayed while I bathed, retiring at once into that hidden life which was so real to him. When I was ready to walk on with him he was all animation again, and pointed out to me all the objects of interest."

Clifford had come to Kalawao thinking of it as a hellish place; and indeed he found it distressing to see "none but lepers" for the fourteen days he was there. But he grew to enjoy it as he had not been able to enjoy the overpowering awfulness of India. He liked to watch the Hawaiians sit talking at their doorsteps, pounding *kalo* into *poi*, or galloping on their horses—"men and women alike astride"—between Kalawao village and Kalaupapa. "And one always receives the ready greeting and the readier smile." The "cheerful people, the lovely landscape, and the comparatively painless life were all surprises." There was even a moral beauty about Kalawao that Clifford could respond to. He met, and was impressed by, a "good old blind man in the hospital, who told me that he was thankful for the disease, because it had saved him from so much evil."

Clifford had brought with him a treatment for leprosy "in which I was much interested": gurjun oil, the "produce of a fir tree which grows plentifully in the Andaman Islands (off the coast of Burmah)." He had seen it used to what looked like good effect in India. The oil in its raw condition was brown and sticky; but "shaken up with three parts of lime-water it makes an ointment as soft and smooth as butter." It was to be rubbed on the skin each day, the longer the better; and it could also be taken internally. This treatment, in fact, was not new to Kalawao. It had been tried the previous year, but had not caught on. Clifford got the impression that Damien was no more than politely interested in it, but he hoped just the same that his gift would be given a fair chance to prove itself.

Other gifts for Damien and his work came with Clifford: charitable donations from well-disposed people in England, which were uncrated and handed out from the *Mokoli'i*'s boat to be carried off one by one to Kalawao. "First came an engraving of Mr. Shields' 'Good Shepherd,' from Lady Mount-Temple; then a set of large pictures of the Stations of the Cross, from the Hon. Maude Stanley; then a magic-lantern with Scriptural slides; then numbers of coloured prints; and . . . an ariston from Lady Caroline Charteris, which would play about forty tunes simply by having its handle turned. . . . There were beautiful silver presents from Lady Grosvenor and Lady Airlie, and several gifts of money. And, most valuable of all, there was a water-color painting of the Vision of St. Francis by Mr. Burne-Jones, sent by the painter."

Damien hung the St. Francis—a copy of Burne-Jones' large oil painting, but worth some hundreds of dollars in its own right—in his little upstairs bedroom. He arranged for some of the colored prints to go on the walls of St. Philomena's church. Clifford staged his magic-lantern show, with its pictures from the life of Christ; and Damien explained to the watching crowd what they were seeing. The Hawaiians sang for Clifford: a "lepers' hymn," and, because it was Christmas, *"Adeste Fideles."* On Christmas Day, the people of Kalawao put on an entertainment, acting "little scenes": Belshazzar's feast, and other Biblical spectacles. Between times, Lady Caroline Charteris' ariston played cheerfully. Clifford could not have been more pleased.

Visitors in those years could stay in the Board of Health's guest house; and Damien would come over at night to talk to Clifford, sitting on the veranda steps, answering questions about his life while "the stars shone over his head, and all the valleys glimmered in golden moonlight." Damien would never come inside the guest house; but he invited Clifford to visit him at his own small home. They ate there with Conrardy, Clifford at a separate table, somewhat hesitant about what he was offered by Damien's cook, confining himself for the most part to biscuits and fresh fruits. After dinner, they would climb the steps to the second story, to sit outside Damien's workroom on a narrow balcony festooned with blossoming honeysuckle.

"Some of my happiest times at Molokai," Clifford wrote later, "were spent in this little balcony, sketching him and listening to what he said." Clifford made the effort to see Damien as he was on the leprous surface, as he was in inner truth, and as he once had been. The artist's subject was in his forty-ninth year, coming to the end of his final labor on the roof of St. Philomena's church, and his final battle with leprosy: "a thick-set, strongly-built man, with black curly hair and short beard, turning gray." The signs of the disease were evident—the hands and face uneven with a "sort of incipient boils," the forehead "swollen and ridged," the nose "somewhat sunk," the eyebrows gone, the ears "greatly enlarged." Damien, so Clifford deduced, must have had a handsome countenance, "with a full, well-curved mouth and a short, straight nose; but he is now a good deal disfigured . . . though not so badly as to make it anything but a pleasure to look at his bright, sensible face."

This was the kind eye of the sympathetic artist. Clifford sketched Damien in his balcony seat, often while he was reading his breviary, with Hawaiians gathered round to watch, "their poor faces . . . swelled and drawn and distorted, with bloodshot goggle eyes." In the case of the Hawaiians, the artist did not bother to soften their looks with his pen, something he could not resist doing for Damien. Clifford's finished portrait of the priest, a gentle one, showed him in profile, wearing a straw hat and wire-rimmed glasses, head inclined, the disease suggested rather than clinically rendered, a man homely to look at rather than horrible. Even so,

Damien was wryly mournful at what Clifford revealed to him of himself. "What an ugly face!" he said. "I did not know the disease had made such progress." And when Clifford offered to send a photographic copy of the picture to Pamphile in Belgium, Damien said that perhaps it would be better not to do so, as it might pain his brother to see how badly he was disfigured.

When Clifford came to write a book about his visit to Kalawao, he noted in the introduction that it was a worthy thing, a duty, to honor such men as Damien. He went on to observe that even good people "have generally a little difficulty at first in quite admiring a hero; for heroes are not made to order just on our favorite pattern. None of them are precisely like our grandmothers or our favorite clergymen." Yet he himself, a Protestant prepared to set out cogent arguments against Catholicism as a faith, proposed to admire Damien unreservedly, so he said, announcing to his readers that "what follows afterwards will be unmixed praise of a Roman Catholic saint." And the frontispiece he chose for his book was another portrait he had made of Damien, this time an "imagined" version of the priest twenty years younger, before leprosy, before Kalawao. There were photographs Clifford could have used for reference; but if he saw them, he chose not to bother with them. Rather, he defined for himself the necessary features of the not-yet-hero, showing, so to speak, what Damien must once have been in order to become what he did. This portrait, done in 1888, was dated 1868. It was the hero-to-be made to order by Clifford, for Clifford. Never did the features of a single man reconcile so sublimely strength and sensitivity and renunciatory purpose: the athlete's muscular neck rising from a priest's collar; severely cropped curls capping a well-shaped skull; a mouth somehow opulently ascetic; an eye at once melting and steadfast, on intimate terms with illimitable distances. It was the face of some wakefully dreaming Pre-Raphaelite young immortal, one who would never die—because he had never lived. It could not have been less like Damien.

When Clifford left Kalawao on the last day of 1888, Damien, the good, devoted, contentious, knotty, simple, complex, lonely, aging, dying man, came stumping down to the shore in his tattered and patched black clothes and stood in all his disfigurement as the artist sailed away with his pictures. Clifford had found time in his two weeks at the settlement to paint some landscapes, but never the twilight landscape with figures that his eye arranged for him across the rail of the departing steamer. "As our ship weighed anchor the sombre purple cliffs were covered with white clouds. Down their sides leaped the cataracts. . . . Father Damien stood with his people on the rocks till we slowly passed from their sight. The sun was getting low in the heavens, the beams of light were slanting down the mountain sides, and then I saw the last of Molokai in a golden mist."

XXIX

The turning of the year, from 1888 to 1889, was marked by a formal exchange of good wishes between Damien and his superiors. Bishop Koeckemann sent a meerschaum pipe with his note; and Father Fouesnel sent some tobacco, asking Damien's opinion of it so that he could ascertain his taste and keep him supplied. This was friendly in a small way; but there were large issues still between Kalawao and Honolulu which kept obtruding themselves.

Early in the new year, the question of altering the church building at Kalaupapa came up. It would be improved by some changes; but what should be done was a matter for disagreement. To begin with, the Franciscan Sisters at Kalaupapa had to be considered. They were independent of Damien; and their chaplain, Father Wendelin Moellers, was the priest of Kalaupapa, independent of Damien too, by the designation of the mission's superiors. He should have some say in the matter of the church, and also in the matter of where his own house was built. Damien, as always, had his own strong opinions.

While all this was being worked out, charity money kept arriving. Damien, so Koeckemann noted dryly, was "triumphing," with money "coming for him by the thousands of dollars." Koeckemann said he was prepared to allow Damien to spend it as he saw fit—and indeed Hugh Chapman and many of the other donors were still specifying that the money was to be put to use by Damien personally—but the bishop did write plaintively to Damien that he would prefer to be told what the money was being used for, rather than have to find out about it from the newspapers.

Problems of publicity; problems of obedience, or at least the definition of obedience; the problem of a lack of mutual confidence, in which strict definitions would not have been necessary —in all this, the new year was like the old. And, once the formal good wishes of the season had been passed across the Molokai Channel, Damien and his superiors went back to snapping at each other. First it was the business of the church at Kalaupapa: "Don't be so absolute in your ideas!" wrote Fouesnel. Then it was a long list of supplies that Damien wanted. He asked for them—as always, but now with ultimately pressing urgency—to be sent quickly; and Fouesnel complained that Damien was again dipping his pen in acid. "Don't be so impatient. Sometimes, even often, it is impossible; and you never take that into account . . . 'it's necessary,' 'I need it,' 'send it at once.' And when we have to write to France for it do you think I will get it sooner by throwing myself in the water? Calm yourself, then, and *do as the others do.*" Damien, of course, was doing only what he took to be his duty.

One of the things he wanted from Fouesnel was a new burial pall. The Sacred Hearts Sisters in Honolulu would make it for him, Fouesnel said; but they were busy; it would be slow. And by this time Damien could feel himself dying.

Edward Clifford wrote regularly to ask about Damien's health; and Brother James Sinnett wrote back to say that the gurjun oil was making some improvements: Damien's face was better, and his voice was less feeble. But the oil, as Damien knew, was good for not much more than an "exterior cleansing"; and the disease was inside him, reducing him to nothing.

He very much wanted contact with other people; and perhaps in his last doomed months he still wanted to think for a moment that he did not have leprosy. When Clifford had come ashore, Damien had clasped his hand in welcome. Talking to Conrardy, every so often, Damien would press some gift or other on him, saying: "Keep this for yourself; no leper has touched it." He was more than pleased that the Franciscan Sisters had come to work at Kalaupapa. He used to visit them when he could; and, denied entry to their oratory because of his disease, he used to kneel in prayer in the garden outside, looking through a window at the altar with its crucifix. He particularly wanted them to see and approve the work he was doing on the church buildings. And one day, impulsively, he invited two of the Sisters to eat with him at Kalawao, insisting so strenuously that they did not know how to refuse. They ate under great strain, because Mother Marianne had forbidden them to share food with the diseased; the next day, Damien, remorseful about having imposed himself upon them, went to Kalaupapa to beg their forgiveness.

He wrote to Pamphile on February 12 to say that he was too sick to keep regularly in touch with his family, but that he thought his brother and the others at Tremeloo could very well write at least as often as he did, or more often. No letter came in immediate answer, of course—the mails still took at least a month each way from Belgium—and in the last letter Damien wrote to Europe, in March, to a Catholic Sister who knew his family, he allowed himself to wonder whether the unresponsive Pamphile was ashamed of him for catching leprosy.

Between those two letters, his condition had become much worse. In mid-February, his hands, which had been spared sufficiently for him to go on saying Mass, broke out in painful eruptions; he had a violent diarrhea; he was coughing badly—perhaps pneumonia was adding itself to his leprosy; his breathing was obstructed, so that he was getting only an hour or two of sleep a night, toward morning; and in the daytime the sunlight hurt his eyes. Yet somehow, as James Sinnett wrote to Edward Clifford, he

managed to keep on working. At the end of February, he brought
his will up to date, confirming that everything was to go to his
bishop on his death, and naming a new co-executor.

In March, a leprosy specialist from New York, named Prince A.
Morrow, visited the settlement; and at his request Damien dictated his own case history. Dutton took it down from the beginning, whenever that might have been: the itching on the face at
Kohala; the spots on the skin in the early years at Kalawao; the
pains in the feet and the sciatic nerve trouble at the beginning of
the eighties; then the period after Eduard Arning's diagnosis, with
the progressive "disfigurement of his person in a general and
marked manner."

With Morrow came a Honolulu man named William Brigham,
to take scientific photographs for the doctor. He posed Damien
with a crowd of youngsters from his boys' dormitory, the last
picture of the priest in the world of green grass and open air and
other people. The disease was overwhelmingly present. Damien
was surrounded by it in his dozens of boys. His own left foot was
bandaged; and his right arm was in a sling, the hand heavily
swathed, showing beneath a mantle that covered his shoulders.

Another picture that Brigham took, a solitary portrait, showed
Damien, head and shoulders and upper body, as he finally was: a
leprosy case, dying. Brigham was no friend of Damien and what
he stood for—another antipathetic Protestant, in fact—and his
sharp-lensed camera would not in any event have permitted him
to soften the lines of the sick man's face as Edward Clifford had
done with his artist's touch. Damien's uniqueness of feature—that
face which so struck those who saw it healthy with its strength and
vigor—had become nothing but a generalized record of the disease. And yet there was still a determined selfhood about him,
preserved not in the look of the eyes, from which the life was
already beginning to fade, but rather in the well-worn and unmistakable iconography of the singular man, the singular priest.
There were things that Damien had owned for years, that were
consummately part of him; and these he chose to wear for the
camera: a pair of wire-rimmed eyeglasses, set on the sunken nose,

hooked gracelessly over the elongated ears; and the black hat of a man of religion, battered, its broad brim turned haphazardly up and caught to the crown with pieces of string.

The feast day of St. Joseph, after whom Damien's parents had named him at his birth, fell on March 19. A letter came to Kalawao for Damien, wishing him happiness, and commemorating as well the twenty-fifth anniversary of his arrival in Honolulu to begin his missionary ministry. The writer was one of the Sacred Hearts Sisters who had made the passage from Europe with him. No friendly, informal anniversary greeting came from either Koeckemann or Fouesnel.

Four days after his feast day, Damien went to bed sick. Until then, as Father Wendelin Moellers said, he had been "as usual, active, coming and going"; but March 23 "was the last time I saw him thus." Four days later again, he became definitely bedridden; and he began preparing for death.

The burial pall he wanted had arrived from Honolulu. On March 30, he made a general confession to Moellers, who confessed himself to Damien in turn; then, together, they renewed the vows that bound them to the Congregation of the Sacred Hearts. The next day, he received holy viaticum; and on April 2, Conrardy administered extreme unction to him. He thought only of dying; and yet still he did not die. "Even Saints and Martyrs have to exercise sometimes a little patience," said Rudolph Meyer, who had come down the *pali* to see him. Damien spoke of his good fortune at having priestly colleagues with him, but more at having workers to take his place at the settlement. His colleagues and the Franciscan Sisters were his *Nunc Dimittis*, he said; he was no longer necessary.

For a few days in early April, he rallied. The Sisters visited him; there were Hawaiians about the place night and day, as there had always been; and late in the evening, Conrardy would walk from the church to the house, bringing the holy eucharist to Damien, with Sinnett carrying a lighted torch and ringing a bell. Damien received communion, said Sinnett, like a seraph.

Not so his medicine, according to the new settlement doctor,

Sidney Bourne Swift. "Poor fellow he has been a very bad patient." Dangerously ill for two weeks, Damien had "completely
tied" the doctor's hands, so Swift said on April 11. Until the day
before, when Damien's temperature went up to 105 degrees, Swift
"could not get him to take quinine." Swift thought Damien's condition was "most critical"; but as a doctor he had "never lost hopes
of his recovery."

On Saturday, April 13, Damien was sicker than ever. It was clear
this time that the end was coming. Dr. Swift began to think of
getting his camera ready to take some deathbed photographs. A
little after midnight, Damien took communion; and from then on
his consciousness faltered. On Sunday, Sinnett heard him say that
there were two figures with him constantly, one at the head and
one at the foot of his bed. They were not visible to Sinnett; and
Damien never named them.

Wendelin Moellers had had to go back to Kalaupapa to offer
Sunday Mass. He stayed there overnight. Early on the morning of
Monday, April 15, he got a note from Conrardy at Kalawao to say
that Damien was in his death agony. Hurrying to the sickbed,
Moellers met another messenger on the road who told him that
Damien was dead.

The body was carried to St. Philomena's church; and the Franciscan Sisters came to prepare the coffin. All his outdoor working
life at Kalawao, Damien had worn black; in death, he was dressed
in his priestly vestments. Throughout Monday, he lay in his coffin,
surrounded by the people of the settlement praying for his soul.
On Tuesday morning, Moellers celebrated Mass for him; and then
the funeral cortege moved out of the church to the cemetery: the
cross; a band of the musicians who played at all the Kalawao burial
ceremonies; the members of one of the funeral associations; the
Sisters, women, and girls; the coffin, carried by eight patients, all
white men; then Moellers, the officiating priest; Conrardy; the
acolytes; and then Dutton and Sinnett and the men and boys.

XXX

From the beginning of his life in religion, Damien had gone to great pains to establish his right to earthly exile; and he had put himself in the way of a disease whose distinguishing mark was the dissolution of the flesh, a mortification bridging life and death. Yet, if Damien wanted death, he wanted it as the end of life as a good priest; and even then he wanted it not for itself, but for what it would bring him.

He had chosen long ago the spot for his burial in the graveyard at Kalawao. The coffin bearers laid him to rest amid the two thousand other graves there, facing the altar of St. Philomena, under his pandanus tree.

CHAPTER FIVE

STIGMA

I

When Pamphile heard of Damien's death, he wrote to the mother house of the Sacred Hearts in Paris, a long letter of fraternal reminiscence: how his brother, young Joseph, "Jef," had come to join the Congregation at Pamphile's urging; how Pamphile had taught him Latin; how Damien had taken his brother's place in the Hawaiian mission in 1863. A month later, he wrote another letter, very much the same, this one to the *Times* of London, mentioning a campaign of his own, or at least of his own country, "the projected Belgian memorial of my brother's life and work." Committees had already been formed, said Pamphile, "to collect funds for a 'Damien Institute,' the object of which will be to insure a continuation of my brother's work at Molokai itself. Burses are to be founded in a college that shall be called by my brother's name, and the utmost care exercised in the choice of proper subjects for the glorious but most difficult task of ministering to and nursing the lepers."

Pamphile understood that if anything was to be accomplished in Damien's name, then that name must be known: publicity was essential. He recalled, for the readers of the *Times*, his own publication in a French religious journal of an early letter from Damien at Kalawao, and the rebuke he had received from his brother: "I want," Damien had said, "to live and work here unknown to the world." Such, said Pamphile, was the "simple earnestness and humility of my dear brother's character." Now, however, Damien's death had released Pamphile from any vow of silence on his behalf; and Pamphile was pleased to announce the forthcoming publication in England of Damien's letters, "translated from the French and Flemish, many of them dating back to his childhood, and carefully treasured for years by our mother, who adored Jef, and who died of a broken heart when she heard he had taken the leprosy."

The letters appeared first in a magazine, and were then collected in a book, published in 1889, for which Pamphile wrote the introduction. The book was later republished in an expanded version, giving Pamphile the chance to tell once more the story of the life of the De Veuster brothers. In doing so, he went back in all candor to the Old Testament tale of Jacob and Esau: the archetypal story of fraternal differences and rivalries in preferment for favor. "In case my efforts are crowned with . . . good results, as I hope they will through God's mercy and the generosity of Christians, it will be some consolation to me—whereas my brother, like another Jacob, supplanted me in the ministry of the apostolate—to nourish the sweet hope that I shall contribute, at least in this way, towards insuring the stability of his works."

In 1895, the Sacred Hearts mission at Honolulu asked Pamphile to come to the settlement and work. The most obvious point in favor of the idea was the public edification to be derived from seeing a second brother follow the first in self-sacrifice: something which would be well received in the wider world. It was not a matter in 1895 of recruiting new workers for the settlement. Rather, Pamphile was one element in a plan to get rid of a worker already there. Within the mission, there was a strong wish to be disembarrassed of the man Damien had chosen as his companion in his last months, the stranger-priest Louis-Lambert Conrardy, and to have a member of the Congregation take his place. The feeling was that Conrardy had forced himself upon the settlement, and that his continued presence there was a reproach to the Sacred Hearts Fathers. To bring Pamphile to Kalawao would execute a double stroke, a removal of the reproach and a reinforcement of the Congregation's moral authority.

Conrardy did not want to leave; and he presented a petition with Hawaiian signatures, twenty meters long, to show that the people of the settlement wanted him to stay. But the mission's leaders wanted to be rid of him; the Franciscan Sisters did not like him; and the Board of Health cordially wished him away: he had strong and disputatious ideas about the administration of the settlement, and he kept writing letters that could be read as pejorative, and the letters kept getting into print. Protesting to the last, Conrardy left Kalawao and the islands late in 1895.

The first part of the double stroke was accomplished, and the second part was initiated when Pamphile took up his new duties at the settlement in December. But it turned out immediately that he was a most approximate substitute for Damien. In his first letter home to Europe, to the father-general, he said quite simply that he considered his presence at the settlement almost useless. Experience confirmed this. Pamphile was a quiet, retiring man, a considerable linguist and scholar, but by no stretch of the imagination a rough-and-ready worker in the field like his late brother. And at fifty-eight Pamphile was already almost ten years older than Damien had been when he died. It was hard for a scholar to make a missionary of himself at that age. All his priestly life, Pamphile had been used to the orderliness, the protection—and the convenience—of life in the cloister, with sacristans to look after church buildings, cooks to prepare food, people to mend clothes. Damien had never minded a certain amount of disarray in his church; he would eat anything or nothing; he gave away most of his clothes, and mended what was left with whatever was at hand: hot wax, paper, and string, on one occasion. Pamphile was no energetic and resourceful improviser. If he had not been Damien's brother, no one would ever have thought of him for Kalawao. He was old, and he felt lost. He wanted to go home to Louvain.

But if there were edifying reasons for him to have come to the settlement, there were even stronger reasons for him not to leave. Father Léonor Fouesnel, still provincial of the mission, argued for keeping Pamphile on the grounds that he could not be spared: Father Wendelin Moellers would be left alone at the settlement without a confessor, which would be intolerable. (Fouesnel, remarkably, had never been so earnest about the need of a regular confessor for Damien in the days—the years—of his loneliness.) Beyond that, of course, there were cautionary considerations; and these were put strongly to Pamphile. To go, especially so soon after arriving with a certain amount of fanfare, would be to abandon Damien, to be derelict in duty; and—on top of everything else —it would shame the work of the Sacred Hearts Fathers in public. Pamphile's bishop at Honolulu, Hermann Koeckemann's successor, Gulstan Ropert, who as a young priest in 1868 had gone to share Damien's work in Kohala, wearing Pamphile's clothes, invoked the dead brother to help the living: "I pray to Father Damien every day to inspire his brother with more highly religious ideas."

Pamphile was not at all lacking in religiosity. It was just that he felt himself to be ludicrously misplaced. The more he was pressed to stay, the more he wanted to go; and at last he began talking of leaving not only the settlement, but the Congregation: if he could not go back to Europe as a Sacred Hearts Father, he would go back and become a Capuchin, a Franciscan.

Eventually, early in 1897, after a little more than a year at the settlement, Pamphile was given permission to go home. He left for Europe in the late summer. By September, he was back at Louvain. He arrived there at seven in the evening, the hour at which he had been accustomed to perform his regular adoration before the altar. Without even making his return known to his old colleagues, he went straight to the church and took up the reassuring acts of adoration.

He lived another twelve years, following with mathematical regularity the life of the cloister. In 1909, he celebrated the fiftieth anniversary of his ordination as a priest. Soon afterward, he died of a heart attack: a simple, humble man, good at his work, so his obituarist said, not at all inflated by the fact of his fraternity with the remarkable Damien, and genuinely liked by all who knew him.

II

England as well as Belgium expressed a public interest in the stability of Damien's works. Edward Clifford, home again in London in the late spring of 1889 after his visit to Kalawao, was scheduled to give a public lecture on Damien on May 14. He prepared for it thinking that his subject was still alive. But then, three days before his speech was to be read, the news of Damien's death appeared in the papers; and Clifford's inspirational lecture became a eulogy. Damien's other well-intentioned friend in London, the Reverend Hugh Chapman of St. Luke's, wrote to the *Times* saying that he wanted his fund for work at Kalawao to continue even though Damien was dead. Within a few weeks, public support arose for a fund of a broader kind. The most imposing of patrons agreed to lend their names: the Archbishop of Canterbury; Cardinal Manning; two dukes, an earl, a Baron de Rothschild; and, at the head of the list, His Royal Highness the Prince of Wales. The purposes of the fund included a monument commemorating Damien and his work, to be set up at Kalawao; special treatment for any victims of leprosy who might be found in England; and serious research into leprosy in the colonies of the British Empire, especially India.

Edward Clifford, good Christian and good imperial Britisher, was delighted in advance with all this. "When Father Damien consecrated his life to Christ and buried himself in the leper settlement of Kalawao he little thought that the echoes of his self-sacrifice would not only be the bugle call to quicken the divine life in thousands of souls who lived under grayer clouds than the rich skies of Molokai hold, but that they would rouse an Empire to rid its neglected myriads of the terrible plague which has at last laid him to rest under his palm-tree. But so it is. No one can measure the results of the simplest act performed with a single eye from love to God and man."

Committees were formed; fund-raising events were held: concerts with speeches, dinners with speeches. A special journalistic note of horror was added when the new attention to leprosy in London turned up a diseased meat handler at one of the city's busiest markets. This single case may have helped the fund dispro- portionately. As Clifford remarked, weighing the case of India against the case of London: "It is natural but rather sad that people should be resigned to the fact of 250,000 of our fellow-subjects dying of leprosy, but tremendously agitated when they find that there is an idea that the mutton chop they have bought in the meat market may have been handled by a leper."

The relations of the individual to society, and specifically of Damien to the British world at large, were put in an altered per- spective when, halfway through the fund-raising, the enterprise changed its name from the Father Damien Memorial Fund to the National Leprosy Fund. The Prince of Wales, speaking in January, 1890, made it sound almost as if Damien's moment had passed. "The general question of leprosy," said His Royal Highness, "has had its true character somewhat obscured by the attention which was directed to it by the devoted life and heroic death of Father Damien. The case is bad enough without it being made to appear worse than it is, and it is much to be regretted that the fate of the Martyr of Molokai has been rendered an excuse for a good deal of exaggeration of a kind from which he would have been the first to shrink."

So the movement went on, a conglomerate of genuine charity, instinctive reaction to suddenly apprehended horror, the scien- tific spirit, and British imperial self-interest, with the last of these coming to predominate. When the Prince of Wales said at a ban- quet that he wanted it understood that the establishment of re- search and treatment facilities in England did not constitute an invitation to sufferers from abroad to make their way there, his audience approved: "Hear, hear!" And by the time scientific sur- veys began to show that very likely the contagiousness of leprosy was low, and that leprosy in India, however horrible there, was not a real imperial hazard—meaning that Britain was not directly threatened—a great deal of the agitation associated with Damien's death had died away. Long before those findings were in, the National Leprosy Fund, formerly the Father Damien Memorial Fund, had been wound up.

As for the monument to Damien at Kalawao, Edward Clifford supervised the design and construction of a cross of red granite, with a sculptured portrait head inset in white marble ("nothing like Damien," said Dr. Arthur Mouritz when he saw it). The monument was satisfactorily noticed: a description, with an engraving, "appeared in nearly all the leading Home, Colonial, and American newspapers." Shipped charitably freight-free to Honolulu, the cross was unloaded there in mid-1891.

King Kalakaua had already taken a trip to Kalawao to consider a site for it. But the erection of the monument, the financial responsibility of the Hawaiian government, was delayed. There was not enough money, so Edward Clifford was told. Government revenues were down, because the sugar plantations of the islands were going through hard times, the result of a disadvantageous change in the tariff laws of the United States, where virtually all the annual crop was marketed. The planters, the *haole* élite of the kingdom, were greatly discomfited; the politics of the kingdom became turbulent.

The installation and dedication of the monument waited, in fact, more than two years longer: waiting, in the end, on national questions far more wide-ranging than the price of sugar. The *haole* enemies of Walter Murray Gibson and King Kalakaua in the 1880s continued to be the enemies of Kalakaua's successor, his sister Liliuokalani, who came to the throne in 1891. She was their enemy in return. Ultimately, she came to be regarded by the *haole* business oligarchy as insufferable, the embodiment of bad government; and in January, 1893, a brief and almost bloodless revolution in Honolulu brought down the Hawaiian monarchy. In its place there emerged a provisional government, directed by *haole*, largely Protestant, looking forward to speedy annexation of the Hawaiian Islands by the United States.

The government officials who eventually invited the Catholic bishop to the unveiling of the Damien monument in September, 1893, were apostles of the general righteousness of American imperial expansion. And so, in the 1890s, in the Hawaiian Islands as in Britain, the questions of leprosy and imperial dominion were joined.

III

For the Reverend Doctor Charles McEwen Hyde, the political marriage of the Hawaiian Islands and the United States would be a moral consummation as well. He was as much an imperialist as any American of his day in Honolulu; and he had come to believe that Hawaiians were not fit to govern themselves. He had always wondered about what he called the fiscal irresponsibility of Hawaiians, their unwillingness to work like white men, their lack of interest in things of the mind—"There are no *studious* Hawaiians"; and he speculated about the influence of climate upon human development. He had no doubt, however, that the best in human character could flourish anywhere. Witness what he and others like him had accomplished in the Hawaiian Islands: it was "Yankee push" that developed the sugar plantations; and "missionary push" that was more generally guiding the islands in the right—American—direction. Business growth, Westernization generally, Hyde was sure, would end the idea of "Hawaii for Hawaiians." He had supported the revolution of 1887, which he held, not inaccurately, to have been carried through by the muscle of *haole* workers and tradesmen, the money of *haole* capitalists, and the brains of the *haole* Protestant "mission boys." He looked forward from then on to the fall of the monarchy, and after that to American annexation.

All this, in broad terms, Hyde could justifiably regard as a Protestant victory. And yet, for Hyde the clergyman of Honolulu, the victory was bound to be hollow in a way, because in the very years of the Protestant-American political ascendancy in the islands the

Hawaiians were deserting the Protestant churches. Not surprisingly, a good many islanders saw no point in going on with the worship of a Protestant God whose *haole* ministers seemed to look down on them even as they prayed for them. By the 1880s, Hawaiians had come to perceive that Protestantism, Westernization, and Americanism were all much the same; and that together they meant the end of Hawaii for Hawaiians. To be sure, there was hardly a way for Hawaiians to turn back wholeheartedly to traditional religious and cultural practices: the abandonment of the old *kapu* system was decades in the past, and very few Hawaiians alive toward the end of the nineteenth century would have known what it was like to worship the old gods in the old way, with no Christian God to disapprove. The question was, where to turn? No doubt *haole* Catholic priests condescended to them, just as *haole* Protestants did (the Church to that point, indeed, had not ordained any native Hawaiians as priests). But at least the *haole* priests of the Sacred Hearts Congregation did not have open political designs on the independence of the kingdom. So the Hawaiians of those years who continued to take an interest in Christianity tended to attach themselves to Catholicism—or even to Mormonism: anything but New England Protestantism. Census figures and church statistics told the story. In the Hawaiian Islands, history, Christian religious history at least, was on the side of priests and elders.

Hyde had a rejoinder for this, no more than a partial one, but a good New England Protestant one. To begin with, he suspected that census figures, during the Gibson regime at least, were being manipulated to make the Protestant position look worse than it was. But even with that taken into account, there was no doubting that the Catholics especially were managing to gather the Hawaiians into their fold, by telling them that Catholics were, in Hyde's words, "God's poor, they don't rob & murder the natives as the missionaries do, &c, &c." Hyde's point was that if the Catholics actually did have better control of the "low down" classes than the Protestants, then this was really "an arraignment of the Catholic church as fit for such people and not because it elevated them, which was what we considered desirable for every human being."

Hyde had never been able to bring himself to feel comfortable at the presence of Catholics in the islands. He was always ready to combat their influence in education, his professional specialty. As for his other great pastoral interest, the field of charity, its most spectacular manifestation—the charity of leprosy—was virtually pre-empted by the Catholics. Here Hyde, without perhaps much to say, said a great deal.

His own faith, he asserted, was actively concerned with leprosy. Not a meeting of its ministers went by without the question being discussed. If Congregationalists had had sisterhoods like those of the Catholic Church, then—Hyde had no doubt—Kalawao could have been staffed by them without trouble. In the absence of such sisterhoods, the Protestants of the Hawaiian Islands had concentrated on the public service of charitable giving, only to be rewarded by seeing how the Catholics "appropriated to themselves institutions founded at public expense, or even by the generosity of Protestant Christians"—by which Hyde meant that the Franciscan Sisters ran the Kakaako branch hospital while it existed, the Kapiolani Home for Girls in Honolulu, and the Bishop Home for Girls at Kalaupapa, which Hyde himself had had a part in establishing.

For a Protestant politician-administrator of charity like Hyde, who had a most serviceable sense of the ways in which money might be made to do good, this was galling. He would willingly enough concede that the Sisters in their way were useful to Hawaiians; but still he felt that he was being exposed to a subtly aggressive kind of Catholic imperialism, and a moral imperialism, to boot.

Taking things all in all, then, there was no way for a man such as the Reverend Doctor Charles McEwen Hyde to like a man such as Father Joseph Damien De Veuster. The two men had actually met, in 1885, a year or so after Hyde's private fright over leprosy in his own body, and about the time when Damien's face was beginning to show the marks of the disease. Hyde was at Kalawao briefly, on Protestant church business. He made a point of seeking out Damien and talking to him; and on his return to Honolulu, he wrote a newspaper article which was not ungenerous to the work of the Catholic priest. But always for Hyde there was a holy offensiveness about Damien. The priest was, after all, the outstanding embodiment of a faith which Hyde considered unworthy, and of a charity which had somehow managed to present itself to the world as morally superior to the works of the Protestant church and the pious philanthropists of Honolulu whose good impulses Hyde so earnestly nurtured.

So when Hyde, in the midst of all the posthumous public glorification of Damien, wrote his personal, private letter to the Reverend Gage of California, he spoke strongly, even bitterly. It was not the first or the only such letter he wrote on the subject. But Gage was the only one who published his letter from Hyde. In due course, the published wrath of Robert Louis Stevenson descended on Hyde's head. Stevenson sent a copy of his Open Letter to Hyde; and the Honolulu newspaper 'Elele somehow got a copy as well, printed it in a regular issue, and then reprinted it as a separate broadsheet. Hyde was now almost as much a public figure as Damien; and he had to justify himself in public. And so the long acrimony began.

Since Hyde was a man with his own kind of integrity, seeing no distinction between a public position and a private one, what he said in public self-justification was inevitably personal. At one point in the recriminations over what he had written and what he had meant, and what the truth was about Damien, Hyde made a remark about not being able to warm to the idea of the "sanctity of dirtiness." This was as important as anything Hyde ever said. It was the connecting link in the chain of his disapproval of the "filth" of Hawaiian culture; the leprosy which seemed to him to spring inevitably from that filth; the religion—Catholicism— which seemed best attuned to serve such a debased people; and the Catholic priest who died in the service of Hawaiians, of their disease.

Leprosy was incontrovertibly frightful. To fear and shun it, and to wish its carriers to be gone, was to do no more than subscribe to the teachings of the Old Testament of the Bible by which Hyde lived. This was Hyde's moral justification—part of it, at least—for supporting the revolutions that ended Hawaiian self-government, a misgovernment that only perpetuated leprosy, as Hyde saw things. But, by the same token, it was leprosy that made for Hyde's ultimate difficulty with Damien. To Hyde, who could never permit himself to link sanctity with dirt, the self-surrender of Damien, who made himself a "leper," was not only repellent but somehow morally perverse. Hyde could never have made a sacrifice that matched Damien's.

And if Damien's life and death offered, however unreasonably, a reproach to respectable, secure, Honolulu-based, politically sound, imperially validated Protestant piety, then Hyde proposed to expunge the criticism simply by pointing to Damien's leprosy. Hyde was one of the moral diagnosticians of leprosy. He could not believe that a dirty man could ever be a saint. In Hyde's mind, Damien was dirty, leprous; and because he was leprous he was presumably licentious, a man of sin with no place to stand but the stony ground of a deserved outcast's exile.

This was the most shocking thing that Hyde said in his letter to Gage: that Damien "was not a pure man in his relations with women," and that "the leprosy of which he died should be attributed to his vices and carelessness." When Stevenson forced Hyde into print on his own account, Hyde repeated what he had said to Gage, adducing something like chapter and verse. "That testimony came to me . . . in the course of many years' correspondence and conversation with residents, white and native, on Hawaii and Molokai, government physicians, agents and other officials. Father Damien . . . before going to Molokai, had charge of two other parishes, where it is believed that he caught the disease, and left behind him an unsavory reputation."

This was the sort of assertion that should have been provable, that demanded proof; and Hyde tried actively to assemble positive testimony. Dr. George Fitch would say in private that Damien had syphilis. But he never said it in public, or in writing. And then, according to Fitch's medical theories, everyone who had leprosy was by prior definition syphilitic. Of course, Fitch's theories had no credence in the rest of the medical profession. Besides which, as a point of medical fact, Damien had been carefully examined by that scrupulous medical scientist Eduard Arning at Kalawao in 1885 for traces of any disease "other than leprosy"—this being understood to mean venereal disease—and no trace of anything was found.

As for the unsavory reputation of Damien, Hyde was sure that here he was on safe footing. Apart from what all those reliable witnesses had told him, he himself remembered something about a court case involving a Catholic priest in the Kohala district of the island of Hawaii, where Damien had served before going to Kalawao. The affair had to do with a Hawaiian girl and a breach of morals. Hyde wrote away for a copy of the court records. The case had indeed existed; a priest of the Sacred Hearts mission was indeed the defendant; and he had indeed been before the courts in the Kohala district. But from Hyde's point of view, there were several deficiencies in the record. First, the case had not been pressed to a conclusion. A nolle prosequi had been entered, legally closing the matter. Two further things were wrong. The case occurred in 1880, by which time Damien had been gone from Kohala seven years. And the unconvicted priest's name was not Damien but Fabien. It was a name that sounded something like Damien: close enough, perhaps, to have given rise to unhistorical rumor; close enough as well, perhaps, to have reached the ears of Father Albert Montiton, stationed on the other side of the island, leading him to voice suspicions about Damien's morality when he found himself at Kalawao in 1881. But Fabien was not Damien; and Damien was not Fabien; and Hyde could not make him so. Hyde could not prove his case, because he had no case to prove.

Within the Congregation, not even Damien's severest critics believed Hyde's accusation for longer than it took to consider the facts. Albert Montiton, once he came to know Damien as an "eyewitness," surrendered his earlier suspicions, and made a point of saying so after Damien died. Koeckemann and Fouesnel, concerned though they had to be about the difficulties Hyde's story created for the mission, did not give the insinuation credit.

Arthur Mouritz said simply that it would not have been possible for Damien to carry on an affair at Kalawao. He had no privacy: his house was open to everyone, day and night. And if he had been keeping assignations elsewhere on the promontory, it would certainly have become known. At Kalawao, everyone knew everyone else's business.

What Damien himself had to say about his sexual life was recorded by Joseph Dutton. When Dutton was taking down the details of his illness in March, 1889, about six weeks before he died, Damien told him that he had never had sexual relations.

Finally, if anyone were to have heard about his alleged sexual delinquencies, it ought to have been his confessors. The seal of the confessional would have prevented them from saying anything about it directly. But it might have been noted that Gulstan Ropert, who confessed Damien at Kohala, believed him to be—though no saint—a good man. Albert Montiton, who confessed him at Kalawao, came to the same conclusion. And Columban Beissel, who for several years visited him from Maui to confess him, was later a leader in the campaign to defend Damien's honor against the attacks of Hyde. (One of Damien's confessors, to be sure, could not bring himself to say a word in his favor, in life or in death. This was André Burgerman; but his silence could reasonably be taken as yet another example of his general contrariness.)

Hyde did not emerge from the business well. He came to consider, after a time, that by being forced into the position of attacking Damien in public he had been unjustly made a "leper" himself. No one, or hardly anyone, would lend support to his arguments: only other Protestants, and very few of them. The rest would not touch him. Hyde, so he said, did not want to press his friends to attest to his competency and veracity, if it meant exposing them to "malodorous and scarifying" attacks in the press—the leprous martyrdom of publicity. "No one in this world can know with what stress of pain I have taken the stand I have maintained as a witness for the truth, assailed on the one hand by the arrogant pretentiousness of the Roman hierarchy, and betrayed on the other by the fanciful falsities of sentimental humanitarianism." Having said what must be said, and by no means wishing to retract anything, Hyde rested his case, lonely in righteousness. "I leave it to any candid mind to judge on which side lies the calumny and slander. There let it lie."

But Hyde's attack on Damien's character was not the kind of thing to lie down, least of all at the behest of Hyde. It would not be buried. It kept itself alive for years, well into the twentieth century. William Brigham, for example, by then curator of a museum at Honolulu endowed by the same Charles Reed Bishop whose money helped pay for the girls' home at Kalaupapa, showed his photograph of Damien to a group of tourists and lectured them on the priest's moral defects—"one of the worst of men"—only to learn that his listeners were Catholics and most affronted. And E. C. Bond, son of the Protestant minister at Kohala in Damien's time, finally put into print the fact of the mistaken identity—Fabien-Damien—which was at the bottom of Hyde's accusations.

By this time, Hyde was dead. One of the last of his managed benefactions was the establishment in 1895 of the Henry P. Baldwin Home for boys with leprosy, taking the place of Damien's old dormitories at Kalawao. The new home was endowed out of the profits of sugar plantations owned by the son of a Protestant missionary. It was staffed by Sacred Hearts brothers, and was run by Joseph Dutton for the Board of Health: the charity of the rich and the charity of those vowed to poverty meeting once again on the moral frontier of disease among the Hawaiians. Hyde came to the settlement for the dedication ceremonies, and dined with the Franciscan Sisters, in some small trepidation that he might be badly received. In the same year, there was an outbreak of cholera in Honolulu; and Hyde was one of the volunteer inspectors who patrolled the affected parts of the city. Hyde lived until 1899, ten years after Gage published his letter about Damien. He died having seen the minor revolution of 1887 and the decisive one of 1893 crowned by the annexation of the islands to the United States in 1898. The chief executive of the Hawaiian government after the monarchy fell was Sanford Ballard Dole, son of a Protestant missionary, one of the best of the "mission boys," whose wife Anna led a private life dominated by such a dread of leprosy that she would not go from room to room in her own house without covering the doorknob with a handkerchief.

I V

In the years since Damien's death in 1889, the settlement had been changing. As soon as he was decently interred, new brooms began to sweep clean. Damien had never been a good personal or institutional housekeeper; and it was left to Joseph Dutton, a formidable soaper and scrubber, together with the Franciscan Sisters, who had rigorous rules about hygiene, to put the ramshackle boys' dormitories at Kalawao in order. Damien's own little two-story house was taken apart: the lower story broken up into boards, the upper shifted away from St. Philomena's church and used as a music rehearsal room.

All his belongings—his few clothes, his carpenter's tools, his books, his private journals, the letters people had written to him —were fumigated and sent to Belgium, where most of them eventually went on display in a museum attached to his family's old home in Tremeloo. Dutton and the others began sending away leaves and pieces of wood from the pandanus tree above Damien's grave as souvenirs. In time, the tree aged and died. The tomb itself was kept in good order; but finally the graveyard at Kalawao was declared full and unusable, and a new site was chosen between Kalawao and Kalaupapa.

This was one indication of a major move that was about to take place. The Board of Health had been considering the relations between the two villages. Only a couple of miles apart, they were very different from one another. There had always been a considerable separateness: once, when a joint musical competition was being planned, it was discovered that their clocks were set forty-five minutes apart. With Damien alive, Kalawao village had been the center of the settlement. Now the Board, for various reasons, had come to favor Kalaupapa. "It is thought best," the president of the Board reported to the legislature in 1890, "that the people should be gradually concentrated at Kalaupapa, where there is plenty of room. Streets should be laid out in regular order according to some definite plan, and all new buildings erected thereon. Kalawao, as the buildings decay, should be abandoned as a place of residence, both on account of its inconvenient distance from the landing and its climatic inferiority to Kalaupapa."

As the population began to diminish at Kalawao, the Board was able—finally, thirty years after the establishment of the settlement—to buy out the remaining Hawaiian small landholders who had been part of the scene on the promontory from the beginning. A new set of water pipes was put in to improve the supply at Kalaupapa; and this in turn directed the drift to the village at the landing, along a road that acquired the name of Damien Boulevard.

By the turn of the twentieth century, Kalaupapa was twice the size of Kalawao. Soon, the only people left at Damien's old village were the boys in the Henry P. Baldwin Home. In the late 1920s, the priest of Kalawao talked about the place as "dying"; his congregation was down to about twenty-five, and there were perhaps ten other people, Protestants, living round about. Early in the thirties, the Baldwin Home was relocated at Kalaupapa, and Kalawao village was virtually abandoned. "It is pitiful," wrote a Sacred Hearts father, "to visit this deserted place."

By then, Kalaupapa itself, having absorbed the population of Kalawao village, was growing not bigger but smaller. The reason was simple but momentous: the leprosy epidemic in the Hawaiian Islands was over. At its own mysterious rate, the disease was burning itself out—by no means entirely, but as an epidemic: sufficiently, at last, to reduce the diseased population at the settlement by multiples.

If anything had made this possible, it was not a radically improved system of treatment for individual cases. Leprosy as a disease remained essentially incurable. But rigorous segregation as a public policy seemed to have worked.

In retrospect, the high point, both in the incidence of the disease and in the segregation of sufferers, could be seen in the 1890s, just after Damien's time. When he died in 1889, there were more than 1,100 cases of leprosy at the settlement. The next year, the figure reached 1,213. That was the peak. By 1900, a decline was noticeable. By 1910, the figure was down to not much more than 600; by 1940, to about 350. The disease was no longer renewing itself in the general population.

V

One of the Hawaiians exiled at the height of the epidemic to die at the settlement was Dr. Eduard Arning's experimental subject, Keanu the murderer. Arning was not in the islands to see it happen: he had had an argument with Walter Murray Gibson, and had left for Europe in mid-1886. Arthur Mouritz kept an eye on the case. A few months after Arning's departure, Keanu began to show signs of the disease. By the fall of 1887, he was a "confirmed leper." When Kakaako branch hospital was closed after the revolution of 1887, Keanu was put back in jail at Honolulu. But, as Mouritz said, "no proper accommodation for him existed in the hospital of the prison." He became "a menace to the prisoners . . . therefore it was determined to remove him" to the settlement. With another diseased prisoner, he was taken to Kalaupapa in February, 1889, and locked up in a jail the Board of Health had built there. He died in November, 1892, at the age of fifty-six.

So Arning's experiment had worked, or at least it seemed to

have worked. He had implanted leprous tissue in a human subject, and the subject had got leprosy. Arning presented a scientific paper on the case of Keanu at the First Congress of the Society of German Dermatologists in 1889; and this, together with the reporting of the rest of his careful work, earned him a good reputation in his field. But within a few years, it began to be doubted that his science had really proved how the disease might be transmitted. Leprosy, after all, was epidemic where Keanu had lived all his life; among his relatives, several came down with it. He might have caught the disease not from Arning's implanted leproma, but from something in his own life among his own people. Arthur Mouritz, for one, thought so. He himself tried more than a hundred times to inoculate diseased Hawaiian volunteers with the disease in new areas of their body, and never succeeded.

Dr. Arning did not think Hawaii was the place for basic research in leprosy. Best to carry that on in Europe, where, as Arning said, "there are quite a number of bacteriologists and microscopists besides myself at work on this intricate question, and slowly unraveling knot on knot towards its solution." In Hawaii, "the intense feeling which everything connected with leprosy necessarily evokes in so small and terribly afflicted a community, cannot favour the slow and tedious process of purely scientific work." And then there was another element of difficulty, as Arning put it: "the character of the natives."

The invincible Hawaiianness of Hawaiians remained strong enough after the turn of the twentieth century to defeat an ambitious attempt to do what Arning said should not be done: perform basic research among them. Since annexation in 1898, Hawaii had been United States territory. Hawaiians were American citizens. And when the United States Public Health Service built a Leprosy Investigation Station at Kalawao at a cost of $300,000, the Stars and Stripes flew there. The station was opened at Christmastime in 1909, on the site of Damien's old improvised Goto bathhouses at Kalawao. The new facility was impressive, elaborately equipped, and carefully designed to maintain a scientific level of sterility. Its

very rationale was its downfall. The scientists depended for subjects upon volunteers from among the Hawaiians. Out of the nine
hundred who lived at Kalaupapa, nine were willing to come to the
station. And even this handful did not like being cooped up inside
fences, did not like being turned into untouchables for science's
sake. One by one, they went back to the unscientific Hawaiian
society of the village of Kalaupapa. The station was left with nothing—or rather no one—to investigate. Within just two years, it was
dead; and the elaborate buildings were left to decay, with the
elaborate scientific instruments still inside, measuring nothing. If
progress was to be made toward the understanding and control of
the leprosy bacillus, it would be in the great centers of medical
research, the ones Eduard Arning had talked about.

VI

Between the time of the lazar houses of medieval Europe and
Damien's time at Kalawao, very little had changed in the response
of Western society to the presence of sufferers with the visible
signs of leprosy. The disease stigmatized its victims; they were
turned into "lepers"; they might or might not have the luck to be
charitably noticed.

One of the accomplishments of the twentieth century was to
begin to distinguish the disease from the sufferer; to begin to
separate physical stigma from Old Testamental moral stigma; to
begin to see the "leper" merely as someone who had the disease
of leprosy. In the great centers of medical research, some laboratory progress was made. At the same time, systematic field work
was started in places where leprosy was endemic, and where it
became epidemic. Gradually—everything about leprosy research
was difficult and slow—a comprehensible picture of the disease
emerged.

There proved to be not just one manifestation of leprosy but a
whole spectrum. The worst of these, scientists came to call "le-

promatous." It began with the emergence of the leprosy bacillus, now classified as *Mycobacterium leprae,* in the body in enormous numbers, and proceeded with the invasion and destruction of the skin and mucous tissue of the upper respiratory tract. It resulted in the destruction of facial features, impairment of body functions, bad nerve damage, and the loss of use of muscles. Untreated, the disease might leave its victim deformed, crippled, ulcerated, blinded, his senses devastated, his very ability to breathe threatened.

This was Damien's case. By no means all leprosy was lepromatous. Many cases were self-limiting, self-terminating; they did not begin as lepromatous or become lepromatous. So Damien's case was, medically, exceptional in that it was in the worst of all categories.

Another finding which emerged from twentieth-century research was that leprosy was not highly contagious. The visible awfulness of untreated lepromatous leprosy had obscured this understanding in the minds of normal, unaffected people, who wanted only not to have to see or touch a "leper." But it was true enough: perversely, this most horrible of diseases was hard to catch. *Mycobacterium leprae* was not aggressive. Its ability to attack the human organism was not overwhelming; it was slow to multiply. For most purposes, simple, careful personal hygiene would suffice to ward it off.

Susceptibility varied, apparently with the individual. There was no reason to think that Westerners, white men, were racially less vulnerable than nonwhites. Put them in an intimate environment which favored contagion—typically, an overcrowded place with poor sanitation—and they would get leprosy, in one or another of its manifestations, about as often as members of any "native" population (and more often, it began to seem, than Africans or Indians). Some individual white men would resist the disease better than others. This was a matter of their genetic inheritance, and resistance or lack of it would determine the outcome, together with how prolonged and how intensive their exposure had been

—what scientists came to call the "challenge dose" of *Mycobac-terium leprae.*

Damien's case was that of a white man who subjected himself to exposure—prolonged, repeated, intimate, virtually uninter-rupted—for years. His challenge dose was as high as it could have been. His attitude to hygiene was haphazard. Whatever genetic resistance he had—and it must have been low—was overcome. He got leprosy, and the form it took was lepromatous.

The final separation of the leprosy sufferer from the stigma of his disease would come when there was a medical cure—a treat-ment to prevent the physical stigma from appearing, or remove it once it became visible. The major hopeful medicines of Da-mien's era all came from the East, from a medical tradition in which leprosy was tens of centuries old: the *hoang-nan* pills of the late 1870s at Kalawao, before Damien himself was diagnosed as diseased; the Goto treatment, which he followed so enthusiasti-cally; Edward Clifford's gurjun oil, which he doubted. At the turn of the twentieth century, the East provided the West with another medicament: chaulmoogra oil, which formed the basis of treat-ment for the next forty years. This was still no cure. Then, in the 1940s, one of a newly developed range of Western drugs, the sulphones, turned out to be highly useful in the treatment of leprosy. Its name was diaminodiphenylsulphone, shortened to Dapsone, DDS. Its action was bacteriostatic, meaning that, with proper dosage, the numbers of leprosy bacilli in an affected per-son's body could be brought down substantially to nothing. This meant in turn that even lepromatous leprosy could usually be arrested. It even meant that, with proper caution, it was possible to talk of a "cure" for leprosy.

Not that the availability of a "cure" meant that all cases of leprosy would be cured. What it did mean was that in centers of Western civilization, in prosperous, well-informed societies, peo-ple who contracted leprosy had a chance of being treated as though they had a generally manageable disease of low conta-giousness, by no means requiring lifetime segregation and isolation. And it meant as well that in the remaining centers of epidemic leprosy—essentially, in the non-Western, tropical world—epidemics might be brought under control by widespread use of Dapsone, if there was enough manpower and logistical support to administer the drug wherever it was needed.

In the 1970s, a century after Damien first went to Kalawao, this remained a scientific kind of pious hope. There were still something like ten million cases of active leprosy in the world, perhaps as many as fifteen million (there was no certainty that leprosy was accurately reported). And DDS was not available everywhere, despite the fact that it was very cheap indeed.

Dapsone, DDS, offered, so to speak, the chance to "segregate" leprosy chemically, rather than have leprosy sufferers segregated bodily, physically, made into "lepers." The human being with leprosy could remain, with treatment, a social being. And because the drug helped in many cases to do away with physical stigma, the ancient cultural and moral stigma of the disease might in time die away: social pathology eliminated along with medical pathology.

With DDS—something like a means of genuine control of leprosy available to mankind for the first time—the terms of reference of vocations such as Damien's were changed irreversibly. Damien, of course, had lived and died long before sulphones, and the medical history of leprosy in his era was written in his face. In the twentieth century, even in the era of DDS, religious missionaries, Protestant and Roman Catholic, continued to get leprosy, an appreciable percentage of them: almost 4 percent among Protestant workers in one region of tropical Africa, more than that again among Catholic leprosy workers world-wide in the 1940s. In some sense they, like Damien, must have been willing subjects, ready at least to put their bodies in harm's way. Beyond that, the calculus of inherited resistance, environment, exposure, and the challenge dose produced in them a concentration of *Mycobacterium leprae* sufficient to be identifiable.

In religious terms, this experience would still generally be called

edifying. And yet, inevitably, there was a difference between contracting a disease that was incurable and contracting a treatable
condition. If the physical stigma of untreatable leprosy might, in
the case of a man such as Damien, have been read also as a sign
of holy grace, then DDS treatment had, in substance, brought to
an end the era of the traditional religious heroes—the saints—of
leprosy.

VII

Beyond that, there was the question of how many heroes the
world needed, or rather wanted. The insufficiencies of nineteenth-
century science had left open to Damien and his charity the field
of leprosy, for a priest's life and a heroic death. As Pamphile could
properly say in 1889, "When science has said its last word, the main
comfort and hope of the leper must be found in the sympathy of
an ever-present friend, and in the promise of an immortal and
untainted life beyond the grave." But if there had been a hundred
Damiens all at once, very likely the world would not have valued
each of them as highly as the one, single, marked and identified
Damien. There was a sort of parsimony about the workings of
worldly response to religious heroism, in which one man's object
lesson in charity was somehow worth more than many. Perhaps
this kind of recognized heroism, like many other less noble
phenomena, was subject to laws of diminishing returns; best that
it should be perceived as concentrated in a minimum number of
exceptional individuals. Joseph Dutton had a thoughtful word on
the subject: the world, he said, is busy; it cannot bother with many
heroes.

Perhaps, on the other hand, the world was overvaluing even
Damien. This was the final question: whether he was really a hero,
or more than a hero, a saint. The *Times* of London had been ready
to beatify him on his death. The Reverend Doctor Charles
McEwen Hyde said he was anything but a saint. Robert Louis

Stevenson said he was a man with human failings, but none the less a saint for all that. None of these authorities spoke with the authority of the Catholic Church.

The examination of Damien's sanctity would have to be initiated by his superiors in Honolulu. Bishop Koeckemann and Father Fouesnel were most reluctant to begin. For them, Damien's celebrity had been nothing but a vexation; and posthumous publicity in his name was even more baneful than what had gone before. Damien had lived his last years in the glaring light of world attention. The illumination had hurt the eyes of Koeckemann and Fouesnel. Koeckemann had decided that "Saints look better at a distance." The bishop did not deny Damien his peculiar virtues; he was even ready to describe him as a "particular kind of saint who (I have no doubt) has already been honored by God." But a true Saint of the Church—no. Koeckemann would never concede Damien this kind of sanctity. No matter how admirable his self-sacrifice might have been, his faults were too grievous.

Koeckemann had not attended Damien's funeral at Kalawao (neither had Fouesnel). The bishop did make a funeral oration at Honolulu; but he limited himself to three minutes on Damien's "public" life, and avoided the question of his "personal" attributes. Koeckemann thought this safest on a public occasion; and even in the most private of letters to the father-general he begged to be dispensed from the "disagreeable task" of giving additional evidence that could only be disadvantageous to Damien.

The father-general, for his part, did not want to let the subject drop there. The Sacred Hearts, a young and still small Congregation, had no saints. There was a point in knowing if a case could be made for beginning proceedings to have Damien beatified, and eventually canonized. Koeckemann, sure there was not, dutifully arranged for an inquiry at Kalawao, naming as investigators two priests who shared his views. "I know already," wrote the bishop, "that it will not contain anything remarkable in favor of our hero. . . . We think there is nothing to be gained by pushing the inquiry any further. When Father Damien has been proclaimed hero and

martyr of charity, everything has been said; the rest only compli-
cates matters."

Father Corneille Limburg, chosen by Koeckemann to share the
work of the inquiry, was one of those who admired the dead
priest's self-sacrifice, but who could see nothing extraordinary in
his personal life: just a catalogue of virtues and defects. And his
fellow investigator, Father Wendelin Moellers, at work with the
Franciscan Sisters at Kalaupapa, wanted nothing more than for
the settlement to "sink back into obscurity." In the field, Limburg
and Moellers by no means pushed their inquiry to the limit. Early
in 1890, they interviewed the Franciscan Sisters at the settlement;
and they also got Joseph Dutton to put on paper his impressions
of Damien's character. They did not think it "prudent" to question
"Conrardy and others who might cause scandal by their indiscre-
tions." Moellers did not believe it possible to get reliable evidence
on sanctity from *kanaka*, so none of Damien's Hawaiian parishioners were questioned. Not even the part-Hawaiian Ambrose Hutchison, by then the respected and capable assistant superintendent
of the settlement, a good Catholic, and also an admirer of Damien,
was asked what he thought.

Unsurprisingly, the report from Kalawao was brief and muted.
One of the Sisters noted that Damien's face in death had seemed
to lose its disfigurement; but she agreed that this was common in
leprosy. Joseph Dutton, a conscientious chronicler of things in the
plainest of prose, went into homely detail, cataloguing personal
defects along with virtues, and paying careful attention to the
vagaries of Damien's temperament, which he had experienced at
first hand in the years when the disease was taking strong hold. On
one point, at least, all were agreed: there were no miracles to
report, in a place where miracles, being so much needed, might
perhaps have been expected if Damien were a true saint.

Bishop Koeckemann duly dispatched the report to the father-
general. Nothing came of it; and, of course, that was the intention.
Toward the end of 1890, Koeckemann was allowing himself to
write to one of his missionaries in the field: "Probably no place in
the world concerns itself less about Damien than the islands."

At the settlement itself, in some ways at least, Damien left not much of a mark. Each year, on the anniversary of his death, a procession would wind from St. Philomena's to his grave, where Ambrose Hutchison would make a faithful memorial speech. Other than that, the settlement went its erratic way. In 1890, at the height of the segregation drive, there was a riot at Kalawao. Stones were thrown; some Hawaiians threatened to hang the resident superintendent, a *haole;* and Father Conrardy and Mother Marianne were abused, though without being harmed. There was some suggestion that such a thing could never have happened in Damien's time, because of his moral authority; but that idea could hardly have been seriously supported. In the early 1890s, for a variety of reasons, tempers were high among Hawaiians—and among government officials involved in segregation. Within the space of a few years, there were pursuits, resistances, and fatal shootings on more than one island. It was likely enough that the settlement itself would go through a disturbed period. And, in any case, there had been riots in Damien's time, most of them in the early years, but the worst of all quite late, in 1885, when some girls were being transferred from the settlement to the Kapiolani Home in Honolulu, and their "protectors" objected. A commotion at Kalaupapa landing on the day the girls were put on board ship ended with two fatal stabbings. This sort of thing was never out of the question. Damien never subdued the whole settlement to Christian obedience. That trouble broke out so rarely during his lifetime was fortunate. That it began again so soon after his death was no more and no less than a sign of troubled times. As the epidemic began to recede, the disturbances died away.

Early in the twentieth century, one of the Sacred Hearts brothers at the settlement, Serapion van Hoof, caught a disease that was thought to be leprosy. He reacted much as Father Grégoire Archambaux had done, with despair, and began to talk of leaving the mission, even of marrying. The holy example of Damien was used to dissuade him. Reconciling himself to his fate, he said: "The old man has leashed me here, he wants me to die at the settlement." Van Hoof's case was singular; and it came to be doubted in the end that he really had leprosy. The only other possible case of the disease among the Sacred Hearts in the islands came a quarter-century later, when a suspicious spot appeared on the head of Father Peter D'Orgeval. It was excised surgically; and there was no further sign of it during his long life.

For the rest, the Sacred Hearts missionaries at the settlement, usually six in number—two priests and four brothers, working among far fewer Hawaiians than Damien had served alone or with one companion—lived uneventfully through the brief period of crisis at the height of the epidemic and the long years of decline that followed. They began to talk of their lives principally in terms of monotony. Year by year, one of them wrote, there were "few new horizons"; once "one has communicated his first impressions, there remains little to say." Priests at the settlement, he said, were not like missionaries in—say—Africa, who traveled and had new peoples and places to strike their imagination. Life on Molokai, then, was "prosaic." (A little later than this, Albert Schweitzer, a missionary though not a traveling one, wrote from his leprosarium at Lambaréné about the "terrible prose" of life in Africa.) When Damien's successors reflected on what his life must have been like, they marveled not so much at his ability to handle leprosy as at his ability to withstand boredom and lack of relief.

The leprosy patients of Kalaupapa had their own preoccupations. They worked; and, like Hawaiians everywhere, they made music and took an interest in politics. The Sacred Hearts priests of the declining years of the epidemic remarked again and again that the settlement was not—or was not only—a "necropolis," a city of the dead. There were happiness, and song, and general amusement, as well as the horror of the disease and the certainty of death. Somehow, the darkness of it all was discounted by the Hawaiians, eventually taken for granted. Even the priests managed this shift of vision, perhaps necessary for them if they were to stay and work at the settlement. "One is leprous in the same way that one has blue or brown eyes, and no one pays attention for long to these small details."

Father Wendelin Moellers, who was at the settlement when Damien died, and who stayed on for another fourteen years, described the place in the 1890s, after Damien was gone, much as it might have been described in the 1860s, before Damien came. The settlement, said Moellers, a sharp, unromantic, even disenchanted observer, was like other Hawaiian villages, except gayer, lazier, and more licentious. Leprosy did not repel the *kanaka;* in fact, since he was diseased he did not have to work; the government provided for him; and this made leprosy one of the desiderata of the good life. Few of the Hawaiians, Moellers thought, really wanted to be cured. They would take a little medicine from time to time; but if a treatment was harsh and onerous, they did not want it. The old Hawaiian "immorality" persisted. People lived pell-mell; families were broken up; there were adultery and concubinage. Among a group with nothing to do but eat, drink, sleep, and amuse themselves, "turpitude" was rife. In the Homes there were some good Christians, but no touching and edifying deaths. The Hawaiians were "fatalistically resigned" to disease; they received the last sacraments without enthusiasm. In fact, they did not call for the priest; he had to seek them out. The sojourn of a missionary at the settlement, Moellers concluded, was not a pleasure. The roses of the Hawaiians' self-indulgent life were not thornless for their priests.

Perhaps this could have served also as a description of the settlement when Damien was there. Perhaps it had always been like that, and always would be, whatever the quality of the priest.

Damien, of course, managed somehow to wear those thorns, and others, as a crown. Still, it was hard for his superiors to acknowledge any exceptional merit in him; and they kept finding reasons for not forwarding the cause of his beatification. This went on even after the days of Koeckemann and Fouesnel. Koeckemann's successor as bishop, Gulstan Ropert, who had known Damien since his days as a young priest in Kohala in the 1860s, was no readier than the others to think him a saint. A good man, yes, he said; but a saint is something different. Even the beginnings of the process of beatification would have to wait until everyone who knew Damien well was dead, said Ropert.

Time was arranging that. Koeckemann died in 1892, Fouesnel in the same year, Wendelin Moellers in 1914. Father Albert Montiton made his peace with Damien not long after his departure from Molokai, spoke well of him when he heard of his death, and died himself in 1894. Father André Burgerman lived on and on, at loggerheads with his superiors as always. The obscure disease from which he suffered so long might well have been leprosy: Arthur Mouritz saw him in his old age, and thought he looked like a burnt-out case. Burgerman's temperamental fires still burned. Once, after he had retired from active work and had come to live at the mission in Honolulu, he had an argument with the provincial over coffee, struck him, and split his lip. Nearer to death, Burgerman quieted down greatly. Walking to Mass with the aid of a cane, he would sometimes fall, and would wait patiently for a passerby to help him up. After a life of ecclesiastical pulling and tugging, he died, aged seventy-eight, still a member of the Congregation, in 1907.

Louis-Lambert Conrardy, maneuvered out of his post at the settlement in 1895, spent the next several years arranging a similar life elsewhere. He immersed himself in his vocation at the leprosarium of Shek Lung, in South China, where he worked until his death in 1914.

Mother Marianne Kopp lived until she was eighty; she died in 1918. Some of the Sisters who went with her to Kalaupapa survived longer, and gave testimony about Damien's character to a visitor from the mother house of the Sacred Hearts in 1924. So did the part-Hawaiian Ambrose Hutchison; and then, in 1930, as a very old man, he wrote out in trembling longhand an extended memoir of Damien. He died in 1932.

Joseph Dutton, it seemed, was going to survive forever. His was an extraordinary life. In more than forty years at the settlement, he left Kalawao village only three times, to go to Kalaupapa. For years on end, he did not leave the grounds of the Baldwin Home for Boys, which he ran. Into late middle age, then old age, then extreme old age, he worked without stopping. He had, he said, got into the habit of sleeping only an hour or two a night. "I don't know," he wrote at the age of sixty-five, "whether Mr. Edison was joking when he said sleeping is just a lazy habit." His office was neat as a pin, his account books meticulously kept. He was a prodigious letter writer: his address book had four thousand entries. In his old age, he joined all sorts of worthy societies by mail. He was a formidable American patriot, who flew the Stars and Stripes in front of the Baldwin Home. He became almost as well known in his way as Damien, and one of his finest moments came in 1907, when Theodore Roosevelt's Great White Fleet, announcing America's naval might by a world cruise, saluted him from the Molokai Channel. During World War I, by which time he was in his seventies, Dutton proposed a regiment of Civil War veterans like himself, to go to Europe in the uniform of the Grand Army of the Republic.

Day by day, year by year, decade by decade at Kalawao, he wore the plainest of blue denims. Beyond letting his plain white beard grow long in his old age, his only self-indulgence was to listen to a little music box play Strauss waltzes while he bandaged sores. For the rest, he was a ruthless censor of the world of pleasure, intercepting magazines before they reached his boys at the Home and snipping out all frivolous or carnal pictures, more and more as the years went by. The modern world—what the magazines were made up of—had not much reality for him. He had never seen a motion picture, or ridden in an automobile. Once he saw an airplane at a distance. In 1930, at the age of eighty-seven, his sight failed him, and he was brought to Honolulu for an eye operation. He liked to sit in his hospital bed, listening to radio broadcasts of football games, a sport he had never seen played. He died in 1931.

All these people had had their say about Damien at one time or another; and if the cause of his beatification was ever to be taken up seriously, their testimony would necessarily count for something. If it was possible, from their comments alone, to make a broad judgment, it would be that Damien's exceptional devotion to his work was the source of all his difficulties, with his superiors and with the world of politics in the Hawaiian kingdom. Dutton, who was by no means an uncritical admirer of Damien, saw defects of character, but said that such faults were consumed like straws in the fire of Damien's charity.

The odd thing was that Damien had in him a good many of the characteristics of his closest associates, friend and foe. There was something in him of Burgerman, the doctor-priest of uncertain temper; more than a little of Montiton, the ailing "energumen"; much of Dutton's patient renunciatory strength and narrow unworldly persistence. At the same time he lacked almost completely the expedient practical vision that his superiors at Honolulu in particular needed to sustain the mission socially and politically.

Damien spent most of his life defining himself, and trying at the same time to make his life more than merely self-defining or self-serving. The first authorities he encountered and against whom he contended, those of his immediate family, gave way to the higher authorities he found embodied in the Congregation: new fathers and brothers to measure himself against. And behind them all at last stood God the Father and Christ the Son, who must ultimately be served, served to the end. At Kalawao, Damien found—he was sure—a way to be himself and to be a servant of God, in imitation of Christ. He wanted these to be the same thing: that is to say, he wanted to be a good priest. If his superiors and colleagues—fathers and brothers all, with their own sense of what it was to serve God within the Congregation of the Sacred Hearts —found him hard to get on with, that may have been for many reasons: Damien was a difficult man; they were difficult men; the situation was difficult. Beyond all that, Damien, more than any of his colleagues, was somehow managing to put all of himself—what was wrong with him as well as what was valuable and rare in him —at the service of his fellow man in a way to which many men could respond. The capacity to strike such a response may have to do with the elusive quality of charisma; and the place of the charismatic in an institution such as a hierarchically organized church has never been a comfortable one. Personal drives of the most powerful sort sometimes produce a version of religious duty unpalatable to those responsible for maintaining a prudent equilibrium within the institution. Perhaps that, abstractly, was Damien's case.

"Calm yourself, and *do as the others do,*" Léonor Fouesnel used to tell Damien. But Damien was an unusual man living in a turbulence of holiness. So he emerged as a troublemaker in the eyes of his immediate superiors, who knew him as a person, and as a hero in the eyes of the world, where he was known only for what he did: in any case an oddity, an eccentricity, an embarrassment, an exception to rules—an exceptional man, who remained at the same time perversely most ordinary in his personal ways, the ways of a peasant born and bred. This interplay of the ordinary and the extraordinary was given dimensions of moral tragedy and grandeur by his leprosy, forcing all those who knew him or heard about him, once the world got hold of his story, to ponder the problem of sanctity as Damien's life posed it—whether there might be any such being as Robert Louis Stevenson asserted: a man with his own idiosyncrasies and personal defects, with all the grime and paltriness of mankind, but none the less a hero and a saint.

In any formal sense, all these considerations had to wait until the Church was ready to move. For one reason or another, the Church moved slowly. Koeckemann and Fouesnel had done their best to damp down enthusiasm for Damien after his death. Koeckemann's successor as bishop, Gulstan Ropert, did not believe there was a case for Damien's beatification. His successor in turn, Libert Boeynaems, did not give the matter much attention. Not until the time of Bishop Stephen Alencastre, in the 1930s, did the movement in Honolulu gain strength and become formalized.

Damien had not been without European advocates in the meantime. Father Maurice Raepsaet of the Sacred Hearts in Belgium had worked energetically to make the Damien Institutes a reality. Another Sacred Hearts Father, Ildefonse Alazard, took it on himself to keep Damien's name alive, and for several years toured Europe with an illustrated lecture on leprosy and religious heroism at Kalawao.

Whatever the situation in Honolulu, and whether perhaps it was the old business of saints looking better at a distance, Damien's story touched off a sizable and steady response in Europe. The most concrete of measurements was in the growth of the Congregation of the Sacred Hearts itself. Without question, the dead Damien was producing religious vocations. Since the foundation of the order at the beginning of the nineteenth century, growth had been perceptible but slow, to 451 fathers and brothers in 1870. Over the next twenty years, the figure fell, to 350 in 1890. Then, in the decade following Damien's death, 251 new members entered the Congregation. Wendelin Moellers was right when he spoke of the spread of the order as having its roots in Damien's tomb.

In 1936, a landmark was reached. The Belgian government requested that Damien's remains be exhumed at Kalawao for reburial in Louvain. Amid considerable pomp and circumstance, the transferral was carried out. Two years later, in 1938, beatification proceedings were formally begun. The Church's age-old machinery for this purpose moved painstakingly and ponderously: the positive identification of Damien's remains and his relics; the examination of his writings; the gathering and weighing of evidence in an interminable list of characteristics: Damien's faith, hope, charity in God, charity toward his neighbors, prudence, justice, fortitude, temperance, poverty, chastity, obedience, humility, heavenly gifts, his death, the fame of his holiness, and favors and miracles attributed to him.

Even then, there was a question of priorities within the Congregation. The leadership of the Sacred Hearts had decided by this time to propose some other candidates for beatification: the founder of the order, and several priests who had been put to death during the political upheavals of the period of the Commune in Paris in 1871. One view was that Damien's case should wait upon these others. The martyrs of the Commune had died for the faith before Damien; they should take precedence. As for the founder, he should lead all the rest: first the father, then the sons, so the reasoning went.

So Damien's case continued to go slowly, while the testimony of his supernatural intercession piled up higher and higher—in Spain alone, more than sixty thousand examples of aid to supplicants in the period between the end of World War II and the middle 1960s, and a possible miracle to be investigated. In 1966, the chapter-general of the Congregation, the authoritative policy-making body of the Sacred Hearts, resolved to concentrate exclusively on the cause of Damien as the most rewarding, for the Congregation, the Church, and the world. How long the beatification would take; whether indeed it would ever be accomplished; and whether it would be followed some day by canonization, in an era when the Church itself was showing some parsimony about the naming of saints, no one could tell.

VIII

Meanwhile, in 1959, the territory of Hawaii had become the fiftieth of the United States of America. Federal law entitled each state to name two of its illustrious dead and place their statues in the capitol building in Washington, D.C. In 1961, in the opening round of a lengthy exercise in the politics of recognition, Damien's name was put before the state legislature of Hawaii. It took four years for him to achieve the official designation of greatness, along with Kamehameha, the Hawaiian warrior-king who unified the islands in the late eighteenth century.

Kamehameha already had a statue in Honolulu, a huge piece of nineteenth-century imitation classic in bronze and gilt, giving him the look of a Roman emperor in Hawaiian regalia. This was duplicated, to be set in its weighty brown and gold amid all the white marble shapes of Statuary Hall in Washington.

For Damien, who had no statue in the islands, an international sculptors' competition by invitation was held. The unlooked-for result was that Damien emerged in a statuary form as upsetting to comfortable opinion as the man himself had ever been in life. The sculptress Marisol Escobar produced nothing in the way of conventional pious representation of worthiness. Rather, her statue, unveiled in duplicate at Washington and Honolulu in 1969, was strong, careless of what has usually passed for careful public good taste, idiosyncratic, demanding of attention, even worrisome, disconcerting.

All this made her work in its own way entirely appropriate. Marisol chose, indecorously, to show Damien in the advanced stages of leprosy. Working from the photographs taken of him at Kalawao in 1889, she constructed a broad and lumpy face with ruined features, and faithfully applied the old wire spectacles and the battered black hat with its strings. The hand that held the sturdy walking stick was obviously diseased; the diseased feet were hidden in solid, boxy workman's boots. And the squat, bulky body was draped in a bronze mantle, almost black and with a look of implacable solidity, sloping at the shoulders and falling straight down to the feet, so that Damien appeared to be standing upright, sturdy, inextinguishably alive, in a cloak which had become a burial pall, which had in turn become a coffin, all of which had, somehow, always been part of the man himself.

NOTES

For a key to abbreviations see the Bibliography.

CHAPTER ONE. THE TRAITS OF HIS FACE

I

Page

3 The deathbed scene is detailed in Meyer to Ashley, April 6, 1889 (AH, BH); Fouesnel to Clifford, June 6, 1889 (V et D); Moellers to Bousquet, April 17, 1889 (R); Emerson to Swift, October 25, 1889 (AH, BHLB); Mulhane, 98–99.

I I

5 *Other men and women of religion:* Wright, *Imperial,* 88–90; Thin, 145; Tebb, 293 *ff;* Tardieu, 69; Carr, *passim; Damien Institute,* 10, 1 (1904), 4.
The special fate of Damien: Case, 117.

I I I

6 For the history of medicine, see Ackerknecht; Singer and Underwood. For Hansen, see Rokstad.
Leprosy the most frightful disease: Skinsnes, "Leprosy in Society," *passim.*
Transmitted along hereditary lines: Times, December 29, 1866.
Consternation: Wright; Mackenzie, *passim.*

7 *Contagion . . . capable of passing between races::* Sydney *Mail,* February 20, 1892.
"Half a century of territorial conquest": Brown, 5.

8 *Free trade in disease:* Mackenzie, 933–934; Mulhane, 43.
"Indian lascar": Wright, *Imperial,* 119–120.
"Militarily speaking": Brown, 7.
Inoculation with leprous material: Rokstad, 67.

I V

10 *"A scene of loathesome and despairing riotousness":* Times, May 13, 1889.
    "Highly sensational and objectionable": Emerson to Swift, October 25, 1889, AH, BHLB.
    Thousands of Londoners bought copies: Tauvel, 177.
11 *"One of the noblest Christian heroes":* Times, May 13, 1889.

V

12 *"Dear Brother":* Stevenson, *Open Letter.*
13 *One notable sufferer interested in the fate of another:* Dutton, 111.
    "There are Molokais all over the world": Stevenson, *Letters,* III, 155.

V I

All quotations in this section are from Stevenson, *Open Letter.*

CHAPTER TWO. I AM GOING IN YOUR PLACE

I

For Damien's background and early life, see *Life and Letters;* Tauvel; Jourdan; V et D.
21 *"I hope that my turn will come":* Damien to Parents, July 17, 1858, L.
22 *"Because to forbid your son":* Damien to Parents, December 25, 1858, L.

I I

For Damien's preparation for the priesthood, see Tauvel; Jourdan; V et D.

I I I

26 The register containing Damien's signature is in R.

I V

27 *Writing from Paris at the turn of 1861:* Damien to Parents, January 16, 1861, L.
    "A sudden trembling": Damien to Parents, April 25, 1861, MSL.

Page

28   *"I believe it would be as advantageous"*: Damien to Parents, August ____, 1861, L.
Pamphile's first Mass: V et D.

V

29   Damien in Paris: Damien to Parents, April 25, 1861, MSL.

VI

31   *"You are young"*: *Times*, June 29, 1889.
The photograph of Damien: Damien to Parents, October 30, 1863, L.

VII

33   *"It would be impossible for me to tell you"*: Damien to Parents, March 22, 1864, MSL.

VIII

34   *"You will remember"*: Damien to Pamphile, August 23, 1864, MSL.
35   *"Here I am a priest"*: Damien to Parents, August 23, 1864, MSL.

IX

36   *"The advice of veterans"*: Damien to Bousquet, ____, 1864, MSL.
37   *"I regret not being a poet"*: Damien to Pamphile, August 23, 1864, L.
38   *"A little sermon"*: Damien to Bousquet, October 23, 1865, R.

X

38   *"Instead of a tranquil and withdrawn life"*: Damien to Bousquet, November 1, 1864, R.
Strength of body: Damien to Favens, October 23, 1864, V et D.
Zeal: Pouzot to Favens, October 27, 1864, R.
39   *"This is my home"*: Van Heteren to Joachim, ____, 1866, R.
"I am always in the best of health": Damien to Pamphile, March ____, 1865, V et D.
"Nothing but a log": Damien to Bousquet, October 23, 1865, R.
Hospitality: Damien to Parents, October 24, 1865, L.

Page

40   *"We eat what Providence sends us":* Damien to Pamphile, July 14, 1872, L.

41   *"As it is the custom of the country":* Damien to Très révérend père, December 20, 1866, MSL.

XI

42   *"Fine face":* Favens to Bousquet, August 10, 1865, R.
     A man of quick decision and action: Favens to Bousquet, February 5, 1866, R; Favens to Bousquet, December 11, 1866, R; Damien to Favens, June 21, 1869, MSL.

43   *"Every Sunday about ten o'clock":* Archambaux to Bousquet, November 11, 1887, R.
     Protestant and Catholic missionaries: Kuykendall; Yzendoorn, *passim.*
     Damien did not like Calvinists: Damien to Mon révérend père, March 5, 1867, MSL; Damien to Mon révérend père, August 25, 1868, MSL.

44   *Things were working the other way:* Damien to Bousquet, September ____, 1870, R.
     Sectarian pleasures: Damien to Pamphile, March ____, 1865, V et D.

XII

44   Damien takes out his handkerchief: Marie-Stanislas to Mon révérend père, November 2, 1864, V et D.
     He studied Hawaiian: Damien to Parents, August 23, 1864, MSL.

45   *"I like our poor* kanaka": Damien to Parents, October 24, 1865, L.

46   *"Corruption is so precocious":* Damien to Bousquet, December 20, 1866, R.

47   *"Let us suppose":* Damien to Pamphile, December 22, 1866, L.
     "The charlatan looks for the cause": Damien to Pamphile, December 22, 1866, L.

XIII

48   *"Black thoughts":* Damien to Bousquet, September ____, 1870, R.
     Isolation: Damien to Bousquet, October 23, 1865, R; Damien to Bousquet, December 22, 1866, V et D; Damien to Mon révérend père, March 24, 1868, MSL.

49   *"Please plead the cause":* Damien to Mon révérend père, January 28, 1868, MSL.
     Pamphile's missionary vocation: Damien to Pamphile, August 23,

Page
49
1864, L; Favens to Bousquet, February 5, 1866, R.
His brother's life was an evasion of responsibility: Damien to Pamphile, December 22, 1866, V et D.
50 *"At first glance":* Damien to Pamphile, October ____, 1867, L.
"What is the good": Damien to Pamphile, ____, 1870, MSL.
"In his heart": Damien to Pamphile, December 22, 1866, L.
51 *"I asked for my brother":* Ropert to Mon révérend père, April 26, 1893, R.

XIV

51 *Damien fell ill:* Damien to Pamphile, September 22, 1870, L.
Le bon petit gros Damien: Damien to Révérends pères, October, 1868—January, 1869, V et D.
52 *"Where are you then":* Damien to Pauline, July 14, 1872, L.

CHAPTER THREE. GOD'S ATHLETE

I

56 *Pathetic pleas:* Bertrand to Dumonteil, September 5, 1872, R; Favens to Bousquet, April 23, 1873, R.
Ashore at the settlement: Maigret Journal, May 10, 1873, UH; Damien to Bousquet, August ____, 1873, R; *Missions Catholiques* 1873, 476.

II

56 *Damien already knew about leprosy:* Damien to Parents, January ____, 1869, V et D; Damien to Mon révérend père, August 16, 1871, MSL.
A kind of burning: In March, 1889, Damien dictated an account of his disease to Joseph Dutton. Dutton made several typescript copies. One is in HHS.
"An inner voice": Damien to Bousquet, August ____, 1873, R.
58 St. Francis Xavier: Brodrick, *passim.*
St. Francis of Assisi: Moorman, *passim.*
60 *"We lepers":* Damien to Pamphile, November 25, 1873, V et D.

III

60 Leprosy in 1873: See the biennial *Reports* of the Board of Health to the legislature of the Hawaiian kingdom.

Page
60

"*A most consoling and inspiring effect*": Ka Nūpepa Nūhou, April 15, 1873.

61   *A letter to be read:* Hawaiian Gazette, May 14, 1873. *A dozen well-meaning gentlemen:* Pacific Commercial Advertiser, May 24, 1873.

"*We care not*": Ka Nūpepa Nūhou, May 13, 1873.

Protestant and Mormon activity on leprosy: *Hawaiian Gazette,* May 21, 1873; *Ka Nūpepa Nūhou,* May 23, 1873; Damon, 50 *ff.*

The only topic of conversation: Favens to Bousquet, May 28, 1873, R.

62   "*Without detracting from the devotion*": Favens to Bousquet, May 28, 1873, R. All quotations in the remainder of this section come from the same letter.

IV

63   *A powerfully-worded statement:* Bishop to Hall, June 12, 1873, HD; *Pacific Commercial Advertiser,* June 14, 1873.

65   Hawaiian minister goes to Kalawao: Alexander to Hall, June 7, June 25, 1873, BH.

V

65   "*Father-general of the poor*": Damien to Bousquet, August 8, 1873, R.

Damien was leaving the settlement: Rogers to Hall, August 22, 1873, BH.

66   *The provincial wanted to go ashore:* Favens to Bousquet, October 8, 1873, R.

One of the Sacred Hearts fathers from Maui: Bouillon to Bousquet, September 14, 1874, R.

67   Permission to be at Kalawao: See letters in HD between October and December, 1873; also Favens to Bousquet, December 10, 1873.

VI

67   "*Like a great blue morning glory*": Birò, 147–148.

"*Grand, gloomy and bleak*": Stevenson, *Letters,* III, 153.

68   "*The whole face of the abyss*": Stoddard, *Lepers,* 18, 33; also Stoddard, *Diary,* 38–39.

The *pali* trail: Bouillon to Bousquet, March 3, 1878, R; Kaeo to Emma, August 18, 1873, HMCS; Summers, 185.

Kalawao was heavily populated: Creighton, 94.

Page
69 *"Swells and flings itself upward":* Summers, 159.
   A changeful landscape: Saxe, 25.
   "A tongue of land": Stoddard, *Lepers,* 19–20.
70 *"The huge furrows":* Leprosy in the United States, 112.

VII

70 *The Board of Health was pleased with Kalawao:* See Board of
   Health *Reports.*
71 Rudolph Meyer: Shaner, *passim.*
   The Hawaiians sent to Kalawao: undated MS in BH.
   "Do you mean": Heuck to Lepart, August 7, 1866, BHLB.
   Louis Lepart: His letters are in BH.
72 Donald Walsh: Stoddard, *Lepers,* 47–52.
   British Army discipline: Pacific Commercial Advertiser, Novem-
   ber 13, 1869.
   "Men and women": Kaeo to Emma, August 20, 1873, HMCS.
   "The sick": Memo by Walsh, April 2, 1867, HD.
73 *"No. 4 house":* Memo by Walsh, May 30, 1867, HD.
   "By what means": Memo by Walsh, May 30, 1867, HD.
   "They must not fancy": Heuck to Lepart, March 17, 1866, BHLB.

VIII

74 *Leprosy was the latest:* Mouritz, *Path; Brief History, passim.*
   "Ma'i pākē *ship": Ka Nūpepa Kū'oko'a,* March 16, 1865.
   Leprosy among *haole:* Thompson, 288.
75 *Make your will: Ka Nūpepa Kū'oko'a,* July 28, 1866.
   General ignorance on this subject: Friend, July, 1873, 64.
76 Hawaiian attitudes to leprosy: *Ka Nūpepa Kū'oko'a,* December 2,
   1865; Kaimiola to Board of Health, November 13, 1866, BH; Rags-
   dale to Hall, July 1, 1873, BH; Neilson to Carter, February 25, 1881,
   BH; *Hawaiian Gazette,* January 22, 1889; Rae to Board of Health,
   April 13-May 10, 1870, BH.
   "The day following the visit": Kaeo to Emma, August 18, 1873,
   HMCS.
77 *"The most thorough indifference":* Board of Health, *Report,* 1868,
   2.
   Racial nightmares: Ostrom to Mott Smith, April 9, July 10, 1877,
   BH.
78 *"The roots of this thing":* Emerson to Wilder, March 28, 1879, BH.
   His sugar plantations would be set afire: Notices in BH, October,
   1881.

Page
78

Nathaniel Emerson liked Hawaiians: Emerson to Meyer, January 3, 1889, BHLB.
He would not touch them: Jacks, 71.
Physical examinations by raising the rags: Report by Fitch, July 15, 1882, HD.
The white Protestant minister: Undated MS in BH; Bouillon to Bousquet, June 21, 1875, R.

IX

80   *"Thou welcome the hour":* Kaeo to Emma, July 7, 1873, AH.
      "Last night": Kaeo to Emma, August 11, 1873, AH.
81   *"I was dressing":* Kaeo to Emma, July 27, 1873, HMCS.
      Kaeo allowed to return to Honolulu: Board of Health Minutes, June 27, 1876, BH.
      Damien and Kaeo: Kaeo to Emma, July 15, August 15, 1873, AH.

X

82   *"The Puhala tree":* Mouritz, *Path,* 232–234.
      "He saw in the hospital": Van Heteren to Mon père, August 6, 1874, R.
83   *"All my repugnance":* Damien, copied in Favens to Bousquet, May 28, 1873, R.
84   *"Be careful":* Favens to Damien, May 20, 1873, R.
      "I am not yet a leper": Damien to Pamphile, November 25, 1873, L.
      The smell of the crowd: Damien to Bousquet, August 8, 1873, R.
      "Sometimes, confessing the sick": Damien to Pamphile, November 25, 1873, L.
      "In the morning": Damien to Parents, November 25, 1873, V et D.
85   *"Ordinarily they listen":* Damien to Bousquet, December 17, 1874, V et D.
      St. Philomena's church became too small: Damien to Maigret, July 28, 1873, R.
86   *The native Hawaiian Protestant minister:* Holokahiki to Hall, December 25, 1873, BH.
      "The Papist teacher": Ka Nūpepa Kū'oko'a, January 17, 1874.
      "In tears": Damien to Bousquet, December 17, 1874, V et D.
      Two hundred graves: Damien to Mon révérend père, December 28, 1874, MSL.

XI

86 *"Let me tell you"*: Damien to Pamphile, November 25, 1873, L.
87 *He wore himself out:* Damien to Bousquet, August ____, 1873, R;
Damien to Mon révérend père, July 16, 1874, MSL.
André Burgerman: *Annales des Sacrés Coeurs*, 1907, 350.
Burgerman falls down *pali:* Burgerman to Germain, June 1, 1878,
R; Damien to Mon révérend père, March 16, 1874, MSL.
88 Burgerman's church: Burgerman to Damien, February 24, 1874,
V et D; Damien to Mon révérend père, March 16, 1874, V et D;
Damien to Mon révérend père, June 24, 1874, MSL.
"It is good": Favens to Bousquet, November 5, 1874, R.

XII

89 *"I feel it"*: *Hawaiian Gazette*, June 18, 1873.
"I mean to make": Ragsdale to Hall, July 7, 1873, BH.
G. W. Woods: Woods, *passim.*
90 Ragsdale's illness: Meyer to Gulick, November 5, 1877, BH;
Damien to Elby, November 22, 1877, MSL.

XIII

91 Burgerman as superintendent: Bouillon to Bousquet, March 3,
1878, R; Meyer to Damien, November 29, December 7, 1877, V et
D.
"This priest": Damien to Bousquet, ____, 1876, MSL.
Damien as superintendent: See letters in BH for late 1877 and
early 1878; and in HD for the same period.
92 *"A great rebel"*: Damien to Wilder, January 25, 1878, HD.
"For his being a reverend gentleman": Damien to Dayton, January 25, 1878, HD.
"The Govenor is failing fast": Strawn to Wilder, January ____,
1878, BH.

XIV

93 Burgerman as doctor: Damien to Bousquet, February ____, 1879,
R; Petition, May 10, 1878, BH.
Damien to help support Burgerman: Moncany to Damien, October 8, 1878, R.
"In slavery": Moncany to Bousquet, September 12, 1878, R.
"My great pain": Damien to Favens, December 21, 1878, L.
94 *"Please keep secret"*: Damien to Favens, December 26, 1878, L.

Page
94
> *"They give too much medicine"*: Emerson to Wilder, July 1, 1879, BH.
>
> Moncany to Bousquet, September ____, 1879, R.

95 *Send me a good child of the Congregation:* Damien to Bousquet, February 4, 1879, R.
> *"Severe measures"*: Moncany to Bousquet, February 9–10, 1880, R.
> *"He has threatened me"*: Damien to Emerson, July 13, 1880, BH.
> *"Friendly conversation"*: Emerson to Wilder, July 13, 1880, BH.

96 *"Nothing, its only in the blood"*: Untitled MS by Ambrose Hutchison in HD.

XV

97 *"I have some enormous spots"*: Burgerman to Damien, November 22, 1877, R.
> *"It is said that both are leprous"*: Moncany to Bousquet, February 28, 1878, R.
> *Damien, looking back years later:* Dutton typescript, March 10, 1889, HHS.

98 *"As he sadly supposed"*: *Report of the Special Sanitary Committee,* 10.
> *"My health is very good"*: Damien to Bousquet, February 4, 1879, R.
> *"In any case"*: Moncany to Bousquet, September ____, 1879, R.
> *"My own health"*: Bemiss, 8–9.
> *"A good piece of news"*: Moncany to Bousquet, April 6, 1880, R.
> *"Smooth and rather thin"*: Woods, 5.

XVI

99 Building material: Favens to Bousquet, September 14, 1875, R.
100 *"Over-animated and tempestuous"*: Maigret to Bousquet, March 1, 1877, R.
> *"He remains a priest"*: Moncany to Bousquet, July 5, 1880, R.

XVII

100 Liliuokalani: *Hawaiian Gazette,* September 21, 1881; *Pacific Commercial Advertiser,* September 24, 1881.
101 *Strong as a Turk:* Koeckemann to Associés, October 21, 1881, R.
> *"Much fanfare"*: Damien to Koeckemann, September 27, 1881, MSL.
> *"Above all petty cliques"*: *Hawaiian Gazette,* September 21, 1881.

Page
102 *"He resuscitates"*: *Pacific Commercial Advertiser*, September 21, 1881.

XVIII

102 *"Reputation put under suspicion"*: Damien to Koeckemann, December 31, 1881, V et D.
"Father Albert and I": October 17, 1881, L.
103 *"Everything would go well"*: Damien to Koeckemann, December 6, 1881, V et D.
Damien asked the bishop to define authority: Damien to Koeckemann, November 16, 1881, MSL.
"In concert": Koeckemann to Damien, January 30, 1882, V et D.
104 *"I renew to you"*: Damien to Koeckemann, May ____, 1882, V et D.
105 Damien doing medical work at the hospital: Damien to Gibson, August 19, 1882, HD; Damien to Koeckemann, August 31, 1882, V et D.
"I will willingly leave Molokai": Damien to Koeckemann, August 31, 1882, MSL.
"Is it true": Damien to Koeckemann, September 9, 1882, MSL.
106 Damien and Montiton in 1883: Their letters are collected in V et D.

XIX

107 *Sacred Hearts mission could scarcely tolerate*: Favens to Bousquet, December 21, 1874, R.
"As for Father Albert": Moncany to Bousquet, August 20, 1879, R.
"Because he runs after everyone": Favens to Bousquet, April 30, 1884, R.
108 *"Énergumène"*: Moncany to Bousquet, May 9, 1879, R.
"I do not want to live at war": Damien to Koeckemann, August 31, 1882, MSL.
109 *"The fox will die in his skin"*: Moncany to Bousquet, May 9, 1879, R.

XX

109 *Personal Rule*: The original of Damien's Règlement Personnel is in the Damien museum at Tremeloo.
110 A new presbytery: Damien to Mon révérend père, December 26, 1878.

Page
110

"*Nothing could suit me better*": Damien's Compte des Dépenses, 1878, V et D.

More than eight hundred leprosy victims: Board of Health *Report,* 1880, *passim.*

"*A bit of meat*": Stoddard, *Lepers,* 63; see also Stoddard, *Diary,* 16–17.

"*Fragments of harness*": Stoddard, *Lepers,* 74 ff.

"*Hardly a systematic driver*": Stoddard, *Diary,* 25.

Damien drove across the Protestant cemetery: Kaahaihauu to Wilder, August 19, 1878, BH.

111 Meyer's horses: Notes by Julliotte, 1924–1930, R.

Amputated a gangrenous foot: Board of Health *Report,* 1884, Stallard report, xliv.

"*Women . . . roariously drunk*": Hutchison MS, HD.

112 The dance house: Archambaux to Bousquet, September 8, 1876, R.

"*The hilarious feasters*": Hutchison MS, HD.

"*Because of the infirmities*": Damien to Bousquet, February 4, 1879, R.

113 Damien and orphans: Damien to Pamphile, January 31, 1880, V et D; Hutchison, V et D; Stoddard, *Lepers,* 72; Damien to Koeckemann, April 9, 1883, MSL.

The interior of St. Philomena's: Stoddard, *Lepers,* 75–76; see also Stoddard, *Diary,* 15.

"*A vigorous, forceful, impellant man*": Hutchison MS, HD.

114 "*He brought from his cottage*": Stoddard, *Lepers,* 39.

XXI

114 *In the opinion of . . . G. W. Woods:* Woods to Damien, July 29, 1887, BH.

Only two Hawaiians killed themselves: Hayselden to Meyer, August 10, 1886, BHLB; Meyer to Wilder, December 4, 1891, BH.

115 *Willing to contract leprosy:* Mouritz, *Path,* 141 ff; Thompson, 285.

Hinting at deeper truths: Board of Health *Report,* 1884, Mouritz report, lxvi.

Around the hospital: Mouritz, *Path,* 168–169.

116 The funeral society: *Report of the Special Sanitary Committee,* 6–7.

Funerals: Limburg to Bousquet, December 8, 1888, R; Stoddard, *Lepers,* 61; Board of Health *Report,* 1884, xliii.

The day after Ambrose Hutchison arrived: Hutchison MS, HD.

117 *Obscenities on the walls:* Stoddard, *Diary,* 10.

"*Disrespect paid to the moral law*": Damien to Gibson, November 23, 1882, HD.

Page
117

"The memory of your past infidelities": The original of Damien's revised Règlement Personnel is at Louvain.

XXII

119 *It only takes a month from Belgium:* Damien to Pamphile, January 18, 1883, L.
"Sometimes I envy": Damien to Mother, March 15, 1876, V et D.
"The other day": Damien to Pamphile, January 31, 1880, L.

XXIII

120 *"Good man of religion"*: Fouesnel to Bousquet, November 16, 1883, R.
121 "Dikken Jef": Damien to Mother, January 30–31, 1880, V et D.
"As for me": Damien to Pamphile, January 18, 1883, L.

CHAPTER FOUR. A PECULIAR GOLGOTHA

I

125 *He asked in Japan: Pacific Commercial Advertiser*, September 24, 1881.
"Physchological medicine": Kalakaua to Trousseau, June 19, 1888, BH.
Kapiolani corresponded with Damien: Photocopies of these letters are among the uncatalogued MSS in R; they are translated in Jourdan, *Heart.*
126 Walter Murray Gibson: Kuykendall, III, *passim.*
Board of Health appropriations for leprosy: These can be followed in Board of Health *Reports.*
128 Kakaako: Board of Health *Report,* 1886, *passim.*
Offensive foreshore: Board of Health *Report,* 1884, Stallard report, xxvii *ff.*
129 Sisters of Charity: Jacks, *passim.*
Gibson . . . was flirting with Catholicism: Adler and Barrett, *passim.*
Appropriations for Catholic schools: Koeckemann to Bousquet, January 14, 1886, R.
Léonor Fouesnel decorated: Documents dated November 9, 1885, R.
Mother Marianne decorated: Jacks, 56–57.

Page

129
    Gibson, Dominis, Kalakaua decorated: Koeckemann to Bousquet, May 13, June 11, 1885, R.

130 Episcopalians and Freemasons: Koeckemann to Bousquet, February 13, 1885, R.
    "The old fox": Koeckemann to Bousquet, July 2, 1883, R.

II

130 *"The most burdensome tax"*: Board of Health *Report*, 1880, 59.
    "An almost bottomless pit": Board of Health *Report*, 1890, 60.

131 *"Everywhere among us"*: Board of Health *Report*, 1882, 48.
    Haole with leprosy: Saxe, 12.
    One *kōkua* woman: Emerson to Wilder, June 28, 1879, BH.

132 Ambrose Hutchison: Mouritz, *Brief*, 81–84.

132 *"Syphilis was introduced"*: Board of Health *Report*, 1884, 51 *ff*.

133 Damien on leprosy and syphilis: His report, the MS of which is in HD, was published as part of *Appendix* to Board of Health *Report*, 1886.

134 *Hawaiian culture as corrupt and diseased:* Board of Health *Report*, 1888, 17, 1890, 5.
    "No cleanly wantonness": *Hawaiian Gazette*, February 28, 1883; see also Hyde to Clark, March 10, 1883, HMCS.

III

135 *"Accustomed as I was"*: Hyde, *Father Damien*, 6–7.

136 *"Could I safely"*: Hyde, *Father Damien*, 7.
    "If you take hold": Hyde, *Father Damien*, 11; see also Hyde to Smith, December 30, 1884, HMCS.

137 *"I have been warned"*: Hyde to Clark, February 15, 1884, HMCS.

IV

138 *"Ultimate, frigid fact"*: Board of Health *Report*, 1890, 5.
    "Rescued from the slough": Board of Health *Report*, 1888, 7.
    Medical treatments for leprosy: These letters in BH discuss possible cures: McCormick to Board of Health, July 13, 1891; Swift to Emerson, January 3, 1889; Williamson to Gulick, February 24, 1895. See also Wilcox to Severance, July 13, 1892, BHLB; and Board of Health *Report*, 1884, xcvi-ii. For Hawaiian treatments, see *Ka Nūpepa Kū'oko'a*, March 31, 1866; Meakapu to Gibson, February 9, 1886, HD.

Page
138
    "Expect to find an arcanum": Board of Health *Report*, 1884, Arning report, *passim*.
139   Eduard Arning: Bushnell, "Arning," *passim*. Correspondence on Arning's appointment is in BH.
140   *"Let Hawaii continue"*: Board of Health *Report*, 1884, 13.
141   *"Condemned criminals"*: Board of Health *Report*, 1882, 59.
    Keanu: Mouritz, *Path*, 152 *ff*; Bushnell, "Arning," 13.
142   *"But I do believe"*: *Appendix* to Board of Health *Report*, 1886, xliii.

V

For various accounts of the noticeable onset and diagnosis of Damien's leprosy, see *Life and Letters*, 132; Mouritz, *Path*, 234–235, 379; Mouritz, *Brief*, 85; Johnstone, 83–84; Jourdan, *Le Père Damien*, 394; Dutton, 85–86. Note that Damien's own account, recorded by Joseph Dutton on March 10, 1889 (typescript, HHS), does not mention the diagnosis. My version of events is based on primary sources, together with a technical paper by Arning. Shipping lists were used in an attempt—not altogether successful—to trace the movements of those involved between Molokai and Honolulu.
143   *About the end of 1882:* Dutton typescript, March 10, 1889, HHS.
    The condition was bad enough: Damien to Koeckemann, March 20, 1884, MSL.
    Very likely Eduard Arning: Appendix to Board of Health *Report*, 1886, Mouritz report, xcvi.
    Bishop Koeckemann was writing: Koeckemann to Bousquet, September 27, 1884, R; see also Fouesnel to Bousquet, September 23, 1884, R.
    "Looks like a leper": Stoddard, *Diary*, 16.
    "I have taken the arcenica pill": Damien to Arning, October 31, 1884, V et D.
144   *"The typical analgesia"*: Thin, 189–190.
    Damien scalded his foot: Mouritz, *Brief*, 85.
    Arning visited Kalawao: Hayselden to Mouritz, April 23, 1885, BHLB.
    "Evidence of other diseases": Mouritz, *Path*, 235; see also Damien to Koeckemann, April 27, 1885, V et D.
145   *"He was active"*: Mouritz, *Path*, 229–231.

VI

146   Arning making casts: Bushnell, "Arning," *passim*.

VII

146   *"Because without having forgotten"*: Damien to Parents, February 2, 1885, V et D.
148   *"Being trouble with a kind of nerf disease"*: Damien to Pamphile, January 31, 1885, V et D.
149   *"Anticipated from my first arrival"*: Damien to Sister Marie-Gabrielle, March 25, 1886, V et D.
150   *"The first germs of the disease"*: Damien to Bousquet, August 26, 1886, R.
      "It is the memory": Damien to Koeckemann, October 29, 1885, MSL.

VIII

150   *"I have never seen"*: Mouritz, *Path*, 243.
151   *"Fr. Damien took no precautions"*: Mouritz, *Path*, 237.
      John Wilmington: His memoir of Damien is in R.
      The cemetery was rocky ground: Mouritz, *Path*, 237–238; see also Meyer to Ashley, June 19, 1888, April 26, 1889, BH; Board of Health *Report*, 1890, 87.
152   Water supply inadequate: Mouritz, *Path*, 243–244; for hygiene, see also Julliotte to Alazard, January 26, 1905, R.
      "He was eating poi": Woods, 8.

IX

153   *"Far from robust"*: Bouillon to Germain, August 19, 1876, R.
      "In different degrees": Archambaux to Bousquet, September 8, 1876, R.
154   Medical examination by Arning: Fouesnel to Bousquet, September 25, 1884, R.
      "I intend": Damien to Arning, October 31, 1884, V et D; see also Damien to Koeckemann, December 26, 1884, MSL.
      "Murderers": Fouesnel to Bousquet, June 29, 1885, R.
      Authorizing Archambaux' departure: Gibson to Mouritz, January 5, 1885, BHLB.
155   *"Like a madman"*: Fouesnel to Bousquet, January 29, 1885, R.
      Lahaina . . . was full of leprosy: Fouesnel to Bousquet, January 29, 1885, R.
      "This news has staggered us": Fouesnel to Bousquet, September 23, 1884, R.
      Protective steps: Fouesnel to Bousquet, February 13, 1886, R.

X

156 *"Has never been able"*: Koeckemann to Bousquet, October 30, 1884, R.
Damien would not have been able to stand this: Damien to Koeckemann, January 30, 1885, V et D.

157 *"I am disabled"*: Damien to Koeckemann, February 25, 1885, MSL.
"Intrigue," "thunderclaps": Damien to Koeckemann, Fête de Joseph, 1885. (V et D)

158 *A single priest was sufficient*: Montiton to Bousquet, April 24, 1885, R.
Montiton's departure doubled his work: Damien to Koeckemann, April 25, 1885, V et D.
Visit from a Maui priest: Beissel to Bousquet, July 2, 1886, R.
"I often think of you": Damien to Pamphile, November 26, 1885, L.

XI

The correspondence relating to Damien's visit to Honolulu is well discussed in V et D. See also Julliotte notes, 1924–1930, R; and Adler and Barrett, entries for June–July, 1886.

XII

162 *A new treatment*: Damien to Koeckemann, June 16, 1886, MSL.
"Knowledge and experience": Waller to Gibson, January 1, 1885, HD.
Masanao Goto: Correspondence on Goto is in HD.
"A grain of little pills": Damien to Bousquet, August 26, 1886, R.

163 *"50 boxes"*: Damien to Hayselden, July 21, 1886, HD.
"A few propositions": Damien to Gibson, August 4, 1886, HD.

164 *Goto treatment started . . . on a modest* scale: Damien to Gibson, December 8, 1886, HD.
"My right hand": Damien to Hudson, November 23, 1886, L.
"Six months ago": Damien to Weiler, December 30, 1886, R.
Beissel found him looking better: Beissel to Bousquet, September 29, 1886, R.
Mouritz on Goto treatment: MS report by Mouritz, March 17, 1894, HD.

165 *Mouritz saw him one day*: Mouritz, *Path*, 246.

XIII

165 Anne-Catherine De Veuster: *Life and Letters,* 136–137.
   Stories began to crop up: Courrier de Bruxelles, October 21, 1886.
   Copies made their way to the islands: Weiler to Damien, November 26, 1886, L; Koeckemann to Damien, December 8, 1886, V et D.
   Damien could only say: Damien to Pamphile, November 9, 1887, V et D.

166 *He put Pamphile's case:* Damien to Koeckemann, July 26, 1886, R.
   Koeckemann . . . wrote to Pamphile: Koeckemann to Pamphile, July 28, 1886, R.
   Koeckemann to Bousquet, July 28, 1886, R.
   "Being deprived": Damien to Weiler, December 30, 1886, V et D.

XIV

166 *Letters came in quantity:* Flavin to Your Excellency, November 1, 1887, BH; Phillips to Government, May 17, 1890, BH; Emerson to Dutton, October 21, 1889, BHLB; Koeckemann to Bousquet, September 17, 1889, R.

167 *"He says he wants":* Adler and Barrett, entries for July 22–23, 1886.
   "Ira B. Dutton is truly": Damien to Gibson, August 4, 1886, HD.
   "He will be our right hand": Damien to Hudson, November 23, 1886, V et D.
   "He wore a blue denim shirt": Mouritz, *Path,* 285.
   Dutton was forty-three: For Dutton's life, see Dutton; and Case, *passim.*

168 *"It was a new subject":* Dutton, 191.
   "Speaking to him": Meyer to Ashley, November 7, 1888, BH.
   "The principal graveyard": Mulhane, 93.

XV

169 *Chapman set to work: Times,* October 18, November 12, 1886; for the controversy, see *Tablet,* November 6, 13, 1886. This issue is well discussed in Jourdan, *Heart,* 273 *ff.*

171 *"Formulated a serious charge": Pacific Commercial Advertiser,* April 22, 1887; see also *Times,* March 12, 1887.

172 *The government was in trouble:* Kuykendall, III, *passim.*

XVI

173 Condemned as a troublemaker: Fouesnel to Bousquet, May 5, 1887, R.
Damien was writing in distress: Damien to Fouesnel, November 22, 1883, L.
Fouesnel's defects: Koeckemann to Bousquet, July 27, September 29, 1886, R; Moncany to Bousquet, April 21, 1880; see also V et D, where much evidence is collected.
"Sweeten any pills": Beissel to Bousquet, July 2, 1880, V et D.

174 *Damien scolded him for it: Times,* June 29, 1889.
"make him give up": Fouesnel to Bousquet, July 27, 1874, R.

175 *"It is absolutely":* Fouesnel to Bousquet, February 26, 1884, R.
"As I have a sort of passion": Koeckemann to Damien, January 2, 1887, V et D.

176 *"From strangers, gold":* Damien to Koeckemann, January 20, 1887, V et D.
"After gold and incense": Koeckemann to Damien, February 5, 1887, V et D.
"And if you wish to imitate": Fouesnel to Damien, February 14, 1887, V et D.
"The government, the mission, the Sisters": Koeckemann to Bousquet, February 11, 1887, R.

177 *"Falsehoods":* Fouesnel to Bousquet, February 8, 1887, R.
"Very much annoyed": Adler and Barrett, entry for February 15, 1887.
A way out of everybody's troubles: Hayselden to Damien, March 29, 1887, BH.
Hard to retrace his steps: Fouesnel to Bousquet, May 5, 1887, R.

178 *"If you could send me":* Weiler to Damien, February 11, 1887, V et D; see also Weiler to Damien, March 2, 1888, R.
Damien's letters unsealed: Fouesnel to Damien, February 28, April 11, 1887, V et D; Damien to Koeckemann, November 26, 1885, MSL.
Damien's attitude to publicity: Damien to Koeckemann, March 31, 1886, MSL; Damien to Weiler, December 30, 1886, R; Damien to Kavanagh, November 25, 1887, MSL; Damien to Gross, January 10, 1888, L; Woods, 4.

179 *"During the first years":* Damien to Pamphile, January 31, 1880, MSL.

XVII

179 Revolution: Kuykendall, III, *passim.*

XVIII

180 *"The laxity":* Board of Health *Report,* 1888, 16.

XIX

181 *"How long will the authorities":* Fouesnel to Bousquet, April _____, 1887, R.

182 *"Leprous sinner":* Damien to Koeckemann, December 9, 1886, V et D.

A terrible courage: Fouesnel to Bousquet, April _____, 1887, R.

"We count": Fouesnel to Damien, November 21, 1887, R.

"The bishop": Fouesnel to Bousquet, November 21, 1887, R.

"As for me": Archambaux to Bertrand, December 28, 1887, R.

183 *"Cries of despair":* Fouesnel to Weiler, January 12, 1888, R.

The fixed idea: Bouillon to Bousquet, March 9, 1888, R.

Board of Health relented: Emerson to Fouesnel, February 13, 27, 1888, BHLB; Emerson to Meyer, February 27, 1888, BHLB.

"Perhaps it is gone": Archambaux to Damien, April 10, 1888.

XX

183 *"Although leprosy has a strong hold":* Damien to Pamphile, November 9, 1887, R.

184 Emerson's Board of Health: Meyer to Emerson, January 22, 1888, BH.

"The skin of the abdomen": Mouritz, *Path,* 246.

"Given up all hope": Mouritz, *Path,* 247.

185 *"Resolved to have nothing":* Fouesnel to Damien, June 12, 1888, R; see also Fouesnel to Bousquet, June 28, 1888, R.

186 *"Pray to achieve":* Jourdan, *Le Père Damien.* 480. The Damien notebooks are at Louvain.

A long and comprehensive report: The MS is in HD; it was published in *Appendix* to Board of Health *Report,* 1886.

187 *"He was imbued":* Mouritz, *Path,* 243.

"Various priests": Koeckemann to Bousquet, April 10, 1889, R.

"Seeming to have gone": Koeckemann to Bousquet, July _____, 1888, R; see also Fouesnel to Chapitre-Général, July 30, 1888, R.

XXI

188 *"Nervo-bilious"*: Mouritz, *Path*, 231.
"5 *churches"*: Board of Health *Report*, 1888, 68–69.
189 *"As always ready"*: Dutton typescript, November 1, 1905, HHS.
"Drive ahead": Dutton to Koeckemann, February 12, 1890, typescript copy in HHS.

XXII

190 *The project became mixed up:* Koeckemann to Bousquet, November 17, 1887, R.
Episcopalian Sisters: Adler and Barrett, entry for February 15, 1887.
Damien's superiors . . . were furious: Koeckemann to Bousquet, February 15, 1887, R; see also Damien to Koeckemann, January 28, 1887, V et D.
191 *Sisters . . . willing to go to the settlement:* Jourdan, *Heart*, 365; Jacks, 77.
Charles Reed Bishop: Kent, *Bishop*, 291–294.

XXIII

191 *He had no friends:* Koeckemann to Weiler, September 19, 1888, R.
Conrardy: Jourdan, *Heart*, 295–296.
192 *Conrardy yearned for a priest's life:* Conrardy to Mon cher monsieur, July 19, 1888, V et D.
193 *"Stranger" priests:* Koeckemann to Bousquet, July 29, 1888, R.
An itinerant Irish priest: This episode is discussed in V et D.
Conrardy to become a member of the Congregation: Koeckemann to Damien, January 23, 1888, V et D.
He wanted wings to fly there: Conrardy to Damien, January 2, 1888, V et D.
Damien saw that: Damien to Weiler, August 20, 1888, V et D.
Damien put his case . . . strongly: Damien to Koeckemann, February 12, 1888, MSL.
194 *Damien . . . had "ordered" Conrardy:* Koeckemann to Bousquet, April 26, 1888, R.
"An inundation of letters": Fouesnel to Damien, May 28, 1888, V et D.
195 *His circular letter:* Koeckemann to Bousquet, June 1, 1888, R.
Making plans with Damien: Julliotte notes, 1924–1930, R.

Page

195

Damien wrote to the Chapter-General: Damien to Weiler, July 26, 1888, R.

"They would end": Koeckemann to Bousquet, July 29, 1888, R.

196 *"Leprosy is our bane":* Ashley to Conrardy, September 10, 1888, BHLB.

In a later-published letter: Conrardy to Imoda, June 27, 1888, R.

197 *"How many times":* Conrardy to Friend, November 7, 1888, V et D.

XXIV

197 Father Wendelin Moellers: Fouesnel to Bousquet, November 20, 1888, R.

Limburg: Limburg to Bousquet, December 1, 1888, R.

XXV

198 *"A terrible storm":* Woods, 14.

The wind shook Dutton awake: Note by Dutton, October 2, 1907, R.

199 *"Fortunately, my hands":* Damien to Hudson, May 17, 1888, in uncatalogued MSS, R.

"The face puffy": Limburg to Bousquet, December 1, 1888, R.

XXVI

199 *He died in November:* Fouesnel, circular, November 16, 1888, R.

XXVII

200 *Someone once asked Damien:* Clifford, 91.

"Called away": Damien to Harper, December 28, 1886, R.

"A natural remedy": Damien to Hudson, August 8, 1888, in uncatalogued MSS, R.

"Providential agent": Damien to Clifford, February 28, 1889, V et D.

201 *"I am getting old":* Damien to Kuehn, October 3, 1888, in *Damien Institute,* November, 1903, 176.

"We become generally feeble": Damien to Gross, January 10, 1888, L.

XVIII

All quotations in this section are from Clifford.

XXIX

207 *Formal exchange of good wishes:* Fouesnel to Damien, December 3, 1888, R; Koeckemann to Damien, January 2, 1889, R.
Church building at Kalaupapa: Fouesnel to Damien, February 5, 1889, R; Koeckemann to Damien, January 28, 1889, R.

208 *"Triumphing":* Koeckemann to Bousquet, February 11, 1889, R.
Find out about it from the newspapers: Koeckemann to Damien, February 11, 1889, R.
"Don't be so absolute": Fouesnel to Damien, January 28, 1889, V et D.
"Don't be so impatient": Fouesnel to Damien, March 18, 1889, V et D.
Damien's face was better: Sinnett to Clifford, January 4, 1889, V et D.
"Exterior cleansing": Damien to Clifford, November 11, 1888, V et D.

209 *"Keep this for yourself":* Conrardy to Gross, June 17, 1888, V et D.
Franciscan Sisters: Jacks, *passim.*
He wrote to Pamphile: Damien to Pamphile, February 12, 1889, L.
The last letter Damien wrote: Dutton, 100.
His hands . . . broke out: Sinnett to Clifford, February 21, 1889, V et D.

210 *Dutton took it down:* Typescript by Dutton, March 10, 1889, HHS.
William Brigham: His photographs of Damien are reproduced in this book.

211 *A letter came:* Judith to Damien, March 18, 1889, V et D.
"As usual": Moellers to Bousquet, April 17, 1889, R.
"Even Saints and Martyrs": Meyer to Ashley, April 11, 1889, BH.

212 *"Poor fellow":* Swift to Emerson, April 11, 1889, BH.
Death: Moellers to Bousquet, April 17, 1889, R.

XXX

213 *The spot for his burial:* Moellers to Bousquet, April 17, 1889.

CHAPTER FIVE. STIGMA

I

217 *When Pamphile heard:* Pamphile to Weiler, May 18, 1889, R.
The projected Belgian memorial: *Times,* June 29, 1889.

218 *A book, published in 1889: Life and Letters.*
In case my efforts: Tauvel, xv.

219 *Conrardy did not want to leave:* Ropert to Bousquet, November 19, 1895, R.

Page
219
Disputatious ideas: Meyer to Ashley, March 13, 1889, BH.
Conrardy left Kalawao: Ropert to Bousquet, June 30, 1893, March 6, 1894, R.
In his first letter to Europe: Pamphile to Bousquet, December 5, 1895, R. Other letters by Pamphile are in L.
Fouesnel . . . argued for keeping Pamphile: Fouesnel to Bousquet, February 11, 1897, R.
220 *"I pray":* Ropert to Bousquet, July 21, 1896, R.
Become a Capuchin: Ropert to Bousquet, July 21, 1896, R.
Pamphile was given permission: Ropert to Bousquet, March 9, 1897, R.
So his obituarist said: Annales des Sacrés Coeurs, September, 1909.

II

221 *Clifford's inspirational lecture: Times,* May 15, 1889.
Hugh Chapman: *Times,* May 14, 1889.
The most imposing of patrons: Times, December 10, 1889.
"When Father Damien": Clifford, 175–176.
222 *"It is natural":* Clifford, 149.
"The general question": Times, January 14, 1890.
"Hear, hear!": Journal of the Leprosy Investigation Committee, August, 1890, 14–15.
Leprosy in India: Choksy, 26.
223 *Clifford supervised the design: Journal of the Leprosy Investigation Committee,* July, 1891, 5.
"Appeared in nearly all": Journal of the Leprosy Investigation Committee, December, 1891, 78.
There was not enough money: Wilcox to Clifford, January 31, 1893, BHLB.
Revolution of 1893: Kuykendall, III, *passim.*
Leprosy and imperial dominion: Morrow.

III

224 *He had always wondered:* Hyde to Alden, October 28, 1878, HMCS.
"There are no studious Hawaiians": Hyde to Clark, April 16, 1878, HMCS.
Influence of climate: Hyde to Alden, November 27, 1877, HMCS.
"Yankee push": Hyde to Clark, April 8, 1880, HMCS.
"Hawaii for Hawaiians": Hyde to Clark, January 8, 1878, HMCS.
"Mission boys": Hyde to Alden, July 1, 1887, HMCS.

Page
225   *Attach themselves to Catholicism:* Hyde and Oleson to Smith, July 28, 1888, HMCS.

  Census figures were being manipulated: Hyde to Smith, February 14, 1885, HMCS.

  "God's poor": Hyde to Smith, February 23, 1895, HMCS.

226   *The presence of Catholics:* Hyde to Clark, December 17, 1881, HMCS; Hyde to Smith, November 15, 1888, HMCS.

  "Appropriated to themselves": Hyde, *Father Damien,* 12.

  He felt that he was being exposed: Hyde to Clark, January 19, 1884, HMCS.

227   *He wrote a newspaper article:* Hawaiian Gazette, September 16, 23, 1885; see also Fitch to Damien, August 30, 1885, R.

  " 'Elele": Ka Nūpepa Elele, May 10, 1890.

  "Sanctity of dirtiness": Hyde to Smith, May 10, 1890, HMCS.

228   *"That testimony":* Hyde, *Father Damien,* 20–21.

  Damien had syphilis: Bishop to Gilman, March 5, 1891, HMCS.

229   *The case had indeed existed:* Hyde to Smith, September 20, November 21, 1890, HMCS.

  Fabien: Yzendoorn, 220; see also Schousten to Bousquet, July 12, 1881, R.

230   *It would not have been possible:* Mouritz, *Path,* 241.

  He had never had sexual relations: Dutton typescript, March 10, 1889, HHS; see also Julliotte to Jourdan, May 21, 1933, R.

  The campaign to defend Damien's honor: Pacific Commercial Advertiser, August 20, 1905.

  "Malodorous and scarifying": Hyde, *Father Damien,* 5.

231   *"No one in this world":* Hyde, *Father Damien,* 22.

  William Brigham: Bishop to Gilman, February 16, 1903, HMCS; New York *Freeman's Journal,* November 7, 1903.

  E. C. Bond: Hawaiian Gazette, June 30, 1905; Pacific *Commercial Advertiser,* August 20, 1905.

  Hyde came to the settlement: Jourdan, *Heart,* 423.

232   *Such a dread of leprosy:* Joesting, 253.

IV

232   *Sweep clean:* Board of Health *Report,* 1890, 120; Dutton, 202; Meyer to Emerson, June 18, 1889, BH; Note by Thomas, October 12, 1899, R; Note by Dutton, 1905, HHS.

  Leaves and pieces of wood: Fouesnel to Bousquet, May 28, 1896, R; Hutchison MS, HD.

  Graveyard full: Meyer to Emerson, May 30, 1889, BH; Board of Health *Report,* 1890, 87.

233   *"It is thought best":* Board of Health *Report,* 1890, 46.

Page

233

Population began to diminish: Limburg to Erhard, September 30, 1897, R.

"Dying": D'Orgeval to Mon révérend père, March 29, 1928, R.

"It is pitiful": Bens to Prat, October 12, 1934, R.

234 *A decline was noticeable:* See relevant Board of Health *Reports.*

V

234 *Arthur Mouritz kept an eye:* Mouritz, Path, 154.

235 *He had implanted leprous tissue:* Bushnell, "Arning," *passim.*

Inoculate diseased Hawaiian volunteers: Mouritz, *Path,* 156.

"The intense feeling": Arning to Emerson, May 10, 1886, BH.

Leprosy Investigation Station: Bushnell, "United States," *passim.*

VI

236 *Stigmatized its victims:* Skinsnes, "Leprosy in Society," *passim.*

A whole spectrum: Browne, *Leprosy;* Cochrane and Davey, *passim.* Discoveries in the field are generally reported in *Leprosy Review* and *International Journal of Leprosy.*

239 Protestant missionaries: Grey and Dreisbach, *passim.*

Catholic missionaries: Jourdan, *Heart,* 384 *ff.*

VII

240 *"When science has said"*: Times, June 29, 1889.

The world, he said, is busy: Dutton to Cattebeke, November 29, 1906, HHS.

241 *"A particular kind of saint"*: Koeckemann to Raepsaet, July 27, 1891, V et D.

His faults were too grievous: Koeckemann to Bousquet, December 13, 1889, R.

Funeral oration: Koeckemann to Bousquet, August 23, 1889, R.

"Disagreeable task": Koeckemann to Bousquet, September 17, 1889, R.

"I know already": Koeckemann to Bousquet, February 6, 1890, R.

242 *"Sink back into obscurity"*: Moellers to Gaetan, August 12, 1889, V et D; Moellers to Bousquet, November 12, 1890, R.

"Conrardy and others": Limburg and Moellers to Koeckemann, January 23, 1890, R.

"Probably no place": Koeckemann to Bouillon, November 25, 1890, R.

Page

243   *A riot at Kalawao:* Evans to Board of Health, October 3, 1890, BHLB.

"*The old man*": Schulte to Erhard, May 23, 1910, R.

244   *Lived uneventfully:* André to Mon révérend père, March 23, 1909, R.

"*Few new horizons*": André to Mon révérend père, December 19, 1904, R.

"*Necropolis*": André to Très révérend père, November 12, 1906, R.

"*One is leprous*": Julliotte to Palmace, October 8, 1903, R.

245   *Like other Hawaiian villages:* Moellers to Tauvel, July 23, 1894, R; see also Julliotte to Très révérend père, December 8, 1904, November 30, 1906, R; Jacks, 120.

246   *Process of beatification would have to wait:* Julliotte to Jourdan, May 21, 1933, R.

Time was arranging that: Obituaries appear in *Annales des Sacrés Coeurs.*

Argument with the provincial: Limburg to Bousquet, September 22, 1902, R.

He died, aged seventy-eight: Julliotte to Bousquet, September 3, 1907, R.

Conrardy: Jourdan, *Heart,* 314.

Mother Marianne: Jacks, *passim.*

Ambrose Hutchison: Hutchison MS, HD.

Joseph Dutton: Dutton, *passim.*

He left Kalawao village: Case, 131.

247   "*I don't know*": Dutton to Alexander, July 25, 1908, HHS; see also André to Mon révérend père, February 2, 1905, R.

A ruthless censor: Dutton to Cattebeke, March 31, 1907, R.

248   *Consumed like straws:* Typescript by Dutton, November, 1905, HHS.

249   The Church moved slowly: Franck to Prat, March 22, 1927, R; Limburg to Alazard, August 8, 1899, R; see also discussions of the Chapitre-Général, collated in R.

250   Ildefonse Alazard: See his notebook in R.

Roots in Damien's tomb: Moellers to Très révérend père, April 23, 1899, R.

VIII

For this section, see the files of the Hawaii Statuary Hall Commission in AH; and the Damien statue itself, in the Capitol Building in Washington, D.C., and the replica in Honolulu.

BIBLIOGRAPHY

The basic primary source materials for the life of Damien are in the various manuscript collections of the Congregation of the Sacred Hearts. At the archives of the mother house in Rome, identified in Notes by (R), are the surviving letters of the Hawaiian mission, arranged by author. There is also a separate collection of Damien material, including some original letters. A guide to these holdings has been published: Amerigo Cools, "Répertoire des Archives des Pères des Sacrés Coeurs concernant L'Océanie," *Journal de la Société des Océanistes*, 25 (1969), 345–357. More original correspondence is at the provincial archives of the Congregation in Louvain, identified in Notes by (L). A third sizable group of Damien letters, once lodged with the Congregation in Honolulu, has apparently been lost. Fortunately, before this loss occurred, careful copies of all Damien's letters had been made in connection with the beatification proceedings. In cases where it has been impossible to locate an original, use has been made of the copies in a three-volume typescript collection housed at the Rome archives: "Le Père Damien—Vie et Documents," identified in Notes by (V et D), and of a set of manuscript copies at Louvain, identified in Notes by (MSL). The official collections of source material, as published for use by the Church in connection with the beatification, are: *Beatificationis et Canonizationis Servi Dei Damiani De Veuster, Missionarii, Sacerdotis Congregationis SS. Cordium de Picpus, Positio Super Causae Introductione* (Rome, Guerra e Belli, 1954), and *Beatificationis et Canonizationis Servi Dei Damiani De Veuster, Missionarii, Sacerdotis Professi, Congregationis SS. Cordium Jesu et Mariae (Picpus), Positio Super Virtutibus* (Rome, Guerra e Belli, 1966).

Extensive documentation on leprosy in the Hawaiian Islands is in the Archives of Hawaii at Honolulu, identified in Notes by (AH). The relevant files are: Board of Health (BH); Board of Health Minutes (BHM); Board of

Health Letter Book (BHLB); Hansen's Disease (HD). The Board of Health of the Hawaiian kingdom published biennial *Reports* to the legislature, containing basic data and current thought on leprosy. Special reports on leprosy were also published from time to time, principally the following: *Report of the Special Sanitary Committee on the State of the Leper Settlement at Kalawao* (Honolulu, n.p., 1878); *Leprosy in Hawaii* ... (Honolulu, Daily Bulletin, 1886); *Supplement: Leprosy in Hawaii* (Honolulu, *Daily Bulletin*, 1886); *Leprosy in Foreign Countries* ... (Honolulu, Daily Bulletin, 1886); *Appendix to the Report on Leprosy of the President of the Board of Health to the Legislative Assembly of 1886* (Honolulu, Pacific Commercial Advertiser, 1886); *Copies of Report of Dr. Eduard Arning to the Board of Health* ... (Honolulu, Hawaiian Gazette, 1886); *Report of the Special Committee on the Leper Settlement at Kalawao, Molokai* ... (Honolulu, Gazette Publishing, 1888). Also useful in this regard is a report by the United States Senate Committee on the Pacific Islands and Puerto Rico, *Leprosy in Hawaii* (Washington, Government Printer, 1902).

Also in AH are the files of the Hawaii Statuary Hall Commission, the body charged with overseeing the design and construction of the Damien statue.

In the document collection of the Hawaiian Mission Children's Society Library, Honolulu, identified in Notes by (HMCS), the following files were useful: Emma-Kaeo Letters (a companion collection is in [AH]); Elias Bond Letters; Sereno E. Bishop Letters. HMCS also has microfilm and Xerox copies of the letters of Charles McEwen Hyde to the American Board of Commissioners for Foreign Missions, originals of which are in Houghton Library, Harvard University.

In the document collection of the Hawaiian Historical Society, Honolulu, identified in Notes as (HHS), the W. D. Alexander Papers contain some materials from Joseph Dutton.

At the University of Hawaii, identified in Notes by (UH) is the manuscript journal of Bishop Louis Maigret, Vicar-Apostolic of the Hawaiian Islands at the time of Damien's arrival.

Much has been published on Damien's life and death. A preliminary checklist of titles, "Liste des livres, brochures, articles, etc., sur le Serviteur de Dieu R.P. Damien De Veuster SS.CC. dans la bibliothèque du Secrétariat-Général de la Congrégation des Sacrés Coeurs," prepared by the Congregation's archivist, Reverend Father Amerigo Cools, runs to about fifty typescript pages. Of the many full-length biographies published so far, few can be regarded as historically sound and adequate in their use of source materials. One of these is *Le Père Damien: Apôtre des Lépreux* (Braine-le-Comte, Zech et Fils, 1931), by Vital Jourdan, a member of the Congregation. A revised version, using newly located source material and with a bibliography, was published in English translation as *The Heart of Father Damien* (Milwaukee, Bruce, 1955). By far the most popular life, in English at least, has been John Farrow's *Damien the Leper* (New York, Sheed & Ward, 1937), which has been through many printings. It is interesting reading, but is not based on solid research, and contains many invented incidents and conversations.

The following newspapers and periodicals yielded useful material:

> *Annales Des Sacrés Coeurs*
> *Courrier de Bruxelles*
> *Damien Institute*
> *Friend*
> *Hawaiian Gazette*
> *International Journal of Leprosy*
> *Journal of the Leprosy Investigation Committee*
> *Ka Nūpepa Elele*
> *Ka Nūpepa Kū'oko'a*
> *Ka Nūpepa Nūhou*
> *Leprosy Review*
> London *Tablet*
> London *Times*
> Missions Catholiques
> New York Times
> Pacific Commercial Advertiser
> San Francisco *Chronicle*
> Sydney *Mail*

The following sources, which emerged from a much wider range of material consulted, were directly useful. The list includes unpublished papers, articles from the periodical press, scientific monographs, religious works, and general publications. In the Notes, these works are cited in shortened form.

Ackerknecht, Erwin H. *A Short History of Medicine.* New York, Ronald, 1955.
Adler, Jacob, and Gwynn Barrett, eds. *The Diaries of Walter Murray Gibson.* Honolulu, University of Hawaii, 1973.
Bemiss, J. H. *A Few Cases of Leprosy.* New Orleans, L. Graham, 1880.
Besnier, Ernest. *Sur la Lèpre.* Paris, G. Masson, 1887.
Bird, Isabella L. *Six Months in the Sandwich Islands.* Honolulu, University of Hawaii, 1966.
Brodrick, James. *St. Francis Xavier.* London, Burns and Oates, 1952.

Brown, A. M. *Some Comments on Leprosy in its Contagio-Syphilitic and Vaccinal Aspects.* London, Hirschfeld Brothers, 1888.

Browne, Stanley G. *Leprosy.* Acta Clinica No. 11. Geneva, Documenta Geigy, 1970.

————. "Leprosy: The Christian Attitude," *International Journal of Leprosy,* 31 (1963), 229–235.

Bushnell, O. A. "Dr. Edward Arning: The First Microbiologist in Hawaii," *Hawaiian Journal of History,* 1 (1967), 3–30.

————. "The United States Leprosy Station at Kalawao," *Hawaiian Journal of History,* 2 (1968), 76–94.

Carr, John. *A Fisher of Men: The Venerable Peter Donders, C.SS.R.* Dublin, Clonmore and Reynolds, 1952.

Case, Howard D., ed. *Joseph Dutton, His Memoirs.* Honolulu, Star-Bulletin, 1931.

Choksy, N. H. *Abstract of the Report of the Leprosy Commission In India.* London, Baillière, Tindall and Cox, 1893.

Clifford, Edward. *Father Damien: A Journey from Cashmere to His Home in Hawaii.* London, Macmillan, 1889.

Cochrane, R. G., and T. Frank Davey, eds. *Leprosy in Theory and Practice.* 2nd ed. Baltimore, Williams & Wilkins, 1964.

Committee on Leprosy and Department of Health, State of Hawaii. "Recommendations for Treatment of Leprosy in Hawaii." Typescript, n.d.

La Congrégation des Pères des Sacrés Coeurs dite de "Picpus." Paris, Letouzey et Ané, 1928.

Consulat Royal de Belgique, Honolulu. "L'Exhumation des Restes Mortels du Reverend Père Damien Deveuster, SS. CC. . . . ." Typescript, dated 1936.

Creighton, R. J. "The Leper Settlement on Molokai," *Honolulu Almanac and Directory* (1886), 90–96.

Damon, E. M. *Siloama: The Church of the Healing Spring.* Honolulu, The Hawaiian Board of Missions, 1948.

Daws, Gavan. *Shoal of Time: A History of the Hawaiian Islands.* New York, Macmillan, 1968.

De Becker, Raymond. *De Groote Melaatse: De Ziel van Pater Damiaan.* Antwerpen, Vlaamsche Boekcentrale, 1957.

Dedication of the Kapiolani Home for Girls, the Offspring of Leper Parents, at Kakaako, Oahu, by their Majesties King Kalakaua and Queen Kapiolani. Honolulu, Advertiser Steam Print, 1885.

Delaney, John J., and James Edward Tobin. *Dictionary of Catholic Biography.* New York, Doubleday, 1961.

Douillet, Jacques. *What Is a Saint?* London, Burns and Oates, 1958.

Dutton, Charles J. *The Samaritans of Molokai: The Lives of Father Damien and Brother Dutton Among the Lepers.* New York, Dodd, Mead, 1932.

Farrow, John. *Damien the Leper.* New York, Sheed & Ward, 1937.

Feeny, P. *The Fight Against Leprosy.* London, Elek Books, 1964.

Feldman, William H. "Gerhard Henrik Armauer Hansen: What Did He See and When?," *International Journal of Leprosy,* 33 (1965), 412–416.

"The First Hawaiian Leper," *Friend,* February, 1890, 12.

Foster, Burnside. "Leprosy and the Hawaiian Annexation," *North American Review,* 167 (1898), 300–305.

Fox, G. Newberry. *God the Builder.* London, The Leprosy Mission, 1972.

Francis of Assisi. Paschal Robinson, tr. *The Writings of Saint Francis of Assisi.* London, J. M. Dent & Co., 1906.

Gray, Herman H., and John A. Dreisbach. "Leprosy Among Foreign Missionaries in Northern Nigeria," *International Journal of Leprosy,* 29 (1961), 279–290.

Gussow, Zachary, and George S. Tracy. "Stigma and the Leprosy Phenomenon: The Social History of a Disease in the Nineteenth and Twentieth Centuries," *Bulletin of the History of Medicine,* 44 (1970), 425–449.

Hathaway, Joseph C. "Leprosy in Hawaii," *Hawaii Medical Journal,* 29 (1970), 429–437.

[Hyde, C. M.] *Father Damien and His Work for the Hawaiian Lepers: A Careful and Candid Estimate.* Reprinted from the *Congregationalist,* August 7, 1890.

———. "The Leper Settlement on Molokai," *Friend,* September, 1895, 66–67.

Jacks, L. V. *Mother Marianne of Molokai.* New York, Macmillan, 1935.

Joesting, Edward. *Hawaii: An Uncommon History.* New York, Norton, 1973.

Johnstone, Arthur. *Recollections of Robert Louis Stevenson in the Pacific.* London, Chatto & Windus, 1905.

Kent, Harold W. *Dr. Hyde and Mr. Stevenson.* Tokyo, Tuttle, 1973.

———. *Charles Reed Bishop: Man of Hawaii.* Palo Alto, Pacific Books, 1965.

The King Kamehameha I and Father Damien Memorial Statues. Washington, U.S. Government Printing Office, 1970.

Kuykendall, Ralph S. *The Hawaiian Kingdom.* 3 vols. Honolulu, University of Hawaii, 1938–1963.

Leprosy and Libel: The Suit of George L. Fitch against the Saturday Press. Honolulu, Saturday Press Print, 1883.

Life and Letters of Father Damien, the Apostle of the Lepers. London, Catholic Truth Society, 1889.

Macken, Thomas F. *The Canonisation of Saints.* Dublin, M. H. Gill & Son, 1910.

Mackenzie, Morell. "The Dreadful Revival of Leprosy," *Nineteenth Century,* 26 (1889), 925–941.

Mission to Lepers. *These Ninety Years.* London, Mission to Lepers, 1964.

Molinari, Paul., S.J. *Saints: Their Place in the Church.* New York, Sheed & Ward, 1965.

Moorman, J. R. H. *Saint Francis of Assisi.* London, S. C. M. Press, 1950.

Morrow, Prince A. "Leprosy and Hawaiian Annexation," *North American Review,* 165 (1897), 582–590.

Mouritz, Arthur A. *A Brief World History of Leprosy: Hawaii: U. S. America: Philippines: Malaya: Fiji: China: India: Europe.* Revised edition. Honolulu, A. Mouritz, 1943.

————. *"The Path of the Destroyer": A History of Leprosy in the Hawaiian Islands and Thirty Years Research into the Means by Which It Has Been Spread.* Honolulu, Star-Bulletin Press, 1916.

Mulhane, L. W. *Leprosy and the Charity of the Church.* New York, D. H. McBride & Co., 1896.

Rokstad, Ingvald. "Gerhard Heinrich Armauer Hansen." *International Journal of Leprosy,* 32 (1964), 64–70.

Ryrie, G. A. "The Psychology of Leprosy," *Leprosy Review,* 22 (1951), 13–23.

Saxe, A. W. *Report on Hawaiian Leprosy . . .* Sacramento, Day & Joy, 1881.

Schweitzer, Albert. *African Notebook.* Mrs. C. E. B. Russell, tr. Bloomington, Indiana University Press, 1939.

————. *On the Edge of the Primeval Forest.* New York, Macmillan, 1931.

————. *Out of My Life and Thought: An Autobiography.* C. T. Campion, tr. New York, Holt, Rinehart & Winston, 1949.

Shaner, Susan. "Rudolph Wilhelm Meyer." Unpublished paper, University of Hawaii.

Singer, Charles, and E. Ashworth Underwood. *A Short History of Medicine.* 2nd ed. New York, Oxford University Press, 1962.

Skinsnes, Olaf K. "Leprosy in Society. I. Leprosy Has Appeared on the Face," *Leprosy Review,* 35 (1964), 21–35.

————. "Leprosy in Society. II. The Pattern of Concept and Reaction to Leprosy in Oriental Antiquity," *Leprosy Review,* 35 (1964), 106–122.

————. "Leprosy in Society. III. The Relationship of the Social to the Medical Pathology of Leprosy," *Leprosy Review*, 35 (1964), 175–181.

————. "Leprosy in Society. IV. The Genesis of Lepra-Angst," *Leprosy Review*, 39 (1968), 223–228.

Skinsnes, Olaf K., and Robert M. Elvove. "Leprosy in Society. V. 'Leprosy' in Occidental Literature," *International Journal of Leprosy*, 38 (1970), 294–307.

Skinsnes, Olaf K. *Leprosy Rationale.* 2nd ed. New York, American Leprosy Missions, Inc., 1971.

Stevenson, Robert Louis. *Father Damien: An Open Letter to the Reverend Doctor Hyde of Honolulu.* Sydney, n.p., 1890.

————. *The Letters of Robert Louis Stevenson.* Sidney Colvin, ed. 4 vols. New York, Scribner, 1911.

Stoddard, Charles Warren. *Charles Warren Stoddard's Diary of a Visit to Molokai in 1884, with a Letter from Father Damien to His Brother in 1873.* San Francisco, The Book Club of California, 1933.

————. *The Lepers of Molokai.* Enlarged edition. Notre Dame, Indiana, Ave Maria Press, 1893.

Summers, Catherine C. *Molokai: A Site Survey.* Honolulu, Bernice P. Bishop Museum, 1971.

Tardieu, Frézal. *Missions Catholiques des Îles Sandwich ou Hawaii.* Paris, Bureaux des Annales des Sacrés-Coeurs, 1924.

Tauvel, Philibert. *Father Damien: Apostle of the Lepers of Molokai, Priest of the Congregation of the Sacred Hearts.* London, Art and Book Company, 1904.

Tebb, William. *The Recrudescence of Leprosy and Its Causation: A Popular Treatise.* London, Swan Sonnenschein & Co., 1893.

Thin, George. *Leprosy.* London, Percival and Co., 1891.

Thompson, J. Ashburton. "Leprosy in Hawaii: A Critical Enquiry," *Mittheilungen und Verhandlungen der Internationalen wissenschaftlichen Lepra—Konferenz zum Berlin im October 1897.* Berlin, Verlag von August Hirschwald, 1897.

Wellmann, Klaus F. "Notizen zur Geschichte des Aussatzes im Königreich Hawaii." *Sudholts Archiv,* 52 (1968), 221–256.

Woods, G. W. *Reminiscences of a Visit, in July, 1876, to the Leper Settlement of Molokai, having special reference to Rev. Father J. Damien Deveuster.* N.p., n.d.

World Health Organization. WHO Expert Committee on Leprosy. *Fourth Report.* WHO Technical Report Series. No. 459. Geneva, 1970.

Wright, Henry Press. *Leprosy: An Imperial Danger*. London, J. and A. Churchill, 1889.

————. *Leprosy and Segregation*. London, Parker & Co., 1885.

Yzendoorn, Reginald. *History of the Catholic Mission in the Hawaiian Islands*. Honolulu, Honolulu Star-Bulletin, 1927.

INDEX

Ahuimanu, mission college, 34
Airlie, Lady, 204
Alazard, Father Ildefonse, 250
Alencastre, Bishop Stephen, 249
Anglican missionaries, 42
Archambaux, Father Grégoire,
    153–156, 181–183, 191, 195, 196, 243;
    death, 199–200; in Kalawao, 153–154,
    182–183
Arning, Eduard, 154, 171, 210, 234–236;
    as Damien's physician, 143–144, 229;
    studies of leprosy, 139–142, 146, 162,
    234–235

Bacillus leprae, 6, 139, 141
Beissel, Father Columban, 164, 165,
    181, 182, 198, 230
Bishop, Bernice Pauahi, 191
Bishop, Charles Reed, 191, 231
Board of Health (Hawaii), 89, 90, 91,
    106, 110, 130, 139, 162, 166, 167, 191;
    and Burgerman, 93–95; and
    Damien's ministry, 65–67, 92, 111,
    177; Kalawao controlled by, 70–71,
    73, 76, 77, 81, 114, 115, 126–127,
    129–131, 180, 182, 184, 219, 232–234;
    personnel changes, 180
Boeynaems, Bishop Libert, 249
Bond, E. C., 231
Bouillon, Father Aubert, 56
Braine-le-Comte, Belgium, 21, 22
Brigham, William, 210, 231
Burgerman, Father André, 98, 105,
    106, 108, 155–157, 173, 191, 195, 230,
    246, 248; Damien's friction with,
    87–88, 90–91, 93–97, 99–100;
    leprosy, possible, 97, 106, 107, 155,
    181, 246
Burne-Jones, Edward, "Vision of St.
    Francis," 204

Calvinist missionaries, 43–44
Catholic Church in Hawaii, 225–226;
    see also Sacred Hearts,
    Congregation of
Chapman, Hugh B.: funds raised for
    Damien, 169–170, 175, 177–179, 185,
    208; and National Leprosy Fund,
    221, 222
Charteris, Lady Caroline, 204
Chaulmoogra oil, 238
Clifford, Edward, 208, 209, 210, 222,
    223, 238; in Kalawao, 202–207;
    lecture on Damien, 221; portraits of
    Damien, 205–206
Conrardy, Father Louis-Lambert,
    192–197, 205, 209, 211, 212, 242, 243,
    246; in Kalawao, 195–197, 218–219

Damien, Father (Joseph De Veuster):
    as athlete, spiritual, 57–58;
    beatification, 250–251; birth, 6, 19;
    character summarized, 248–249;
    Clifford visits and describes,
    202–207; Clifford's portraits of,
    205–206; controversy on, religious
    and political, 172–179; death, 3–4, 9,
    212–213; deathbed photograph, 3, 5,
    10, 212; decoration from Hawaiian
    government, 100–102, 129; early life,
    19–21; funds raised for, 169–171, 175,
    177–179, 185, 207–208; funeral,
    212–213; and Goto treatment for
    leprosy, 162–165; in Kakaako
    hospital, 160–163; lameness, 104, 106;
    leprosy, 5, 7, 97–98, 121, 143–159,
    164–166, 183–187, 198–201, 208–211,
    237–240;
        letters: to father-general of
        Sacred Hearts, 38, 98, 149–150;
        to his parents, 22, 27–28, 33–34,

Damien (cont'd)
  letters (cont'd)
    51–52, 98–99, 118, 146–148; to
    Pamphile, 34–35, 37–38, 50, 84,
    86–87, 101, 118–119, 121, 148–149,
    152, 158, 166, 179, 183, 184, 209;
    to Pauline, his sister, 52;
    published, 217–218;
  meditations and resolutions,
    notebook, 185–186; memorial
    fund (National Leprosy Fund),
    221–223; as missionary, 34–52;
    missionary work, preparation
    for, 29–32; in Molokai, see
    Kalawao; monument at
    Kalawao, 221, 223–224; name,
    choice of, 58; ordained, 34;
    Personal Rule, 109, 117;
    presentiment about Molokai,
    56–57; press reaction to, 60–61,
    101–102; reburied in Louvain,
    250; relics of, preserved, 232;
    religious vocation, choice of,
    21–23; with Sacred Hearts
    Fathers, Louvain and Paris,
    23–26, 29; as saint, investigation
    on, 240–242, 245–251; sexual
    immorality alleged, 102–103,
    228–230; statue in Washington,
    252; strangers offer to help,
    166–167; vows, ceremony of,
    26–27; voyage to Hawaii, 32–
    34
Damien, St., 58
DDS (Dapsone), 238–240
Dole, Sanford Ballard, 232
Dominis, John, 129, 130
D'Orgeval, Father Peter, 244
Dutton, Ira Barnes (Brother Joseph),
  167–168, 184, 210, 212, 230, 240, 242,
  248; Damien described by, 189–190;
  in Kalawao, 167–169, 192, 198, 199,
  231, 232, 246–247

Edward, Prince of Wales (Edward
  VII), 221, 222
'Elele (newspaper), 227
Emerson, Nathaniel B., 78–79, 133,
  138; and Burgerman, 94–96;
  president of Board of Health,
  180–181, 184

Emma, Dowager Queen, 72, 76,
  80–82
Escobar, Marisol, 252
Évrard, Father Clément, 36, 37, 38,
  57

Fabien, Father, 229, 231
Favens, Father Modeste, 66, 87, 97,
  173
Fitch, George, 132–133, 136, 141, 143,
  151, 228–229
Fouesnel, Father Léonor, 55, 60,
  107–108, 129, 144, 181–183, 187, 192,
  194–197, 200–201, 207, 211, 219–220,
  230, 245, 246, 249; in controversy
  on Damien, 172–178; Damien
  characterized by, 120; forbids
  Damien to visit Honolulu, 159;
  hostility to Damien, 174–178, 185,
  186, 208, 241; on leprosy, 155–156
Francis of Assisi, St., 58, 114
Francis Xavier, St., 29, 32, 58–59
Franciscan Sisters, see Sisters of
  Charity

Gage, H. B., Hyde's letter to, 11–14,
  227–232
Gibson, Walter Murray, 136, 139–140,
  154–155, 162, 167, 184, 186, 223, 225,
  234; in controversy on Damien,
  177–178; leaves Hawaii, 179–180; and
  leprosy in politics, 126–130, 171–172;
  opposes Damien's visit to Honolulu,
  159–161; opposes Goto treatment in
  Kalawao, 163–164; visits Damien, 161
Goto, Masanao, 171, 180; leprosy
  treatment, 162–165, 184, 187, 238
Grosvenor, Lady, 204
Gurjun oil, 203–204, 208, 238

Hamakua, Hawaii, 40, 51; see also
  Kohala-Hamakua
Hansen, Gerhard Henrik Armauer, 6,
  8, 139, 141
Hawaii (Hawaiian Islands): Catholics
  honored by government, 129–130;
  Damien as missionary, 34–52;
  Damien honored by government,
  100–102, 129; leprosy in, 60, 63–64,
  73–79, 130–135, 233–234; leprosy in
  politics, 125–130, 171–172;

Hawaii *(cont'd)*
missionaries sent to, 30–34, 42–44, 55–56; as state, 251; sugar industry, 126, 223; U.S. annexation of, 223–224, 232, 235
Hawaiian Evangelical Association, 63–64, 75
Hawaiian Gazette, 101, 134
Hawaiian language, 44–45, 148
Hawaiian people, 34, 45–48; attitude toward leprosy, 75–79, 115, 245; immorality, Christian views of, 46–47, 134–135; medicine, traditional, 47–48; Protestants turn to Catholicism, 225
Hayselden, Fred, 180
Honolulu, 33, 34, 60, 65, 74; Damien permitted to stay in, 159–161; Damien serves mass in, 105–106; Kakaako, *see* Kakaako hospital; Kapiolani Home, 136, 190, 226, 243
Hoof, Serapion van, 243–244
Hutchison, Ambrose, 96, 111–113, 116, 132, 242, 243, 246
Hyde, Charles McEwen, 135–137, 162, 191, 224–232, 240; Damien meets, 226–227; leprosy, contact with, 135–137; letter against Damien, 11–14, 227–232; Stevenson's reply to, 13–16, 227, 228

Jaussen, Bishop Tepano, 30

Kaeo, Peter Young, 89, 93; Damien meets, 81–82; letters, 72, 76, 79–82, 90
Kahuna (medical priests), 47–48, 52, 76, 81, 125, 133
Kakaako hospital, Honolulu, 128–129, 136, 142, 155, 159, 180, 183, 190, 226, 234; Damien in, 160–163; dismantled, 191; Goto treatment in, 162–163
Kalakaua, King David, 100, 125, 129, 130, 162, 172, 179, 193, 223; coronation ceremony, 134–135; visits Damien, 161, 163
Kalaupapa, Molokai, 68, 85, 90, 100, 158, 182, 209, 234, 236; Bishop Home for Girls, 191, 197, 198, 226, 231; changes after Damien's death,

232–233, 244; church, 93–94, 99, 110, 113, 156, 207, 208; Damien and Montiton dispute over, 102, 103, 106
Kalawao, Molokai, 4, 6, 55–56, 60–61, 67–75, 131–132, 142, 230, 241–242; Archambaux in, 153–154, 182–183; buildings, number of, 188–189; Burgerman in, 87–88, 90–91, 93–97, 99–100; changes after Damien's death, 232–234, 243–245; children in, 112–113; Clifford in, 202–207; conditions described, 72–73, 82–83, 114–117, 245; Conrardy in, 195–197, 218–219; Damien goes to, 56–57, 59–63; Damien praised for going to, 61–62; Damien segregated in, 65–67, 158–159; Damien's monument, 221, 223–224; Damien's work in, 62–63, 82–96, 109–121, 150–153, 183–184, 188–191, 199; Dutton in, 167–169, 192, 198, 199, 231, 232, 246–247; Goto treatment in, 163, 187; government appropriation for, 126–127, 130–131; Hawaiian royalty as patrons, 125; Henry P. Baldwin Home for Boys, 231, 233, 246–247; immorality in, 111–112, 245; Kaeo's descriptions of, 72, 76, 79–82; *kōkua* (helpers), 77, 114–115, 131; leprosy settlement established, 70–72; Liliuokalani visits, 100, 101, 125; memorial anniversary services for Damien, 243; missionaries in, 61–62, 64–65, 78–79; Montiton in, 102–109; orphanage, 190–191; Pamphile in, 218–220; religious services, 112, 113; riot, 243; St. Philomena's church, 55, 61, 84, 85, 110, 113, 198, 199, 204, 212; Siloama church, 61, 64; Stevenson visits, 13, 67–68; *Times* article on, 10; U.S. Public Health Service Station, 235–236
Kaluaaha, Molokai, 88, 93
Kamehameha, King, statue in Washington, 251–252
Kapiolani, Queen, 125, 170
Kapiolani Home for Girls, Honolulu, 136, 190, 226, 243
Kauai, 180–181
Keanu: dies of leprosy, 234–235;

Keanu (cont'd)
    leprosy experiments with, 142, 146,
    162
Kilauea (volcano), 37–38
Koeckemann, Bishop Hermann,
    100–101, 107, 130, 143, 156, 165, 166,
    181–182, 185–187, 193–197, 207, 211,
    220, 230, 242, 245, 246, 249; in
    controversy on Damien, 172–178;
    Damien's correspondence with,
    103–106, 150, 157, 160, 175, 182,
    193–194, 208; hostility to Damien,
    185, 192–195, 241
Kohala, Hawaii, 40, 44, 51, 56, 57, 58,
    87, 220, 229, 230, 231
Kohala-Hamakua (district), 38–39, 42,
    46, 48–49, 57
Kōkua (helpers of leprosy victims),
    77, 114–115, 131, 181
Kona, Hawaii, 107
Kopp, Mother Marianne, 129, 161,
    190–191, 209, 243, 246
Kūʻokoʻa (newspaper), 61, 75, 86

Lahaina, Maui, 95, 153–155, 181
Lepart, Louis, 71–72
Leprosy, 130–142, 236–240;
    chaulmoogra oil for, 238; as Chinese
    disease, 74; contagiousness, 131–132,
    237; Damien's case, 5, 7, 97–98, 121,
    143–159, 164–166, 183–187, 198–201,
    208–211, 237–240; Damien's
    knowledge of, 56, 83, 133; DDS
    (Dapsone) as cure for, 238–240;
    epidemic ends, 233–234; fear of
    contagion, 7–9; Goto's treatment
    for, 162–165, 184, 187; Gurjun oil for,
    203–204, 208, 238; in Hawaii, 60,
    63–64, 70–71, 73–79, 130–135,
    233–234; Hawaiian attitude toward,
    75–79, 115, 245; in Hawaiian politics,
    125–130, 171–172; incidence of, 131;
    inoculation experiments, 141–142,
    234–235; lepromatous, 236–237;
    religious workers with victims, 5, 9,
    239–240; saints care for victims,
    58–59; scientific study of, 6, 139–142,
    146, 234–237; segregation of victims,
    4, 60, 64, 75, 78–79, 127, 130, 131,
    138, 180–181, 234, 243; syphilis
    connected with, 132–134, 136,
    140–141, 144–145, 229; treatment,

    medical, 138–139, 238; white man's
    responsibility for, 74–79
Liliuokalani, Queen, 129, 223; at
    Kalawao, 100, 101, 125
Limburg, Father Corneille, 197–199,
    242
Louvain: Damien reburied in, 250;
    Sacred Hearts Congregation in,
    23–26
Lunalilo, King William, 60–61, 126,
    130

Maigret, Bishop Louis, 34, 36, 37, 55,
    60, 66–67, 87, 100, 173; and
    Damien's mission to Kalawao, 56,
    62
Manning, Cardinal Edward Henry,
    169, 221
Marianne, Mother, see Kopp, Mother
    Marianne
Maui, 36, 55, 66
Meyer, Rudolph, 71, 72, 90, 91, 92, 111,
    160, 164, 168, 187, 188, 191, 211
Moellers, Father Wendelin, 197, 207,
    211, 212, 219, 242, 245, 246, 250
Molokai, 4, 55, 66, 67, 69; Burgerman
    in, 87, 88; Damien's ministry in
    healthy districts, 65, 67; see also
    Kalaupapa; Kalawao
Moncany, Father Régis, 97, 98, 102,
    173
Montiton, Father Albert, 102–109,
    156–158, 173, 181, 191, 195, 229–230,
    246, 248; Damien's friction with,
    102–105; in Kalawao, 102–109; skin
    disorder, 106–109
Mormons, 42, 225; in Kalawao, 61
Morrow, Prince A., 210
Mount-Temple, Lady, 204
Mouritz, Arthur, 82, 115, 154, 167, 180,
    186, 187, 223, 230, 234, 235, 246; as
    Damien's physician, 143–145,
    150–151, 160, 164–165, 184–185, 188
Mycobacterium leprae, 237, 238,
    239

National Leprosy Fund (Father
    Damien Memorial Fund), 221–223
Neisser, Albert, 139
Newspapers, reactions to Damien's
    ministry, 60–61, 101–102
Nūhou (newspaper), 60, 61, 126

Pacific Commercial Advertiser, 101, 171–172

Pamphile, Father (Auguste De Veuster, brother of Damien), 20–22, 28, 32, 49–50, 57, 174, 206, 240; Damien tells him of leprosy, 149, 183; Damien's letters to, 34–35, 37–38, 50, 84, 86–87, 101, 118–119, 121, 148–149, 152, 158, 166, 179, 183, 184, 209; Damien's letters published, 217–218; death, 220; in Kalawao, 218–220; letters on Damien's death, 217–218; as missionary to Hawaii, Damien replaces, 30–31; with Sacred Hearts Fathers, 23–25; offers to help Damien, 166; typhus, 30, 59, 149

Pelekunu, Molokai, 99

Protestants: attitude toward Damien, 63, 66; Hawaiian converts leave churches, 225–226; isolated from Hawaiian culture, 134–135; in Kalawao, 61, 78–79, 86; as missionaries, 42–44; power of, in Hawaii, 129, 180, 223–224

Puna, Hawaii, 37–38, 40, 42, 46, 48

Raepsaet, Father Maurice, 249–250

Ragsdale, William P., 88–90

Roosevelt, Theodore, Great White Fleet, 247

Ropert, Father (later Bishop) Gulstan, 51, 52, 220, 230, 245, 249

Rothschild, Baron de, 221

Sacred Hearts, Congregation of: and Burgerman's problems, 93–97; in controversy on Damien, 172–179; Damien's relationship with, 96–100, 149–150, 160, 170, 192; Damien's sanctity investigated, 241–242, 249–251; growth of, 250; in Hawaii, 61–62, 66, 91, 93–97, 107, 130, 172, 218, 225, 231; in Kalawao, 243–244; in Louvain, 23–26; in Paris, 26, 29, 31, 58; missionaries sent to Hawaii, 30–34, 42, 55–56; perpetual adoration, ritual, 112; Picpus Fathers, name for, 58

Schweitzer, Albert, 244

Sinnett, James (Brother James), 198, 208, 209, 211, 212

Sisters of Charity, Third Order of St. Francis, 129, 161, 190–191, 226; in Kalaupapa, 197–198, 207, 209, 212, 219, 231, 232, 242, 246

Spreckels, Claus, 172

Stanley, Hon. Maude, 204

Stevenson, Robert Louis, 12–16, 153, 240–241, 249; at Kalawao, 13, 67–68; letter to Hyde, defense of Damien, 13–16, 227, 228

Stoddard, Charles Warren, 68, 69, 143, 168, 179; Damien's work described, 110, 113–114

Strawn, Clayton, 92–93

Sumner, William, 92

Swift, Sidney Bourne, 212

Syphilis, leprosy connected with, 132–134, 136, 140–141, 144–145, 229

Tahiti, 87, 96

Times, London, 170, 221, 240; article on Damien, 10, 11; Pamphile's letter in, 217–218

Tremeloo, Belgium, 19, 232

Trousseau, George, 76, 144

Tuamotu Archipelago, 106, 156

Veuster, Anne-Catherine De, mother of Damien, 19, 31, 51–52, 119, 146, 148, 165

Veuster, Auguste De, *see* Pamphile, Father

Veuster, Eugénie De, sister of Damien, 20, 30, 147

Veuster, Frans De, father of Damien, 19, 22, 28, 51, 119, 148

Veuster, Joseph De, *see* Damien, Father

Veuster, Léonce De, brother of Damien, 148

Veuster, Pauline De, sister of Damien, 20, 21, 30, 31, 50, 52, 119, 148

Wailuku, Maui, 55, 56, 57, 59, 60, 174

Waller, Gilbert, 162

Walsh, Donald, 72–73

Weiler, Father Janvier, 178

Williamson, William, 84

Wilmington, John, 151

Woods, G. W., 89–90, 98, 114, 120–121, 152, 198

ABOUT THE AUTHOR

Gavan Daws lived and worked for many years in Hawaii, where he wrote *Holy Man*. He is the author of several books about the Pacific, and he has also made documentary films and written for the stage. A Fellow of the Academy of the Humanities in Australia, and a member of the UNESCO International Commission for a Scientific and Cultural History of Humankind, he is presently professor of Pacific History in the Institute of Advanced Studies at the Australian National University.